A SEASON WITH THE WITCH

Salem

A SEASON WITH THE WITCH

THE MAGIC AND MAYHEM OF HALLOWEEN IN SALEM, MASSACHUSETTS

J. W. Ocker

THE COUNTRYMAN PRESS
A division of W. W. Norton & Company
Independent Publishers Since 1923

For information about special discounts for bulk purchases, please contact W. W. Norton Special Sales at specialsales@wwnorton.com or 800-233-4830

Manufacturing by Berryville Graphics
Book design by Ellen Cipriano
Production manager: Devon Zahn

The Countryman Press
www.countrymanpress.com

A division of W. W. Norton & Company, Inc.
500 Fifth Avenue, New York, NY 10110
www.wwnorton.com

Library of Congress Cataloging-in-Publication Data

Names: Ocker, J. W., author.
Title: A season with the witch : the magic and mayhem of Halloween in Salem, Massachusetts / J. W. Ocker.
Description: New York, NY : Countryman Press, 2016.
Identifiers: LCCN 2016023647 | ISBN 9781581573398 (pbk.)
Subjects: LCSH: Witches—Massachusetts—Salem. | Wiccans—Massachusetts—Salem. | Halloween—Massachusetts—Salem. | Haunted places—Massachusetts—Salem. | Salem (Mass.)—History—Miscellanea.
Classification: LCC BF1575 .O25 2016 | DDC 133.4/3097445—dc23 LC record available at https://lccn.loc.gov/2016023647

10 9 8 7 6 5 4 3 2 1

To Lindsey, Esme, and Hazel.
My witches three.

CONTENTS

INTRODUCTION: SALEM FOR A SPELL

Salem, Massachusetts, is the strangest city in the United States—and that's a country full of strange cities. Las Vegas comes to mind. So does Los Angeles. North Pole, Alaska, is a good example. But the strangeness of these cities makes sense. We can easily trace the reasons they are odd and understand why they jut out from the map. We can see how a city that has successfully capitalized on a vice would use every form of spectacle to lure more vice-prone visitors to its desert wonderland. Or how a city, the primary industry of which involves actors in costumes amassing colossal riches and fame by pretending for a mass media, would develop into a place skewed from the norm. And we can understand how a small, isolated city with few resources except snow and a high latitude would settle on Christmas as a marketing angle.

But the strangeness of Salem . . . makes . . . no . . . sense.

Sure, 1692 is the reason. But it's not a good reason. The Witch Trials constituted a nine-month episode in the city's four hundred busy years of history. But somehow those measly months created a modern identity and an international reputation for Salem.

The episode itself was strange, of course. I mean, a couple of tween girls playing with eggs panicked an entire region into believing it had been infiltrated by supernatural servants of Satan, escalating to the point that more than 150 people were accused. Most of them were jailed, and nearly two dozen were executed. That's certainly weird enough to merit an exhibit at the local history museum, and could be a defining event for a city, I guess. Certainly it's that bizarre.

Except that it's not unique. Not even close.

In Europe, the quick with torches, stakes, and nooses had been actively hunting witches for at least two centuries before buckled shoes printed New England soil. Estimates place the number of victims of the European witch hunts at anywhere from fifty thousand to two hundred thousand—so at the low end, holy-cow-that's-a-lot and at the high end, holy-cow-that's-a-lot.

In 2011, Vardø, Norway, erected a memorial to the ninety-one victims of its seventeenth-century witch hunt. Lancashire, England, long ago turned its Pendle witches incident, in which ten people were hanged in 1612, into a tourist draw. Torsåker, Sweden, has a witch memorial for the more than seventy victims who were beheaded and burned in 1675. So does Ellwangen, Germany, for a staggering 450 victims in the late 1500s and early 1600s. Zugarramurdi, Spain, has a whole museum dedicated to its witch trials of 1609, in which some seven thousand were accused. There are other memorials and museums all over the continent. They're just hard to find because Salem overpowers the search results, despite not being anywhere near the deadliest, strangest, nor most poignant witch trial in human history. Even all the dramatic stuff like burnings at the stake and dunking chairs never happened in Salem.

The Salem Witch Trials weren't even the first witch trials in America. That dubious bit of monster hunting took place in Hartford, Connecticut, where Alice Young was hanged in 1647 on the spot of what is now the Old State House. Fifteen years later, Hartford would hang another four convicted witches. And that's still thirty years before Bridget Bishop swung in Salem. All told, there were around one hundred people tried for witchcraft in America before the crystal ball dropped on 1692. And that includes Boston, which had shaded its Common a few times with the bodies of accused witches. In fact, Boston's last executed witch was hanged three and a half years before Salem's first.

Nor were the Salem Witch Trials the witch trials to end all witch trials. Witch hunting continued throughout colonial America and Europe for at least another century. Hell, they're happening today. In Africa, India, Latin America, the Middle East, and the Southwest Pacific, men, women, and children are being arrested, tried, tortured, and executed for knowing good recipes for eye of newt and toe of frog. The United Nations estimates that thousands per year are killed for being witches. In 2016. We have robots on Mars and supercomputers in our pockets, and people are still afraid of the hoodoo.

Yet Salem is, alone in this country and on this planet, Witch City. It doesn't make sense. And it gets weirder.

Salem is not defined today in terms of the the Bible-clutching, black-clad Puritans who settled the area and who were both victims and villains in the trials. Instead, it is defined in terms of a cartoon version of what the victims were accused of being: witches, with pointy hats, flying broomsticks, and all.

The Salem police have Halloween-style witch-on-broom silhouettes sewn on the shoulders of their uniforms and painted on the doors of their patrol cars. The local high school mascot is a Wicked Witch of the West–style witch. Every year they graduate whole new classes of Salem Witches. The masthead of the city newspaper features a red cartoon witch. The seal of the fire department is a witch. The orange street signs in the tourist area all have Halloween witches on them. The latest tourism branding campaign for the city involves a conical witch's hat. And that's not counting the private businesses of Salem, where everything from laundromats to cab services to restaurants are themed with flying-broom hags. At some point, dark magic overtook the dark history, and the fantasy became more prominent than the facts. Which, to me, is fine. I'm not judging and, in fact, will defend it. I just bring it up here to say that it's weird.

Now, keep in mind, Salem has four centuries of noteworthy, non-witchy history, so it's not like it doesn't have options. For instance, it was the birthplace, home, and inspiration of author Nathaniel Hawthorne, one of the founding authors of American literature. That's . . . not too shabby. It's also where the National Guard got started. Alexander Graham Bell lived and experimented there for a couple of years and gave one of the first public demonstrations of the telephone in Salem. Parker Brothers was founded in the city by native sons, and it was there that the world was introduced to everything from Monopoly to the Nerf ball. It was also one of the most important seaports in early America, pivotal in trading with the Orient and privateering against the British navy. And, of course, it has been through every American war, including those against the French, the Native Americans, the British, and the South. The Revolutionary War almost started in Salem—Google "Leslie's retreat" sometime. It has enough eggs in its cultural basket to Halloween-prank a whole city, even if that basket has been swapped for a cauldron.

But it gets weirder still.

By digging up the land to ferret out perceived witches, the judges and accusers of the Salem Witch Trials inadvertently prepared the ground for real Witches (capital *W*) three hundred years later.

Today, the city of Salem is the home of actual Witches, men and women who practice Wicca or Witchcraft or a related neo-pagan religion. Nobody knows quite how many Witches have lived in Salem over the decades or are there today. Estimates run from the hundreds to the thousands—the latter estimate would put the number of Witches somewhere around 5 percent of the city's population—across uncounted covens and temples. But regardless of how many Witches live in Salem, the religion is undeniably a prominent part of the city's culture and economy and a powerful draw for Witches across the world.

But wait. Still weirder.

The Salem Witch Trials is the founding event of the American horror genre. What 1776 is to American history buffs, 1692 is to American horror buffs. Salem isn't just a city, it's a space in popular culture—a haunted space in popular culture.

Somewhere along the timeline, the city transmogrified into America's Capital of Creepy. It became a monster mecca. There is no Werewolf City or Vampire City or Zombie City, so Witch City welcomes them all. Today, the city has monster museums and haunted houses, ghost walks and graveyard tours. If you're a fan of the macabre, you put Salem on your travel list.

Especially at Halloween.

Every year, Salem throws a month-long Halloween party. This small city of forty-two thousand swells to more than a quarter million in October. For many, Salem is Halloween Town. Which isn't a bad place to be for a holiday that neared $7 billion dollars in sales in 2015 in the United States.

But don't get me wrong, the witch is still the queen of the monsters in Salem.

Many movies and television series and novels about witches were inspired by, set in, or filmed in Witch City. And for the ones that aren't, no story can get even close to witches without at least name-checking Salem. J.K. Rowling couldn't even create a British world of wizards without doing so in her Harry Potter series. In this era of prime-time horror television—when zombies and vampires and ghosts and psychos dominate the timeslots and channels once ruled by comedians, cops, and lawyers—of course there are witches, and of course Salem is represented. In 2013, the supernatural show *Salem* launched on WGN America, and it is filming its third season as I write this book. I'm sure the show was pitched just on the one word: Salem.

Salem is the weirdest city in the country. It might even be in the running for the world crown. And you know what? I'm going to dive up to my hairline in this odd cauldron. And you're coming with me.

We're going to visit the remaining Witch Trials sites. From graves of judges to proposed execution sites to still-standing houses of trial participants, we're going to explore Salem like it's 1692, overlaying its ghosts across the contemporary landscape of the city like modern-day necromancers. We're going to visit its macabre attractions to see if spooky is different in Salem. We're going to give its non–witch-related sites a fighting chance against an unevenly weighted calendar. We're even going to check out the filming locales of movies and shows that have used Salem as part of their palettes. We're going to see Salem from many different vantage points, even if we have climb above all the pointy hats to do it.

Along the way, we're going to talk to lots of people in Salem—its citizens and leaders, its artists and entrepreneurs, its entertainers and historians. And, of course, we're going to talk to its Witches. We're going to get the perspectives of those who revel in the strangeness of Salem and those who consider it a tacky tourist trap or, worse, a distasteful celebration that plays monkey bars on the victim's nooses.

As for me, I do a little bit more than explore. I pick up my family of four—me, my wife, Lindsey, and my two daughters, Esme and Hazel—and move to downtown Salem for the entire month of October to spend a season with the witch, a time when the city's streets clog with monsters, when festivals and carnivals and parties appear as if magically summoned, when everyone is counting down to the mad monster party that is

Halloween night. Just stepping outside the door will be an official act of research. This book will be more stay-alogue than travelogue.

Salem is odd. And I won't promise you that by end of this book Salem will make sense. I don't want it to. The ingredient list for a spell is much less interesting than the effects of the spell itself. But I can promise a lot of witchery in these pages. A lot of Halloween. A lot of surprises. And a lot of the strangeness that is Salem, Massachusetts.

J. W. OCKER
Nashua, New Hampshire
Salem, Massachusetts

1

WELCOME TO WITCH CITY

A spell had been spoken. Trees had begun to change from Earth-green to Martian-red and Sun-yellow, and they were throwing their leaves down in multi-colored carpets as though preparing for the entrance of some grand royalty. The temperature had dropped to near-winter as crowds of ghosts passed through, rendering the whole land a gigantic cold spot and dispelling any lingering traces of sweaty summer. Monsters had awakened. They cavorted across television screens and down store aisles. They clung to the lawns and facades of otherwise cozy, normal-looking houses. And a countdown to an ancient holiday had started.

I doubt I was the first in New England to utter that magic set of syllables: "It's October 1st!" But when I did that morning in my home in southern New Hampshire, the spell transported me fifty miles away to a place full of magic: Salem, Massachusetts.

I was standing on Chestnut Street, a magnificent stretch of downtown Salem lined by mansions built by wealthy sea captains and merchants in the early eighteenth century. Beside me stood Lindsey, who held our eighteen-month-old Hazel in her arms. Beside her was my other daughter, Esme, two months shy of six years old. She wore an orange shirt with a black cat on it.

A few months earlier, Chestnut Street had been described to me as "one of the prettiest streets of any city, rivaling those of Charleston." I think I agree, with the big difference being that the owners of these stately and historic homes didn't seem to be vying for magazine photo spreads like the tidy homes of Charleston. Chestnut Street seemed lived in. Welcoming, even. Like it wore its history in its bricks and its boards and was okay with the camera catching its wrinkles.

It was move-in day. For the next thirty-one days, we would be Salemites.

Driving in, I hadn't seen an official "Welcome to Salem" sign. The warren of crowded streets that is the city of Peabody just seemed to give way to the warren of crowded streets that is the city of Salem. Other entrances to the city have them—plain, white "Entering Salem" signs that are a far cry from the arch of giant, crossed broomsticks one might expect. But then we saw our first witch. It was a black-clad, green-faced creature with a ratty shock of yellow hair that matched the bristles of the broom she rode. Instead of a wand, she waved a cone of vanilla soft-serve in her hand. She was on the sign of a sixty-year-old ice cream shop called the Dairy Witch. Its tagline was not, unfortunately, "Colder Than a Witch's Teat."

Soon after, it became even more obvious that we had crossed the border into Witch City, as every pole bloomed with orange and green banners, each bearing an ornate black silhouette of a Halloween witch.

This wasn't my first time in Salem. That had been back in October 2004. I was living in my home state of Maryland and was taking a solo road trip of the northeast, hitting spots like Sleepy Hollow, New York, and Providence, Rhode Island. Anywhere that it felt right to be during the autumn season. I only spent a few hours of that trip in Witch City, but it was long enough for something to take root.

I visited again in October 2007. This time I was living in Virginia and was doing a similar autumn road trip, and now I was traveling with Lindsey. Again, the stop was only for a few hours. The year after that, we moved to New England and have made it to Salem maybe twice a year, with one of those visits always in October.

Even so, across all those visits, we had barely done Salem. Our time in Salem was always casual. We were there to waft in its ambiance. But this October, our visit would be different. This time, it would be immersive. This time, we would take advantage of all that it offers. This time, we would risk getting sick of it. And this time, we would see it on Halloween itself.

But it almost didn't happen. Six months before October, everything was booked. Not solid, but to the point of being of no help to me. I tried the few hotels downtown, B&Bs, executive rentals, short-term-lease apartments, vacation rentals, private homes on sharing websites. Certainly, I had constraints. I needed a large chunk of nights that extended over extremely popular weekends. I needed room for my family. It had to be affordable during a time when rates surge. It had to be so close to downtown that the smell of incense from all the Witch shops could buzz me to sleep at bedtime. And I needed it for Halloween night.

I eventually got extremely lucky and was able to piece together a stay across two amazing properties that somehow fit all of my above criteria.

Our digs for the first half of the month came by way of a man dressed as Nathaniel Hawthorne and a puppy with a broken hip.

During the summer, Lindsey and I went on a Nathaniel Hawthorne–themed tour of the city led by Nathaniel Hawthorne himself. Or, a man playing him. The guy's real name was Rob Velella, and I knew him from my previous book, a geographical biography of Edgar Allan Poe called *Poe-Land*. Velella also performs as America's favorite emo author. He's a guy that likes to multi-purpose a moustache.

A friend of his named Jennifer was also on the tour. She lived in Salem. We became cool, and later, when she and her husband Nic needed somebody to watch their puppy Ernie after he broke his hip and couldn't be boarded during their vacation, he came to our house for a week. At some point during the arrangement-making process, our housing predicament came up.

"Hold on," Jennifer said.

Minutes later she'd found us a place to stay for the first half of October with her neighbors, Marshall and Elaine. On beautiful, old Chestnut Street. Marshall owned a business downtown, and his wife Elaine worked there as well, in addition to serving on the board of Historic Salem, an architectural preservation group. The pair moved to Witch City from Washington, D.C., in 2001.

Even if Marshall and Elaine had hated everyone they met, it still might have been worth moving to Salem for their house alone. Their 9,000-square-foot, three-story Federal mansion was built around 1808 by a merchant named Nathan Robinson. The house was huge, blocky, and white, with an impossible-seeming number of windows in its facade. They graciously gave us a suite at the back of the house. More than that, they took a personal interest in the project, and we became friends.

Our home for the second half of October was an old black house divided into two apartments right on Essex Street. Our neighbors there would include Salem Harbor, the Salem Maritime National Historic Site, and The House of the Seven Gables. We were steps away from the streak of blood running across the uneven bricks of the city's sidewalks that is the Salem Heritage Trail. A white historical placard on the side of the house read, "Old Frye Building. Moved here in 1854." It looked like it had been slotted into an empty space, as its side wall faced the road and its front door was about ten feet from the back wall of another house.

It was from these two home bases, which book-ended the downtown area on the west and east sides, respectively, that we explored Salem. After we settled in on the morning of October 1, the first thing I did was crack open the city's "Haunted Happenings" brochure. It was a sixty-page booklet with maps, visitor information, restaurant and attraction advertisements, and a daily schedule of events. On its cover was a man dressed as a furry white demon with horns that the brochure named Lucifer. Events and attractions were scheduled for every single day of October. And almost all of them had the word *haunted* in their names. There was a haunted movie series, a haunted magic show, a haunted street fair, a haunted dinner theater. A Halloween Boo's cruise. Ghost hunts. A Devil's Chase 6.66-mile run. There were the types of events you'd expect anybody to throw around Halloween: pumpkin carving and face painting and apple pressing demonstrations. And there were also a surprising number of macabre theater shows throughout the month, including a musical based on *The Texas Chain Saw Massacre*, a play based on H. P. Lovecraft's story "The Thing on the Doorstep," *The Rocky Horror Picture Show* (of course), and an all-male drag parody called *Golden Girls Live On Stage! The Lost Halloween Episode*. Then there were extremely Salem events such as live séances and magic circles, psychic fairs, and Witch workshops. And lots of places to hear ghost stories told in old, spooky locations. Also an appearance by Molly Ringwald a couple towns over in Lynn.

It was exciting and depressing. No way was I getting to it all, not when I added up all the other sites and attractions I needed to visit, all the people I needed to meet, all the Halloween cocktails I needed to sample, and all the days lost to passing out on the couch from exhaustion.

We spent the rest of the day stocking up on provisions and figuring out the general lay of the land from our Chestnut Street vantage point. Mostly, though, we were killing time until dusk, when the Halloween Parade would start.

That's right. Salem throws a Halloween parade on October 1. That's how Halloween the place is. They call it the Haunted Happenings Grand

Parade. We met at Marshall's office downtown, and he and Elaine showed us a good spot on Washington Street from which to catch it.

It was the parade's twentieth anniversary, and thousands lined the route despite the threat of rain. The parade started out innocently enough, with all the usual townie fanfare. Fire engines and dance academies and high school bands. Junior ROTC. Karate dojos. Bagpipe players. That one guy from every city who dresses as Batman and has built his own Batmobile.

It soon became obvious this was no mere civic parade, though. Covens of Witches marched. A darling school group gathered behind a banner touting Witchcraft Heights Elementary School. The Salem High School mascot lumbered by—an ugly, warty, top-heavy witch. And the audience was lined with children in costumes, participating in an inversion of trick-or-treating where the people walking the parade route handed out candy to the sessile kids.

As the night progressed, the parade shifted from PG to R, with zombies and demons and other monsters joining the celebration. Hockey goalie–masked Jason Voorhees dragged a human-shaped mass of plastic and duct tape behind him on the asphalt. A hearse drove past, its strobe-

Haunted Happenings Grand Parade

lit interior revealing in quick flashes fiends of all faces. A masked asylum nurse faced off with a passerby who tried to cross the parade route. A spectral, robed creature on stilts glided slowly past with no acknowledgment that it was in a parade.

The theme of the Halloween parade was world peace. After all, the literal meaning of Salem is "peace." And that, of course, allowed for delightful moments when trucks decorated like yellow submarines or flower-bedecked VW vans with mechanical bubble blowers were followed by bleeding zombies screaming from cages or tentacle-faced fiends feigning attacks at bystanders. After all, the modern meaning of Salem is "spooky."

This was our scene for the next thirty days. And all because of 1692?

It all felt so strange. And not just that we were at a massive Halloween parade on October 1. It was because I knew that, as soon as the police motorcycles roared past to end the parade, we would walk a few blocks to somebody else's beds and then wake up and do it again. That, were we so inclined, we could dress every day in a different Halloween costume, and it would be OK. That we had a month's worth of experiences ahead of us, each day of which would be haunted by ghosts and monsters and tourists and, of course, witches.

I was both excited and worried by the proposition.

On the one Hand of Glory, I love Halloween. I celebrate it as a season as opposed to a single evening, a season that starts on the first cool day in September (even earlier than Salem's) and which ends when all the jack-o'-lantern souls are doused on Halloween night. I love that every candy aisle in every store is suddenly a carnage of gummy body parts and chocolate grotesques. I love the way round orange pumpkins and tall yellow cornstalks become the dots and dashes of the season's Morse code. I love how we find the colors of decay suddenly beautiful as the leaves die in conflagrations around us. I love that horror movies are on every channel and in every theater. I love that haunted house attractions exist. I love Bing Crosby singing about the Headless Horseman and Michael Jackson dancing with zombies. I love how the carefully tended lawns of spring and summer yield foam tombstones and plastic skeletons in the fall. And, of course, even though they were left out of the *Monster Mash*, I've always loved a good Halloween witch. Or an evil one.

So spending the Halloween season in a place like Salem could mean that this Halloween was going to be the best I'd ever experienced.

On the other Monkey's Paw, I was worried I might be repulsed by Salem after this experiment. After all, Disney World is a blast, but at some point you've bumped into one too many adults in felt ears or seen one too many registered trademark symbols stamped into plastic or realized that inside that jovial-looking Pluto costume is a sweaty college kid having an existential crisis. You give that too much thought and things can get uncomfortable. And I was about to give Salem a lot of thought.

We made it back to our temporary Chestnut digs before the rainstorm hit, giving us the perfect ambiance in which to finish off the night with the tail end of a Stephen King movie marathon on AMC—although *Salem's Lot* was, unfortunately, not on the playlist.

The next day was Friday, October 2, when we would start Salem, and our odd October, in earnest.

2

ON A WITCH HUNT

Parsonage Site

I was standing in a small grassy yard flecked with fallen leaves and encircled by a rustic wooden fence. One either side of me was a square hole, each about forty feet long, twenty feet wide, four feet deep, and lined with stones. It was as if some giant with a cloven hoof had stamped the ground around me.

Esme had jumped down into one of the holes and was playing with a rock, and Hazel was tottering at the edge of the other. The blue historical sign nearby called the humble little spot "one of the most important sites in Colonial American history."

It was our first full day in Salem, and we were treading on a lot of ghosts.

This was it—it, it, it—the exact spot where the Salem Witch Trials all started. In this small area no bigger than a back yard. The holes were the excavated foundation of the local parsonage, one being the foundation of the original 1681 parsonage and the other a 1734 addition. Right. The Devil entered Salem through a minister's house.

Samuel Parris was a businessman before he found himself a distressed spiritual leader in the middle of a distressing spiritual warfare. And perhaps even the catalyst for it. In the books, he's sometimes characterized as a disillusioned businessman for whom pastorhood was a fallback occupation. Other times, he's portrayed as a man returning to God's service, the thing he always wanted to do before his father's death pushed him out of school and into the family business.

He was born in London and came to Boston to matriculate at Harvard. When his father died, he left school to take over the family plantation in Barbados, where Parris had spent his youth. Eventually, he returned to Boston and continued in business, but soon decided to join the cloth instead of selling bolts of it.

He arrived in Salem in the summer of 1688. He was in his mid-thirties and was taking a troublesome position that had been held by three others over the previous fifteen years, troublesome because the village, like many other Puritan communities, was often divided to the point of lawsuits over the choice and pay grade of its minister. Nevertheless, into that two-story parsonage, the foundation of which my family was exploring more than three hundred years later, he moved his household. Its members were his wife Elizabeth; his three young children Thomas, Betty, and Susannah; his orphaned niece Abigail Williams; and their slaves, among them two Native Americans named John and Tituba.

Three and half years later, in January of 1692, Betty and Abigail, nine and eleven years old respectively at this point, were playing a fortune-telling game in the house. They dropped an egg white into a glass of water, possibly looking for the blob to coalesce into a shape that would predict the occupation of their future husbands.

But what they saw lava-lamping in that albumen terrified them: a coffin. Neither, it seemed, wanted to marry an undertaker. They began acting strangely, contorting into weird shapes, dropping lifelessly to the ground, becoming unable to speak or speaking only in unintelligible syllables, screaming over pangs and tortures from invisible tormentors. Weeks later, their condition was unchanged, if strangely inconstant, so Parris took them to the local physician. Dr. William Griggs diagnosed them as "under an evil hand." And this evil hand was a busy one. Whatever afflicted those two girls then caught on with more of the town's girls and some if its adults. These afflicted would go on to accuse more than 150 people of Satanic shenanigans and cause the death of 20 of them—more if you count those who died in prison. All because of a bit of raw egg and the principles of chaos theory.

But the parsonage site is important for other reasons, too. It was once the home of a Witch Trials victim. George Burroughs was the community's second minister. He left town after a few financial arguments with members of his flock. He was seventy miles away in Wells, Maine, when the trials started. But he was remembered, accused, dragged back, tried, and executed. The minister who directly preceded Parris, Deodat Lawson, also lived there. He would go on to write the first of about 1.7 billion published accounts of the Salem Witch Trials, although one of only a few that were firsthand.

It is also where a neighbor and respected member of the community, Mary Sibley, tried to do some magic of her own to help the two afflicted children. While the parents were away and with the help of the Parris family's slave, John, she took urine from the two girls and baked it into a cake on the parsonage hearth. They then fed it to the family dog. When Parris learned of the countermagic, he was apoplectic, publicly chastising Sibley in front of the church and writing in the church record book that, "The Devil hath been raised among us," as if the children's odd behavior was a mere knocking, and Sibley's witch cake had thrown the door wide open.

The site almost has more importance to the trials than its small size can contain. Tituba, one of the family slaves, also lived there, and it was she, maybe more than any other person, whose acts caused what should have been an unfortunate but small-scale American witch trial to escalate into the most infamous of them all.

Tituba was one of the original three people accused by the children in

February, the other two being Sarah Good and Sarah Osborne. All three women were easy targets due to their low status in the community, but Tituba was particularly vulnerable because she had a sheen of the exotic about her. She was Native American, possibly from Barbados. More than likely she had captivated Abigail and Betty and other girls in the village with some New World mojo to pass a boring night or two, so it was natural for some of the girls to throw blame at her, perhaps out of intense Puritan guilt for their sinful curiosity. However, when Tituba was questioned at the local meetinghouse, she, alone of the three woman, readily admitted to being a witch. More than that, she named names, described occult ceremonies and demonic strategies, and laid out the creaky skeleton of a dark conspiracy to infiltrate the God-fearing community that would serve as the template for the Salem witch mythology going forward.

She also, alone of those three women, survived the trials. That was generally the way it went. Admit to being a witch and you were useful to the crusade and had a chance at redemption. Deny it and be purged from the community, life itself, and any hope of God's kingdom. A little rope goes a long way.

But in the end—or, I should say, in the beginning—it was two girls

Salem Village Witchcraft Victims' Memorial

and a winter night. That's how it started. All of it. The atrocity. The tragedy. The horror. All culminating centuries later in the modern phenomenon of Witch City. Right on the spot where my two girls were playing.

Except that we weren't in Witch City. We were next door, in Danvers, about five miles north of Salem. Its nickname is Oniontown.

The Witch Trials started in Danvers, and half the story takes place there. Actually, the Witch Trials of 1692 took place all over Essex County. Victims were accused in many of the surrounding towns. If you ever find yourself in Topsfield, about ten miles north of Salem, head to its common, where you'll find a boulder engraved with the names of Mary Easty, Elizabeth Howe, and Sarah Wildes, all hanged in Salem for being witches. The stone was covered with hundreds of little, green inchworms on our visit, exactly as a witch memorial should be. In Marblehead's Old Burial Hill is a tombstone-shaped cenotaph dedicated to Wilmot Redd, another victim. Her memorial lies on the shores of a pond named in her honor, a pond where, when we visited, locals were racing remote-controlled sailboats for the spectator gravestones.

In Amesbury, a good thirty miles north of Salem, at the end of a cul-de-sac on North Martin Road, is a stone inset with a plaque that once marked the house of Susanna Martin, "an honest, hardworking Christian woman accused as a witch, tried, and executed at Salem, July 19, 1692. A martyr of superstition." We pulled up to the memorial, and within three minutes, a man exited a neighboring house and approached us. His name was Jim, and he assumed that we were descendants of Martin. I went with that.

He dutifully handed us a pair of stapled pages. It was a letter from an author named Stephen Hawley Martin who had written a book about Susanna Martin. It was addressed to the "Keeper of the Stone." That was Jim. Jim told me he pressure-washed it, trimmed the grass around it, and cleaned up any offerings left there. "Except the coins. The neighborhood kids usually grab those." He told us people come at all hours to place flowers and shocks of corn on Martin's memorial. "I know because they always set off my motion lights."

The letter claimed that the author was Martin's seven-times-great grandson and asked Jim to point interested parties to his book, *A Witch in the Family*. It also mentioned that the stone wasn't in its original place, but had been moved when the interstate was built.

The town of Andover got it the worst, as far as the number of accused goes, and had a mini–witch trial within the Salem Witch Trials. More people were accused of witchcraft there during the Witch Trials than in any other town in Essex County, and three of the people executed were from Andover. Andover also bears the strange distinction of being home to the only surviving gravestone of a person whose death was directly attributed to witchcraft in the trials. Most of the afflicted escaped with only pin-pricks and minor bites. Timothy Swan was thirty when he died, tortured to death by demons, if the accusers were correct. His gravestone is in the Old Burial Ground in North Andover.

So there are traces of the Salem Witch Trials all over the North Shore. But Danvers has much, much more than just traces. And that's because, in the seventeenth century, Danvers was Salem. Or at least part of it. Just not a very well incorporated part of it.

Salem was a bifurcated community at the time of the trials. The area known today as Danvers was called Salem Village back then, and it was the backwoods of Salem. They had about five hundred people at the time, mostly farmers. The downtown area on the coast, Salem Town, is what grew into modern-day Salem. About 1,500 people lived in Salem Town during the time of the trials. It was a place of merchants and seamen.

The geographical and economic divisions caused a lot of friction between the two Salem communities, a friction that many consider the most important element in precipitating the Witch Trials. The residents of Salem Village watched their neighbors filling their hands with gold from trade while their own were merely dirty from farming. They were more susceptible to attacks from natives because they were closer to the wilderness, yet they still had to send their men five to ten miles away for security details in town. It took them a long time to even get their own church so that they wouldn't have to trek those same miles every week for services. Salem Village wanted to be its own community, but Salem Town didn't want to lose the taxes the village paid nor lessen the area of the town, so Salem Village stayed a part, if a marginalized and unwilling part, of Salem.

Today, Danvers is a town of twenty-five thousand people, but history is thick there, especially Witch Trials history. Many houses with direct connections to the trials still stand in its neighborhoods. Graves of trial participants dot its cemeteries. The First Church of Danvers traces its lineage back to the original village church. The town erected a Witch Trials monument. And, of course, it has the parsonage excavation site.

But the first site I visited in Danvers, months before we moved to Salem, was the local Danvers library. I needed to talk to a man named Richard Trask.

There are a lot of Salem Witch Trial experts. A lot. But there is only one Richard Trask. Born and raised in Danvers, and tracing his lineage back to two Witch Trial victims, he's been the town archivist since 1972, overseeing original manuscripts and public records and books, including the largest collection of printed materials on the Witch Trials in the country. He pointed them out as we sat down at a table together in the imposing Georgian Revival building where he works—lots of spines with the words *witch* or *devil* blaring boldly from them, almost like I was in the library's horror section. He's also been extremely active in preserving and commemorating the lessons and legacy of the trials in a town that has traditionally preferred silence to memorialization.

Interestingly enough, he became the town archivist by suggesting that the city create the position. In graduate school, he undertook a study on how to develop Danvers's historic assets. He recommended a number of things, from preserving certain houses to establishing a historic district to creating an archival center. The city followed his recommendations and created the archival center. And then Trask took the position of archivist.

"It was really about historical preservation. And in those days I was extremely idealistic. I didn't think money was important and figured that people would cooperate to establish an archive, which even today is somewhat unusual for a New England community, which tend to avoid pooling historical assets. They like to be possessive of their own stuff, even if they can't take care of it. But it just so happened that the stars were right and a number of institutions and agencies in Danvers were willing to do something that at another time they might not have been."

That included the town clerk handing over public records and the First Church depositing its archives there. Now, the Danvers Archival Center holds both public and private records as well as artifacts, including about a dozen gravestones that have made their way to the surface of people's yards over the years. Like I said, thick with history.

For the longest time, the two words that sprang to my mind when I heard the name Danvers weren't "witch trials." They were "insane asylum." Before I'd learned about Danvers's previous incarnation as Salem, my only knowledge of the area was that it was the location of the infamous Danvers State Insane Asylum, a massive, elegant, red-brick building erected in 1878 to house the unfortunate of mind and condition. The Danvers State Insane Asylum was a Kirkbride building, meaning it was designed according to principles of therapy, developed by psychiatrist Thomas Story Kirkbride, in which the very architecture of the hospital and the lay of the surrounding land contributed to healing. That philosophy yielded awe-inspiring castles crammed with the sick and indigent. By the early 1990s, the Danvers institution had been abandoned after a slow death due to financial problems and lack of support from both the local and medical communities. Since then, the asylum has been razed and resurrected as condos, although its facade has been preserved, as has the asylum cemetery. I asked Trask about the place.

"For decades it loomed above Route 1 on a hill up there for everyone to see, so it became somewhat famous. The hill, by the way, was owned by the father of one of the witchcraft judges, John Hathorne." Today, the signs still call it Hathorne Hill. "Marion Starkey, when she wrote *The Devil in Massachusetts* in 1949, called the hospital a fitting memorial to the witchcraft." *The Devil in Massachusetts: A Modern Inquiry into the Salem Witch Trials* was the first modern book on the Witch Trials, and it jumpstarted an international interest in the trials that hasn't waned, most notably inspiring Arthur Miller's *The Crucible*. Her exact description of the asylum was, "an unintended but highly appropriate monument to the whole sorry business."

"Tell me about the excavation of the parsonage," I said. "That was 1970, right? Two years before you were the town archivist."

"Yes. The parsonage was, again, during a time when I was wet behind the ears. I'd read books on archeology and thought it'd be great to find ground zero of the witchcraft."

Trask had this great habit of calling everything about the Salem Witch Trials "witchcraft." In doing so, whether on purpose or not, he sidestepped all the baggage that comes with such phrases as "Witch Trials" or "Witch Hysteria" or "Witch Delusion" or "Witch Panic" or the half dozen other phrases I've heard that attempt to describe the events of 1692 in a way that is both accurate and evocative. The word *witch* itself has become a shorthand term for the victims, even though its use seems to place us on the wrong side of the tragedy. But there's no real way out of this one that isn't contrived. To use the term *witch* is to give too much credit to the accusers and judges. To leave it out somehow misses the dark, shameful soul of the proceedings. The word also just plain gets attention.

"I wrote to a man named Roland Robbins," Trask continued. "He was a window washer who had taught himself archeology, so he was controversial in academic circles. I didn't know it, though. I just knew that he was the guy who discovered important historical sites—the remains of Thoreau's house at Walden Pond, the Saugus Ironworks, Thomas Jefferson's birthplace. I just asked him to come, and he did. It was the start of a three-year project."

And it was a successful three-year project. The site they uncovered was located on private property, but the owner, who was a descendant of Witch Trial victim Rebecca Nurse, was happy to let Trask and friends dig up his backyard. In the end, they uncovered tens of thousands of artifacts, from shards of pottery to pipe stems.

Somewhere around 1990 the town bought the land property and made it a mini-park open to the public. But as amazing as the site is—and it's certainly worthy of the "one of the most important sites in Colonial American history" designation—not many people get to it. That's partly because when people go to Salem, they go to Salem. But it's also because the excavation is hidden behind a residential neighborhood. To access it, we had to locate a small path on Centre Street between two houses.

Even with the small blue sign that directed us down the path ("Samuel Parris Archeological Site, 1681-1784, Vehicles Excluded, Pass at Your Own Risk"), it felt like we were trespassing. A few hesitant steps down the path placed us under the watchful windows of the houses on either side, while the staccato clucks of chickens from an incongruous coop in one of the yards seemed to be warnings of some sort. Soon, though, the path opened onto the grassy area with the holes where we had started our day.

In addition, somewhere in that general area is the site where the black masses were supposed to have been held by the witches of Salem, out in one of Samuel Parris's pastures.

In the mythology that the accusers and confessors communally improvised on the boards of the meetinghouse and the stones of the jails, Satan was a dark man in a high, crowned hat who would force men and women to sign a book in their own blood. Old Scratch would get his human servants to astrally project themselves into the bedrooms of honest men and women to torture them into selling their souls. The ghostly witches would torment their victims every night with pinches and pricks. They would sit on their chests and suffocate the victims like succubi and incubi or soar them above the housetops like they were one of Dickens's ghosts. If the victim turned to the dark side, they got what their heart desired as well as some magical powers—like the ability to turn into animals and monsters—but not powers that did anything against prison bars, shackles, and nooses. They did gain a hidden nipple that could be used to feed blood to their animal familiars, though. Their specters were also somehow vulnerable to walking sticks and blades, which the villagers swung blindly in the direction of the afflicted girls. Led by the Puritan minister/Satanic priest George Burroughs, the witches gathered in Parris's pasture, hundreds at a time, flying on sticks and poles to get together and eat fleshy red bread and drink coppery red wine and plot a takeover of this new world with its vulnerable Christian souls doing the Lord's work in God's country.

A block away from the parsonage site, on Hobart Street, is the Salem Village Witchcraft Victims Memorial. The memorial is a large, sarcophagus-size block of granite topped by an open Book of Life with metal manacles on either side. It looks like a pulpit. If that's the case, its congregation is a set of upright stone slabs topped by a stylized image of a male Puritan. Their "amens" would be the desperate, heroic cacophony of quotes from the victims etched into the slabs:

"Well! Burn me or hang me, I will stand in the truth of Christ," says George Jacobs.

"If it was the last moment I was to live, God knows I am innocent," says Elizabeth Howe.

"The Magistrates, Ministers, Jewries, and the People in general, being so much inraged and incensed against us by the Delusion of the Devil, which we can term no other, by reason we know in our own Consciences, we are all Innocent Persons," says John Proctor, earning himself a starring role in Arthur Miller's *The Crucible*.

The memorial was dedicated in 1992, the 300th anniversary of the Witch Trials, and is located directly across the street from where the Salem Village meetinghouse actually stood. In the very meetinghouse that held all the preliminary questionings before the trials moved downtown in June and became deadly. It was on that spot that Tituba described the Satanic side of Salem in such vivid detail. Where judges Hathorne and Corwin played bad cop/bad cop with the accused. Where Abigail Williams saw a phantom Martha Corey in the rafters suckling a demonic yellow bird between her fingers. Six of the eight statements of terrified defiance etched into the memorial were spoken on that spot.

Today that spot is lined by houses, and I can only assume that the residents are unable to forget the history that their foundations press down upon. Every time they look out of their front windows, they see a Puritan behind a pulpit condemning them.

Trask, of course, had a part in the memorial. He and a woman named Marjorie Wetzel fundraised for it and corralled a local architect named Robert Farley to help design it. The original plan was to erect it at the parsonage excavation, but that the site wasn't prominent enough.

"One day I was walking to work down Hobart Street," Trask said. "I looked across the street from the former site of the meetinghouse and saw a nice, flat area. It was so obvious that the memorial should go there. Later, I discovered that when the meetinghouse was no longer functioning, around 1702, they actually moved it across the street to the location of the present-day monument, where it stood for about 10 years before it fell down. The phrase used in the records was, 'decayed and became mixed with the soil.' So I just thought, 'Wow.'" They dedicated it on the day that the first witchcraft victim died, which was in jail. Three thousand people attended the ceremony.

At the intersection of Hobart and Centre Streets, directly between the parsonage site and the memorial, are two more Witch Trials sites. One is the current incarnation of the First Church of Danvers, which traces its lineage back to the church of the Witch Trials. The pastor that replaced Parris moved the congregation to this spot from the meetinghouse site. At the back of the sanctuary in the current building is a plaque in memory of George Burroughs, the only minister executed as a witch at the trials.

On the other side of the street, at 199 Hobart, is a private home that dates back to the trials and was, at the time, a tavern and inn called Ingersoll's Ordinary, where some of the hearings took place and where participants and visitors gathered throughout the questioning for food and drink. Ingersoll's made a nice little profit off the hearings, a fitting precedent for modern-day Witch City.

Next, we drove to some of the minor Danvers Witch Trials sites. We saw the homes of victims, like that of the aforementioned Sarah Osbourne, who died in jail before she could be tried. The homes of accusers, like those of Sarah Holten and Thomas Haines, the latter of which is the current home of Richard Trask and his wife, who spent twenty years restoring the place. The homes of surviving accused, like that of Sarah Bishop (no relation to Bridget Bishop, who wasn't as fortunate). Most of the houses are private residences today.

We also hit a couple of graveyards, mostly because I can't pass up an old New England graveyard, but also because so few of the final resting places of the trials' main participants are known today. We visited the Wadsworth Burying Ground on Summer Street just to see the tombstone of Samuel Parris's wife, Elizabeth, who died three years after the trials. Although her family's part in the trials was huge, her role seems nonexistent (at least according to available records), as do those of her other two children, who seemed immune to whatever ailed their sister and cousin. Her gravestone was small, with the classic New England winged skull on it. The epitaph was composed by her husband, who signed the bottom of the stone with his initials.

We went to the Putnam Family Cemetery. Almost every graveyard in Danvers is full of Putnams, and the family figures prominently in the Witch Trials. When you read about the subplot of the trials being used as a means of stealing land and as vengeance for old disputes, it's the Putnams that you're mostly reading about. Their surname was all over the court filings. Twelve-year old Ann Putnam was one of the afflicted, as was her mother, also named Ann. Thomas Putnam, the head of the household, pressed charges like they were buttons on a free vending machine. Witch hunting was a family business for them for a while. However, Ann Junior stands out among the accusers for a heartbreaking statement of apology she wrote a decade and a half after the trials to be read before the church. She was one of the few involved who would publically show remorse, as most people wanted to forget the whole debacle or blame the scapegoat-horned Devil for fooling them all.

The graveyard is adjacent to a Massachusetts state police station, up an unmarked path into a small wood. Right—a copse of corpses beside the cops. The graves of Ann, Ann, and Thomas are also unmarked. A hump of earth in the corner to the left as you enter is all that's left of their graves, which is still more than most of the Witch Trial victims ever received.

We had one more stop in Danvers, an important stop, but first we hit a few small but potent memorials in nearby Peabody. Peabody was also originally a part of Salem.

To get to Salem on Route 128 North, you'll take exit 26 at Peabody. The ramp off that exit deposits you at an intersection across from a short stone fence with a sign that says, "1821, Proctor's Tomb." I had taken this exit over the years without paying it much mind, but this time my wife dropped me off nearby, wishing me luck as I Froggered across the busy intersection at Lowell Street and dove onto the median on the other side of the wall. There, marking Proctor's tomb, was a large rectangular block . . . with nothing at all inscribed on it. It was a bit of a letdown, especially since the sign bore the surname of one of the more famous of the Salem Witch Trials' victims.

When John Proctor was accused, it made the mob pick at their pitch-fork tines uncomfortably. He was wealthy and well-connected but somehow completely vulnerable to the writhing of the young girls of the village. And I don't mean that in a *The Crucible* kind of way. It's one of the reasons the Salem Witch Trials are touted as unique among witch trials. Everybody was vulnerable, no matter their reputation or station or location. You're a covenanted church member? Accused. A minster? Accused. The wife of the governor of the state? Accused. Proctor's body was thrown in the crevice on Gallows Hill like the rest of the victims. Also, like the bodies of many of the victims, his was supposed to have been rescued under cover of night by family to be buried anonymously and respectfully on his own land. Which today is a median on an off-ramp.

We found more of the story to the west down Lowell Street, which parallels Proctor Brook for a ways. There, on Quinn Square, is a stone inset with a plaque dedicated to John Proctor. The memorial was placed in 1902 near where his home would have been and then replaced in 1992.

The short tribute to him ends with the phrase, "A Martyr to the Truth." That truth, of course, being a strange one: I am not a witch.

Memorials to two more martyrs to that very same strange truth can be found even further west down Lowell Street, on the edge of Crystal Pond. There, a lonely pair of matching gravestone-like slabs stand. They commemorate Giles and Martha Corey. His memorial calls him, "Irascible, Unyielding." Hers, "Pious, Outspoken." Martha was hanged, but Giles, well, he's the number twenty you hear whenever somebody stutters between nineteen and twenty when they're talking about the number of Witch Trials victims. That's because the eighty-year-old Giles wasn't convicted, nor was he hanged. He was crushed—pressed for information.

Because he wouldn't enter a plea of either guilty or not guilty to being a witch, they tried to induce one by dropping him in a pit on his back, laying a board across him, and slowly placing heavy stones on his chest. And that's "slowly" as in "for two days." But instead of lobbing a plea, Giles's famous reply was, "more weight." It's said that as his tongue lolled out of his mouth, the sheriff poked it back in with his walking stick, the better for him to confess with. Eventually, the stones broke his rib cage and flattened his vital organs. They categorized his death as a suicide. It's often

Giles and Martha Corey Memorials

considered one of the more powerful of the many heroic last stands of the Witch Trial victims.

But here's one place of too many where the Witch Trials get murky.

Before he was a martyr who refused to acknowledge the validity of the trials, he was an accuser . . . of his own wife. That's how much of a mess the trials were. John Hale, a Beverly minister with firsthand experience at the trials, wrote later that, "We walked in the clouds and could not see our way." Accusers became accused, accused became accusers, neighbors and families turned on each other, husbands against wives, grandchildren against grandparents—humans became inhuman to become godly. And Giles is a great example of the thin line between villain and victim. His highest achievement before accusing Martha of kissing Satan's behind had been beating a servant to death. Nevertheless, he and his wife have quaint memorials on the banks of an idyllic little pond full of swans, like the matching gravestones of a loving couple who lived to an old age and died peacefully in bed surrounded by their progeny.

Everything we saw throughout our day in ex-Salem was passive. Memorials, private homes, gravestones, as if the items just popped up while nobody was looking and are content to continue being overlooked. But last on our list is the only site in Danvers actually run as a tourist attraction, although "run," "tourist," and "attraction" are all loose words for the Rebecca Nurse Homestead.

When we pulled into the grassy field that was the homestead parking lot, there were only two or three other cars present. Around us, the handful of rustic buildings on the property seemed deserted, except for a single man sitting in a camp chair and flinging a dirty tennis ball from a plastic, wand-like launcher for an energetic Labrador to retrieve.

We wandered uncertainly toward the buildings.

"Can I help you?" The man with the launcher asked, slinging the ratty green sphere high in the air with a jerk of his wrist.

"We wanted to see the homestead," I said, uncertain of what exactly it was that I was asking for.

"Okay. You can wander around for free, but if you want to go inside the buildings, you'll need to pay admission. Candace is leading a tour right now, so just poke your head around the house over there so she knows you're here."

It was an extremely down-home greeting. I looked at the cars in the field/parking lot to make sure they bore New England tags.

I angled toward the house to do what he said, but Esme piped up. "Can I throw that to your dog?"

"Sure."

"What's his name?"

"Bear."

Esme does this a lot. Her favorite hobby is placing me in awkward situations with strangers by being the outgoing person that I'm not. This time, though, it was fortuitous. The man's name was Don Perry, and he was the president of the Rebecca Nurse Homestead. I'd actually exchanged a few tentative emails with him over the summer.

The Rebecca Nurse Homestead was the home of one of the victims of the Witch Trials. Rebecca is the woman whose accusation changed the entire tenor of the trials. The first few were easy targets. John Proctor and George Burroughs hadn't yet been accused. Nurse, however, was a seventy-one-year-old covenanted church member who everybody respected. She was actually found not guilty at first, but the verdict was reconsidered at the request of one of the judges. When she was accused, everybody started getting worried. When she was convicted, everybody started getting scared. And when she was hanged, the world turned officially upside-down. It meant the noose fit everyone's throats. Thirty-nine people signed a petition attesting to her non-witchiness. But the Putnams, long before they were the hill of dirt I walked across, had been in land disputes with her family for a while and pushed what was already a wildly careening machine in her direction.

The Nurse homestead was settled in 1678 and turned into a museum in 1909. Over the years, the lot dwindled from 300 acres to its current 16 acres, and it has been run by various organizations. Today, it's kept by a group of Revolutionary War reenactors, the Danvers Alarm List Company, one of the founding members of which was, naturally, Richard Trask, who also acted as the site's curator for twenty years.

While we waited near a small gift shop building, Perry quizzed me on a few things to see how good my research was. "Do you know where the real Gallows Hill is?" "What about the former site of Giles Corey's home?" "Have you been to Silly Town yet?" That was his nickname for Salem.

Eventually, he had to take Bear to McDonald's for a cheeseburger, so he turned us over to our tour guide, Candace Clemenzi. Clemenzi was a native of Danvers whose grandparents had been caretakers on the property. "I pretty much got dropped off here as a child, and I've since taken up the mantle," she told me.

Our tour group consisted of my family and two other people. Clemenzi led us first to a dark building that looked pretty old. Except that it wasn't. It dated back to the 1980s. The building was a life-size replica of the Salem Village meetinghouse, something similar in appearance to what would have stood on the spot across from the Danvers Witchcraft Memorial back in the seventeenth century. Inside, it was small, cramped, and topped by a gallery. As Clemenzi talked, I tried to imagine the bitter winters when all that the congregation had to warm themselves with were blankets on their backs, dogs at their feet, and the pastor's hellfire at their faces. Or the children standing in the middle of the building, shaking and screaming and pointing at invisible witches in its rafters.

Next, Clemenzi walked us over to Rebeccas Nurse's home. I asked her a few questions.

"Did I hear Don say that you live on-site?"

"Yes, I'm the resident caretaker. I live over in that part of the Nurse home." She pointed to the far end of the large, red building.

"That sounds sort of awesome."

"This time of year, not so much. We get a lot of people peeking into the windows, knocking on doors, not realizing somebody lives here. It's like living in a fishbowl during October. Can't wait for the month to be over." It's a sentiment I would hear many, many times over the course of the month.

The Rebecca Nurse Homestead may be named after its most famous resident, but the house has been lived in by generations of families and has always had somebody living on the property, up to Clemenzi herself. As a result, the house has been added to over the years. It's now a Frankenstein's monster of time periods, going all the way back to the original 1600s structure. Almost every time we crossed a threshold we were in a different century. In the original portion of the house, Clemenzi walked us through the horrible, horrible life of a colonialist, where strong drink and hope of a better eternity was all that got you through the day. With so many wolves in the woods, even taking a piss at night was a life-threatening act. I'd accuse people of being witches too, if that were my lot in life. Also vampires, space aliens, and ghosts.

After the tour ended, we peeled off, leaving Clemenzi to answer questions from the remaining pair. The section of the homestead I'd been looking forward to the most was the family graveyard. It's near the back of the property, separated from the buildings by a small field. As we walked to it, we passed a family of turkeys picking their way through the tall weeds, seemingly unperturbed that we were a mere two months away from Thanksgiving.

The Nurse rotyard is small and filled with people who lived on the property over the centuries. Rebecca Nurse is believed to be buried at one of the eroded footstones, her body rescued from the unhallowed ground of Gallows Hill. No one's sure about that, of course, but a tall monument in the middle of the graveyard pays her homage and is inscribed with a stanza written by John Greenleaf Whittier specifically for the monument:

O, Christian martyr! who for truth could die,
When all about thee owned the hideous lie!
The world, redeemed from superstition's sway,
Is breathing freer for thy sake today.

Nearby is a smaller stone monument inscribed with the names of the thirty-nine people who valiantly and vainly defended her innocence with a written petition despite overwhelming spectral evidence.

A few steps away from the Rebecca Nurse memorial is a what looks like the usual early New England headstone—thin, slate-like, with a winged skull engraved on the crown. Except that it's almost shiny in its newness. That flat, upright piece of dark stone marks the only known grave of a Witch Trials victim. Maybe. Beneath the grass lie the bones of a person believed to be George Jacobs. It is his final resting place in both senses of the term, the conventional sense and the sense in which it wasn't his first resting place.

And it was there because of Richard Trask. I promise his name rarely comes up in the rest of the book.

George Jacobs was seventy-two when he was given his violent pension on Gallows Hill on August 19, 1962. His story was similar to many of the other Witch Trial victims, although his has good color. Under questioning, he declaimed, "You tax me for a wizard. You may as well tax me for a buzzard." He was also immortalized as the subject of a striking 1855 painting by Thompkins Harrison Matteson, in which Jacobs is depicted deep in the chaos of the court, his granddaughter throwing accusations at him while the poor afflicted are ministered to and the judges look sternly on as if they knew they were posing for a painting.

But where in life he didn't stick out too far from the other Witch Trial victims, Jacob certainly stands out in death. Jacob's bones should be lodged in the soil of Gallows Hill or scattered by carrion creatures or anonymously buried on whatever remains of his family homestead like those of the rest of the Witch Trial victims. However, his afterlife zagged a bit, as sometimes happens with corpses.

Tradition says that Jacob's son did rescue his body and bury it on the family land. Sometime in the 1950s, the land having long since changed hands and the grave lost to posterity, a developer discovered ancient human remains. They were believed to be those of George Jacobs. The bones were placed in a winter crypt at a local cemetery, where bodies wait until the New England ground thaws for a proper burial. However, in Jacobs's case, his bones just took up shelf space since he had no any family to claim him.

In the late 1960s, Trask heard about the remains, so he asked for permission to take photos. While there, the cemetery caretakers pawned off the bones on him. "You like history? Here, take these." So he did. And that's how George Jacobs became Richard Trask's roommate.

"Wait, what? Where did you keep his bones?" I asked him.

"I put them in a glass case that was designed for an antique ship. I had bought it at auction at some point."

"A glass case. Like an exhibit? You exhibited the bones of a Witch Trials victim at your house?"

"Well, they were in my room, so nobody could see them."

"Your bedroom?"

"Yes, my bedroom."

"Sorry if I'm asking too much, but that means every night, you'd see this skeleton before you went to bed?" Trask probably thought I was aghast, but this was the coolest story I'd heard in a while.

"I mean, once you've seen bones, you've seen bones," was his reply.

After a few years, Trask decided that he probably didn't need a dead man in his room anymore, so he tried to figure out how to bury the body. From what he told me, that's apparently really hard to do—lots of red tape to get white bones under green grass.

He did figure it out in time for the 1992 Tercentennial of the Witch Trials, where Jacobs was given a spot of honor in the Nurse graveyard, making the Rebecca Nurse Homestead that much more of an important site for Witch Trials history.

You'd think learning a man harbored historic bones in his bedroom would be the end of the conversation, but I still had one big question to ask Trask, "Why isn't Danvers Witch City?"

"In 1692, Salem Village went through a terrible thing. Like when we went through the Vietnam War. For at least a generation after that war, nobody wanted to talk about it. Most of the accusers came from Salem Village, and a good number of the accused did, too. This was a small community, and there wasn't a person there who wasn't affected personally. When it was over, it was just a traumatic thing that they wanted to forget. Something like that passes through generations."

That shows in the current name of the town. In 1752 they finally became independent of Salem Town after decades of trying. The name they were given had no local connection nor any real meaning: Danvers. Anything, as long as it wasn't Salem. A new name, a new beginning. Salem, to them, was a history best forgotten.

"So you're saying Salem, today's Salem, had a buffer that separated it somewhat from the tragedy of the trials."

"Right. It was a community of 1,500 and didn't have the problem of its entire population being involved. So later they had a way of looking at the witchcraft that made it nonthreatening. And that's why today you get postcards with witches riding on broomsticks. Meanwhile, Danvers was saying, 'Boy, I'm glad that's not happening here.'"

"But even in recent times?"

"When I was growing up in the 1950s, it still wasn't considered proper to talk about the witchcraft. It was thought to be shameful. Every institution had failed in this community, the church, the political system, the courts, and even families." He then gave me an example. The parsonage project attracted national publicity during the excavation, so they started having local school groups coming to witness it and learn the history. Trask was bringing one of those school groups in to see the site when two elderly women across the street—he gave me their names and then asked me not to use them—shook their fists at him and said, "Why are you bringing this up?"

"Is it still that way today?"

"Not so much. I think the turnaround was the parsonage excavation. What we tried to do was focus on the victims, who weren't at all saints, but would still not admit to what over fifty people did admit to in order to avoid execution. Which is heroic, on the parts of just average people. So we tried to celebrate the individual who can take a stand." Trask further explained that the shifting focus, combined with the excitement of archeology—finding something that hadn't been seen or touched in hundreds of years—plus the "titillation" of the supernatural elements of the story finally changed Danvers's policy of blindness to the trials. "Still, I've always liked our position on the witchcraft in that we've been able to play it the pure way. Salem's a commercial venture. We're not making any money off the witchcraft, so we can take the high road."

As our interview ended and I started packing up to leave the archives, Trask asked, "Do you want me to show you some witchcraft artifacts?"

Holy cow. Of course, I wanted to see some witchcraft artifacts. I probably would have spent our entire interview in the back room had I known what Trask was hiding in there. He showed me pottery shards and tobacco pipes and animal teeth that had been buried in the ground atop the parsonage. He showed me an original copy of John Hale's *A Modern Inquiry into the Nature of Witchcraft*, the one in which Hale talks about being in a cloud. He showed me a piece of floorboard from the courthouse in Salem, across which played so much of the tragedy. And, most staggeringly, he showed me the original record book of the Reverend Samuel Parris, which came from the archives of the First Church of Danvers. Carefully turning the pages, I watched the trials unfold in real-time through Parris's own pen. Trask specifically pointed out the ominous line, "The Devil hath been raised among us."

3

WITCH WAY TO THE GALLOWS

Witch House

In Danvers, my day of exploring Witch Trials sites started at a hole in a backyard. In Salem, it started at a plaque on a bicycle shop. Truth is, only one Salem structure connected to the trials survives today. So instead of a day like the one we had in Danvers, where we hit place after place after place, I planned to walk the path of the condemned, the gallows walk: from the site of the courthouse to the site of the jail to the site of the executions. Except that unlike the Witch Trials victims, I would stop at Walgreens at the end of my trek for a Coke Zero.

Salem Cycle is at 72 Washington Street. Its sign bears the silhouette of a witch on a broom-cycle: two wheels, handlebars, a broom for the chassis. Beside that window, making for a great juxtaposition in a city bursting with them, is a plaque that memorializes the old Salem courthouse.

According to the plaque, the courthouse stood there in the middle of Washington Street for forty years, starting in 1677. It was in that courthouse, 15 years later, that the Salem Witch Trials were held. In other words, that ugly stretch of asphalt rolled thinner every day by the wheels of passing cars is where the phrase "Salem Witch Trials" has the most meaning, if still not much accuracy.

In May of 1692, Massachusetts Governor William Phips established the court of Oyer and Terminer to get to the bottom of the whole witchcraft mess. Meaning to "hear and determine," courts of Oyer and Terminer were ad hoc courts for judging specific cases. That could be murder, treason, and in the case of Salem, illegal exchanges of the soul for worldly goods.

Its first session was held in that Salem courthouse on June 2. A group of nine judges of prominent standing oversaw the task that had started in that rustic meetinghouse in Salem Village.

What happened next is well-known, but not so well-documented. The Salem Witch Trials, taken as a nine-month historic event—from the first night of kids vs. demons to the awkward dissolution of the court—is one of the most well-documented events in colonial history. Almost one thousand original documents survive to present day, including warrants and hearing transcripts and complaints and summonses. But a big blank spot is the actual Salem Witch Trials themselves, the five months of the Court of Oyer and Terminer. Most of the original documentation was lost over time—it has even been surmised that some of the documents may have been destroyed by participants and their descendants out of shame.

However, based on what documents did survive, as well as first- and secondhand accounts, it seems as if the chaos of the Salem Village hearings carried over into the Salem Town court. Accusers twisting their bodies in what at this point had become well-practiced motions, spectral witches visiting the courtroom, confused defendants, judges predetermining fates, audience members throwing items at the accused. Here is where Rebecca Nurse was found not guilty by the jury, but then, on suggestion of the chief justice himself, had her Wheel of Destiny re-spun and forcefully wrenched to a halt at "execution by hanging."

Nineteen innocent people learned how their lives were to end on what is now a retail strip, with only a brass plaque to carry the burden of remembrance. However, the spot has a positive side. The Salem courthouse was also the site of the less famous Superior Court of Judicature, Court of Assizes, and General Gaol Delivery. This court was established by the governor after dissolving the first one when he realized things were out of control. Which was right about the time when his own wife was being targeted by the accusers.

The second court started in January of 1693, and it was specifically instructed to not allow spectral evidence of any sort to be a deciding factor. From that point on, evidence had to be directly visible to all involved. If you couldn't stick an Exhibit A tag on it, it wouldn't be recognized by the bench. That meant no more witch ghosts and no more mosh pit children. With that category of evidence itself going spectral, reason could have its turn at the bar. Five months later, all of the 150 accused save three were found not guilty. And those three weren't even condemned to execution. Thus ended the Salem Witch Trials. In history, at least.

Had the old Salem courthouse survived or been preserved, it would be a satisfyingly mixed symbol. Of course, it's all paved over now. And that made it easier to walk to the next site on my gallows walk. It was only one thousand feet away, and was somehow even less exotic.

Heading north on Washington Street, I took a right on Federal Street and followed that almost to where it ends at St. Peter Street. That put me in a parking lot. Behind me, on Church Street, was the Salem Place Mall, a small indoor shopping center, the other side of which faces the Essex Street Pedestrian Mall. The marquee of its tiny cinema advertised mainstream fare, but also such independent and locally produced oddities as *The History of Halloween*, *The True 1692*, and *Vampires of New England*. To my right, along St. Peter Street, was a pair of churches, St. John the Baptist and St. Peter's Episcopal. The latter had a few gravestones bookending its front steps in patches of ground small enough that either the gravestones must have been mere decorations at that point or the bodies they marked were buried standing up. I'd find out later that the church had been expanded to cover its graveyard, only the stones of which were moved. Behind those churches was another graveyard, Howard Street Cemetery, infamous for being the traditional site of Giles

Corey's flattening, although other scholarship places it closer to where I was standing.

I was facing the front door of Ten Federal Street, a long, brick, six-story building full of dentists and doctors and attorneys. I wanted to get closer to the building, but I had to wait for a large tour group to finish up on the spot I was aiming at. Later, while part of a tour group myself, I would hear a guide explain with stony conviction that working in that building had convinced him of the existence of the paranormal. The modern-looking structure didn't seem to have been around long enough to accrue its own ghosts, but what had sat on the spot centuries before more than made up for it. Finally, the tour group moved slowly away, and I walked up to a small metal plaque near the front entrance. It read:

OLD WITCH GAOL
BUILT 1684
ABANDONED 1813
RAZED 1956
IN 1692, DURING THE
SALEM WITCH TRIALS,
MANY OF THE ACCUSED
WERE IMPRISONED HERE.

That simple square of brass represents an unimaginable amount of suffering. Here stood the Salem prison, the "Old Witch Gaol," a wooden edifice with a stone dungeon beneath. Here is where the accused were kept for trial, and the convicted for execution. They were placed in heavy shackles to inhibit their ability to bewitch. They were charged for their own upkeep, so every day in jail made it a day harder to leave.

As the plaque states, not all of the accused were held here. It was much too small a jail for a colony overrun with servants of Satan. The accused were held everywhere jail space was available—Ipswich, Boston, Andover, other places. But the Old Witch Gaol was the last stop for many of the convicted before Gallows Hill.

In the prison that once stood here, seventy-five-year-old Ann Foster died. She admitted to being a witch to save her accused daughter. Foster spent four months in jail, dying of natural causes in those unnatural conditions. She outlived the Court of Oyer and Terminer but didn't make it to the Superior Court of Judicature. She was one of a handful of indirect victims of the trials. It's difficult to know how many there were. People were still in jail from the Witch Trials for a long time after the trials ended—innocent or not, they couldn't afford to pay their prison bill.

In the prison that once stood here, Elizabeth Proctor gave birth to a son. She named him John, after her husband, who had been executed five months before. She would have been on that gallows alongside him had it not been for the pregnancy, and her first moments of joy at the birth of her child would have been mingled with the knowledge that she could no longer avoid the gallows. Fortunately, events were already underway that would eventually free her, her son, and the rest of her cellmates.

In the prison that once stood here, Dorothy Good spent time before doing nine months in a Boston jail. The accusation of Dorothy Good was when the trials should have ended, just a few weeks after they began. The accusation of Dorothy Good is when everyone should have looked sheepishly at their shoe buckles, the accusers frozen mid-dance, the judges awkwardly clearing their throats, suddenly engrossed in their notes. Dorothy Good should have been a potent antidote to the hysteria. She was four years old when she was chained up in the prison, almost the same age as Esme.

Dorothy was the daughter of Sarah Good, who was one of the first three accused and one of the first executed. The little child was examined for weeks. She told the questioners that her mother had given her a black snake and that it had bitten her, producing a small red welt, her magic nipple from the Devil. She admitted to being a witch, doing exactly what the adults were pushing her into. She just wanted her mother. It took months for Dorothy's father to raise the money to free her. Decades later he would attest that the ordeal stunted her mentally.

Back to the wall plaque, particularly striking to me was its fourth line, "Razed 1956." Unlike the old Salem courthouse, the Witch Trials jail survived into the modern era, long enough that Salem should have known better than to demolish it.

The prison was abandoned in 1813 because Salem got a brand new jail, one which stands today, just steps down St. Peter Street and backing up to the Howard Street Cemetery. It's said that it once housed Albert

DeSalvo, the infamous Boston Strangler, one of whose victims was found at 224 Lafayette Street, about a mile away. These days, it's not a jail anymore either, having been shut down in the 1990s due to unsafe conditions. Since that time it has been abandoned and then refurbished to house restaurants and condos. But its exterior, with its gray block walls and distinctive cupolas, still bears the look of a formidable old jail.

In 1863, the Old Witch Gaol was purchased by Abner Cheney Goodall and remodeled as a private residence, address 4 Federal Street, with the timbers and frame of the old prison incorporated into the design. In 1935, descendants of Goodall opened the home as a tourist attraction. Two decades later, it was demolished for office space. "Most of the timbers were sold for firewood," the tour guide told me, his horror both practiced and sincere.

Wandering around the Salem shops, you'll at some point come across a little yellow self-published booklet called *Gallows and Graves*. Written and illustrated by Marilynne K. Roach, it's an excellent primer for all the mysteries surrounding the Salem Witch Trials execution site. I bought the booklet, but I didn't need to use it too much. I got to talk to Roach directly.

As I mentioned before, there are a lot of Salem Witch Trials experts. And every year there are more. There's just something about the Salem Witch Trials that makes people want to tell their own versions of it, to make their own sense of it. And it is extremely suited to re-telling, like a fairy tale—the Brothers Grimm kind, not the Disney kind.

I chose the experts I talked to carefully. I didn't want to be schooled in the history, really, as any one of them could have done that without even flicking open a reference book. Instead, I wanted to learn more about what pulled them to the topic in the first place. I contacted Roach because the angles she takes in her Salem books are unique. The books would still be relevant, even if someone ever accomplished the impossible feat of publishing The Definitive Telling of the Salem Witch Trials.

Watertown is thirty miles southwest of Salem. I was meeting Roach at a large box of a house. Cheery yellow, trimmed in white and green. Obviously a historic New England house even without the dark plaque above its door proclaiming the fact. Known as the Edmund Fowle House, these days it's the headquarters of the Historical Society of Watertown, of which Roach is president.

"That's twenty-seven years of my life in your hands," was the first thing she told me. I was holding a thick black book called simply, *The Salem Witch Trials.*

However, before we got to the witches, she gave me a quick, mandatory tour of the house. With a birth year of 1772, it's the second oldest house in that city. For the first year or so of the Revolutionary War, it was the headquarters for the executive branch of the Massachusetts government. That means some pretty important buckled shoes stamped the wooden boards creaking under my weight. Like those of John Adams. And Samuel Adams. And Paul Revere.

It was also the site of the first treaty signed between a mewling-baby United States and a foreign power, the Mi'kmaq and St. John's tribes from up in what's now Canada. A facsimile of the treaty lay on a table in the house. The Native Americans signed with hieroglyphs.

Along the way, Roach told me she was born and raised in Watertown, and then she pointed out the front window at a large brick building across the street. "And I went to that school." Roach was Watertown through and through. She'd never even gotten a driver's license. All of which made me wonder why she was so into Salem.

Eventually, we sat down at a table on the first floor to talk some darker history. "So, witches. Why are you a Salem Witch Trials historian?"

"I went to school to be an illustrator. At the time the employment agency woman laughed at me and said, 'A Bachelor of Fine Arts qualifies you to stay home and have babies.' It was the '60s."

Roach didn't want to hang her certificate above a crib, so she hefted her portfolio down to New York City and went door-to-door looking for a picture-book deal. She eventually landed one, for a book about the mouse that lived in Thoreau's cabin on the banks of Walden Pond. The publisher ended up publishing her story, just with a different illustrator. "And that's how I became a writer."

"So then how did you switch to history?"

"I visited Salem."

Going through her family's genealogy, she found herself in the 1600s, which brought in the Witch Trials. So, naturally, she segued from her family tree to the gallows tree. On May 27, 1975, she took the train to Salem.

She visited what was then called the Essex Institute (since merged into today's Peabody Essex Museum, or PEM) to see the Witch Trials artifacts it had on display, as well as The House of the Seven Gables, the Witch House, and the Salem Witch Museum.

"I found inaccuracies in some of the exhibits and presentations I'd seen in Salem, and, as I stood on the Common across the street from the Witch Museum, I thought, 'Maybe there's a book in it.'"

And so it was her turn to tell the story. Thus began her work on the large black tome in front of me, *The Salem Witch Trials,* a detailed daily timeline of the events of the Salem Witch Trials. It's an astounding work. The version holding the table down between us was 700 pages and, for it, Roach took regular trips to Salem over three decades.

"I actually used to be kind of embarrassed that I was researching the Witch Trials," she told me.

"Why's that?"

"There wasn't a lot of scholarship on it back when I started. Marion Starkey's *The Devil in Massachusetts* was out, but that overall wasn't a factually correct work. Enough came out over the decades while I was writing my book to make it respectable, but not in the beginning." She told me that when she first went to the Essex Institute, they had her fill out a form to explain why she was there. "I just wrote, 'local history.' I didn't want to say 'the Witch Trials.' Now, if you Google me, you come up with the Witch Trials."

"Right. I mean, you went on a very popular television show last year."

She had been on Comedy Central's *The Daily Show* with Jon Stewart the previous year for her book *The Six Women of Salem,* which focused on just six of the hundreds of people involved in the trials—Rebecca Nurse, Bridget Bishop, Mary English, Ann Putnam Sr., Tituba, and Mary Warren, a cross-section of accused, accusers, executed, and survivors.

"I don't have cable, so I didn't know who Jon Stewart was at the time. I made excuses, I couldn't afford to go to New York, it was winter, it was snowing, my mother was ill. But they arranged everything."

"But here you are with a new book. It's a great angle, but it's still a 300-year-old topic in a, by now, saturated field of publishing. Yet you get onto one of the more relevant TV shows running, one that focuses mostly on current topics of national and global interest—with punch lines. And here you are saying, 'Witches.'"

"And you know what's funny? They didn't do it in October. It was January. Martin Luther King Jr.'s birthday."

"But how did it happen?"

"I think it was because of Jon Stewart's father."

While in the make-up chair, Stewart came by to greet her and she asked him the same question I asked her. "He's very interested in history, and he remembered a childhood vacation on Cape Cod where his father took the family to historical places in Massachusetts. He remembered the whole trip fondly, although I'm not even sure if he made it to Salem."

I like that explanation, but it could also have been that the Salem Witch Trials are just of near-universal interest and are always relevant as both a metaphor and a cautionary tale for most of what's happening in society at any given time on any given piece of the planet.

"How has Salem changed since that fateful day for you in 1975?"

"Well, put it this way. The second trip I took that year was in October, the day before Halloween. I pretty much had the place to myself."

The condemned men and women of the Witch Trials traveled west down what's now Essex Street, which today is still Salem's main drag and cleaves the city in two. I backtracked down Washington, past the courthouse site and then turned right onto Essex, where a bronze statue of Elizabeth Montgomery of *Bewitched* fame perches on a broom.

For the first few blocks it was mostly retail. A comic book shop, a witch-themed consignment store, the everpresent Witch shop. About three blocks down Essex, though, I stopped.

At 310 Essex Street is a black house, ancient-looking, with a jagged roofline. It sits under the limbs of an old maple tree, the branches of which were bursting with red and orange fire. A rustic sign on the front lawn read, "Witch House." Regardless of why you're coming to Salem, the Witch House, at least its exterior, is exactly the type of site you're expecting from Witch City. It looks like it should have a garden of carnivorous plants in front of it, with the skeletons of Hansel and Gretel staked in the middle as scarecrows.

No witch ever lived in this house, but it is the only structure in Salem left with a connection to the trials. As the condemned passed it in the summer of 1692, they had reason to look away. This was the home of Jonathan Corwin, one of the Witch Trials judges.

Corwin was born in Salem and was also a magistrate at the Salem Village hearings. His father was a successful merchant, and that carried on to the son. Corwin bought the house in 1675 when he was in his twenties and lived in it for forty years. It stayed in the Corwin family until the mid-1800s. In 1948, it opened as a museum.

Inside, the house is less ominous-looking. Its large rooms span multiple floors yet still feel cramped, because the spaces are filled with both visitors and a nice-sized collection of period furniture and other artifacts.

Elizabeth Peterson is the manager of the Witch House. She found herself in the strangeness of Salem when her husband got a job in Boston. "We almost picked Marblehead to live," she told me, "but I'm glad we didn't. I love Salem. It's an eclectic, fun city." She was fascinated enough by her new home city that she immediately looked for opportunities to be involved with its historic preservation, and in 2008, she joined the Witch House as a tour guide. She timed it well.

"When I came on, all of the people on the administrative side of the house were on their way out for different reasons. Eventually, I was the only one left who understood what had gone on before, so I became the manager."

"Why does Corwin's house survive when no other structure related to the Witch Trials does?"

"It's a fine house, a mansion even, for its time. The chambers are large enough to repurpose, so the bones of it were left alone. Over the years it was used as a boarding house and an apothecary. It was a bustling place, just constantly in use. There was never a reason to tear it down."

That is, until the city decided to widen North Street, which runs beside the house, in the 1940s. Fortunately, a group of people from the area raised the funds and put in the work to move the house thirty-five feet away from the road and restore it to an approximation of its seventeenth-century glory. They then turned it over to the city.

"Why is it the Witch House, instead of the Corwin House or the Judge's House?"

"It's just always been called that. For centuries. Long before it was a museum, the people who lived here charged admission. Over the years, people have tried to change it to the Corwin House, but it's never been approved by the city."

"But do people come here thinking it's a witch's house, whatever that means to them?"

"A lot of times. Sometimes they even think we're a haunted house. So we spend a good bit of effort framing that. No matter what brought them to the house, though, hopefully they get a deeper understanding of what the period was about."

"That seemed to me to be the focus of your exhibits, that it was more about life in the seventeenth century than the Witch Trials."

"It's a mix. We're still trying to find the best balance to communicate our research to the public in a dignified way." She told me that when she first started at the house, it was mostly a furniture and architecture tour. They then started to shift the focus of the house more to communicating the fears and worries of the seventeenth-century mind. That way, they could help visitors understand how the academic elite who sat on the bench could have believed in things that to our modern sensibilities seem blatantly superstitious. "They were living in a time that the educated individual believed in an alchemical view of science. They were chasing the philosopher's stone at Harvard. So if the highest level of academia believes in imps and ghost and demons, that's going to feed into your assumptions for how the universe works and how you react to it."

In her time at the house, Peterson has seen visitor numbers grow for the site, from about eighteen thousand a year in 2008 to thirty thousand a year today, with a big chunk of that coming in October. "But that's less true than it used to be. Now we're getting an increased number of visitors in other months, especially in August and September. Interest in the Witch Trials doesn't seem to wane." Of course, as a municipal site, they don't have to rely on admissions. They're managed by the Department of Parks and Recreation, so admission income goes into the department fund and the Witch House budget comes from that.

"Tell me about Halloween itself. Do you have to batten down the hatches here?"

"We do a bit of panic-stricken damage control. We're very protective of the site, so around Halloween we minimize visitation, and only let a few people in at a time. On Halloween, it's all about keeping the house safe."

On arriving at the Witch House, I'd passed the border into the historic McIntire District and began seeing sites like the First Church of

Salem, the Ropes Mansion, the Salem Athenaeum, and plenty of remarkable homes. Here and there, Halloween decorations on the houses and businesses gave my gallows walk a surreal ambiance.

October 1692 was calm as far as the Witch Trials went. By that time, all the executions that would happen had happened. It was during this month that people really started to turn against the trials and confessors started to recant their confessions through the bars of their prison cells. On October 29, the governor would dissolve the Court of Oyer and Terminer. Even if modern Salem didn't already have a reason to throw a massive annual party on October 31, it would still be a good time to do so.

Eventually, after almost a mile of Essex Street, I took a few quick turns and ended up at Witch Hill Road, where I found the gallows I was searching for: Gallows Hill Park.

Gallows Hill Park was established in 1912. As I entered, nothing about its macabre name seemed evident. It was mostly a baseball field surrounded by low, forested hills. Just beyond, a giant, pale, cylindrical water tower loomed over it all, painted with the name of the city and a witch astride a broom, her conical hat forming the A in "SALEM."

Salem Water Tower at Gallows Hill Park

Site of the Witch Trials Executions

Unlike downtown, which was packed with people, the park was almost empty. I could see a few paths entering the forest, so I took one at random and wandered the hills, finding myself at various rocky outcroppings and ledges here and there that would have made for dramatic execution sites. Eventually, I went off trail and cut through the weeds and brambles to the base of the water tower. Somewhere on this hill is where tradition has placed the execution and burial site of the nineteen convicted witches.

There were four different trips to Gallows Hill in 1692. Four different hanging sessions. Each was well-attended by spectators. None ended with any last-second reprieves. The first, on June 10, ended the life of Bridget Bishop. July 19 was the last day of Rebecca Nurse, Susanna Martin, Elizabeth Howe, Sarah Good, and Sarah Wildes. August 19 took with it five souls: the Reverend George Burroughs, Martha Carrier, John Willard, George Jacobs, and John Proctor. The final eight victims of the Salem Witch Trials dropped on September 22: Mary Easty, Alice Parker, Ann Pudeator, Margaret Scott, Wilmot Redd, Mary Parker, Samuel Wardwell, and Martha Corey, whose husband had been crushed three days earlier.

There is debate over the mechanics of the hangings, whether trees were used or a gallows erected. On one hand, no bill of sale for timber for the gallows has ever turned up. On the other, three out of four of the hangings were en masse. A witness to the September 22 executions, the Reverend Nicholas Noyes, is quoted as saying, "What a sad thing it is to see eight firebrands of Hell hanging there." That seems to indicate a more contrived apparatus. But maybe it was a terrifying woodland tableau.

Looking out over the crown of the hill, I tried to imagine trees festooned with jerking corpses or an orderly row of the same on a platform. I tried to imagine the drama that accompanied the hangings. Like when the Reverend George Burroughs, the noose tickling the back of his neck, recited the entire Lord's Prayer perfectly. It was a feat that, according to folklore, a witch couldn't do. The crowds might have let him go that day, and the other seven on the gallows with him, had it not been for the Reverend Cotton Mather, who attended this particular execution. After all, it was a rare event when a minister was found to be a double agent. According to a merchant named Robert Calef, Mather leaped onto his horse and admonished the crowd to remember that the Devil "has often been transformed as an angel of light." It was enough to excuse their bloodlust, and Burroughs and the rest were executed. It was an act Mather doubled down on in his book *The Wonders of the Invisible World*, in which he called Burroughs, "a king in Satan's Kingdom."

I tried to imagine Samuel Wardwell choking on the smoke from the hangman's pipe, which halted his final words and caused the afflicted to cry out that it was the Devil who was shutting him up, for whatever reason. I tried to imagine Sarah Good cursing Reverend Nicholas Noyes, "I am no more a witch than you are a wizard, and if you take away my life God will give you blood to drink." The defiance would inspire native Salem son Nathaniel Hawthorne in writing *The House of the Seven Gables*. A quarter of a century later, Noyes died gagging on his own blood from an internal hemorrhage.

Yet, despite the emotional resonance of the site, no memorials, not even a plaque, for the hanged has ever adorned their dust here. In the late nineteenth century, around the bicentennial of the tragedy, plans were made to erect a large stone tower in their memory, but it never came to fruition. So the victims of the Witch Trials merely get a grisly park name.

But good thing the city didn't erect a memorial. Because the executions didn't happen in Gallows Hill Park.

In the 1920s, researcher Sidney Perley placed the exact location of the hangings at a lower point outside the park, and more recent scholarship—recent as in January 2016, about three months after my own visit—has verified the location. That places one of the most infamous sites in American history at the intersection of Proctor and Boston Streets . . . right behind a Walgreens. It's a spot I've driven past plenty of times as I've left Salem over the years, not giving it a second glance unless I needed a Slim Jim.

Fortunately, by this time I knew about Perley's work, so on my October gallows walk, I visited the actual execution site. I grabbed a Coke Zero from the Walgreens before heading around behind the drug store where the pharmacy pick-up window is. Twenty feet from the window and across a sliver of the store's parking lot is a rocky, wooded outcrop called Proctor's Ledge. This is the execution site that is so infamous in American history. And people drive by it every day to pick up their heartburn medicine.

I waited until there were no white coats in the drive-through window before heading up. A small, ghost-like knot of white plastic tied to a limb marked a slight path up the outcrop. I clambered up.

This ledge is where Burroughs recited, where Wardwell choked, where Good cursed.

Atop the rock, the denuded trees were barely thick enough to hide my presence, and the ground was covered in years' worth of dry, brown leaves. About fifty feet from the edge were low rock fences forming the back boundaries of residential properties. I'm not sure what those homeowners think about their backyards being one of the more infamous death patches in American history, and I totally missed my chance to find out. While I stood there, trying to heft the weight of the spot in my mind, I saw a man washing his car. I waved at him, both arms in the air like a castaway, but he either ignored me for being a stranger in the woods behind his house or didn't see me. He just went inside. Maybe to call the police. Maybe to get a turkey sandwich. Whatever the reason, I whiffed on what potentially could have been the best interview in this book.

Death binds moments to places. There's something about the molecules of a body mixing with the soil of a site that merges the two in memory. And I think that's a big part of why the city of Salem, among all the communities in Essex County, including Danvers, is so much more associated with the Salem Witch Trials. I mean, the official trials took place here, sure, but even more important, even more permanent, the executions took place here. The victims might have been from Salem Village and Topsfield and Marblehead and other places, but they became Salem soil.

According to the press release from the researchers who validated the site, the city is planning a "tasteful plaque or marker" to memorialize the spot. Honestly, I would rather it be, I don't know, somewhat less tasteful, I guess, something that would make people pause after grabbing their OxyContin prescriptions. If I had my way, it would be a large bronze gallows with 19 nooses dripping from it, maybe a bronze rock or two at the bottom for old Giles. I have no place on a memorial planning commission.

Do you want to hear something freaky? Steps from this site is where the Great Salem Fire of 1914 started. Around that time the area was covered in leather tanneries and was called Blubber Hollow because whale fat was an ingredient used in the process. On June 25 of that year, a fire started in the Korn Leather Factory at 57 Beacon Street. That puts the origin of the fire in front of the Walgreens. The fire cut a mile and a half swath into the city, destroying 1,376 buildings across 250 acres. It's estimated that some twenty thousand were homeless and ten thousand jobless as a result of the tragedy. In a city of about forty-eight thousand at the time. Deaths, mercifully, were in the single digits.

It's one of the many chapters in Salem's history that has nothing to do with the Witch Trials. But a little bit of folklore can fix that. Often bandied about is the legend that Giles Corey placed a curse on the city of Salem before he died, that his ghost appears the night before a tragedy in the city. The night before the Great Fire, folks claimed to have seen it in the Howard Street Cemetery, near where he was pressed. All that's lacking from the story is for the fire to have followed the gallows walk itself instead of just cutting across it.

With my own gallows walk not ending atop an actual gallows, I was free to head back downtown. I took Federal Street this time, marveling at the beautiful old houses lining it. A few had "For Sale" signs as lawn ornaments, so I looked up the listings on my phone to find prices north of $600,000. None of the listings advertised, "Steps from the Witch Trials Gallows Walk."

Richard Trask and Marilynne Roach weren't the only Salem Witch Trials experts I talked to. I also looked up Frances Hill. Hill is the author of five books on the Salem Witch Trials, including a novel. Her signature work is *A Delusion of Satan*, but she also wrote a book about the physical sites of the trials called *Hunting for Witches*. What really put her on my list, though, was her accent. I happened to watch an interview of her online and learned that she's British. That meant I had a very specific question to ask her. And I drove two and a half hours into Connecticut to do so.

Hill usually lives in London with her husband, Leon Arden, a novelist from New York City. But during the summer months, they return to the States, where they have a home in New Preston, Connecticut. It was to this house that Hill invited me over for tea and a talk.

Hill was born in London, and after getting her degree in English literature and philosophy, she spent time traveling about the continent and "being rather '60s-ish." She started her career as a journalist on Fleet Street in the late 1960s.

"So, witches. How did you become a Witch Trials expert?"

"Because of my daughter. She was 15 and had seen *The Crucible* on stage and was into Wicca, as fifteen-year-old girls always are. So she wanted to visit Salem. That was 1992."

"And what did you think about the idea of going to Salem?"

"We weren't against it. We just probably would never have thought of doing it ourselves. But we went. And we went into the Salem Witch Museum, and I was just taken. I thought, 'What an incredible episode in American history.' I'd never really thought about it before that, even after watching a performance of *The Crucible*. But then we went to buy a book there and couldn't find a good popular history of the trials. There was only Marion Starkey's *The Devil in Massachusetts*, which is what it is, partially fiction. It was very frustrating. And I thought, maybe I could write the book that I wanted to read."

"And that leads me to the big question that I wanted to ask you specifically. Coming from England, you were surrounded by witch trial sites, but it was a US site that grabbed you and changed your career."

"Well, Salem is just different. And, actually, living in England, I wasn't particularly aware of any specific witch trial sites. I'm aware of them now, as a result of my Salem work, but not before then."

"Do you think that's true in general in England? Nobody really pays attention to witch trial sites there?"

"Yes, I think so. People aren't aware of them. And even if they are, they're not big deals. There's no tremendous story attached to them. I suppose the only real narrative that I know of is that of Matthew Hopkins, the Witchfinder General."

Half a century before the Salem Witch Trials, Matthew Hopkins, who designated himself "Witchfinder General," spent three years running around parts of England, chasing, torturing, and killing witches. It has been estimated that he was responsible for hanging some 300 victims. In fact, Hopkins influenced how the Salem Witch Trials were conducted.

"But other than that," Hill continued, "I'm not aware of any English site with a big story. In general, it was just that a couple of poor people were accused, tried, and hanged, whereas in Salem, my God, there's just no equivalent event in England."

The similarities between Marilynne Roach's Salem story and Frances Hill's Salem story are telling. Neither one was from Salem or connected to the city in any way. Neither were drawn to the subject matter through popular culture. It was a visit to the city, the place itself, that cast them in its spell, that made them want to write multiple books about it. In that way, even though Salem hasn't really preserved the physical trial sites, it might not need them. The character of the city itself is a memorial to the Witch Trials. Many have said that Salem capitalizes on the trials, even exploits the victims, but regardless of the verb, it's evident that had Salem not used the trials as a tourist draw, those nineteen-plus victims might today be as anonymous as any victim of the Witchfinder General.

Today, the city of Salem attempts, and somewhat fails, to focus that commemorative power onto one single site: the Salem Witch Trials Memorial. At the same time that plans were getting underway in Danvers to commemorate the 300th anniversary of the trials, Salem was preparing its own. But its memorial took a much different, more high-profile course toward installation.

Salem started with an international design competition. Nearly 250 artists entered. The design that was chosen was unveiled by playwright Arthur Miller himself, whose 1953 play *The Crucible* is the template for how we use the trials as a metaphor and the cultural gateway through which

Salem Witch Trials Memorial

so many learn about them. When it was unveiled in 1992 at the Witch Trials Tercentenary, the ceremony was presided over by Elie Weisel, the Transylvania-born Nobel Laureate who survived the death camps of the Nazis. His mere presence broadened the scope of the memorial to represent not just the 20 victims, but all victims of witch hunts world- and history-wide.

And after all that process and ceremony and significance, the end result is a memorial that you might inadvernently sit down on to eat a cider donut without realizing what you're dropping crumbs all over.

The Salem Witch Trials Memorial is located off an alley called Liberty Street, where it shares two walls with the Old Burying Point cemetery. The cemetery was established in 1638 and is one of the most important sites in Salem. We'll get to it later in this book because it deserves to be the set piece of a chapter. The memorial pairs well with it, though. It's a rough, low, granite-block wall surrounding a rectangular clearing of grass that is shaded by black locust trees. Protruding inward from the wall at regular intervals are twenty bench-like stones, like horizontal tombstones, each engraved with the name of a victim and their day and method of execution.

At the threshold of the rectangle, almost worn to illegibility by the shuffling feet of 35 years' worth of October crowds, is engraved a series of statements by the victims. "God knows I am innocent." "I am wholly innocent of such wickedness." "Oh Lord, help me." Some of the statements are suddenly and poignantly cut off by the beginning of the wall.

Like that last one, many of the ideas behind the memorial are well-conceived. The graves next door are mute witnesses of the memorial, as so many of the interred were mute witnesses of the trials in life. The black locust trees represent the traditional gallows trees of the executions. The benches are the gravestones that most of the victims never had.

I saw this memorial every day in October, and every day offerings appeared on these benches, a spray of flowers, coins. Once I saw, on the horizontal tombstone inscribed with Susanna Martin's name, a small, smooth stone with a note affixed to it written in purple marker: "Sending love from your 10th great granddaughter."

To me, the memorial is . . . underwhelming. I mean, I get it. It's reflective, a place of peace and mourning in the middle of a city often teeming with craziness, and it is for victims whose last days on earth were spent in chaotic courtrooms and depressing dungeons. As far as that goes, it works.

But the memorial is easy to miss. And that's the opposite of what a reminder is supposed to be. In October, it's also adjacent to the Haunted Neighborhood, which we'll visit soon. Suffice it to say here that it's an avenue of haunted houses and carnival food vendors, awash in chemical fog and the smell of corn dogs, the air boisterous with the blare of barkers over loudspeakers. Maybe not always peaceful and reflective.

So I can easily forgive the tourist who grabs his funnel cake and sits on the memorial stone of Mary Parker of Andover as he awaits his turn through the terrors of the Haunted Witch Village. I don't know much about user-centered design theory, but I do know that the memorial demands to be sat upon.

But I'm certainly being somewhat obtuse and unfair. After all, my inclination is to make memory a forceful thing. I want a bronze gallows with 19 nooses, after all.

That's the story of the Salem Witch Trials as told through the memorials and preserved sites within the city. But, strangely enough, these historic sites and commemorations aren't the protectors and tellers of the Salem Witch Trials narrative. Those roles have been adopted by other organizations in the city. And, man, do they love wax figures.

4

WAX WITCHES

Old Town Hall

Salem has no actual history museum, not in the conventional sense, nor, surprisingly, is there a museum dedicated to the Witch Trials. Again, at least not in the expected sense. There are surviving artifacts related to the trials, everything from documents to actual items owned by the victims, but they are packed away in storerooms and archives, not on display. That's a story we'll get to later.

For now, a quick Google search will give you the proof you need to call me a liar. Your results will turn up a Salem Witch Museum, a Witch Dungeon Museum, a Gallows Hill Museum, a Witch History Museum, a Salem Museum, and a Salem Wax Museum, all within walking distance of each other downtown.

But Salem has an extremely elastic definition of the word "museum."

The closest any of the above museums get to being an actual museum is the Salem Museum. However, a more accurate description of that would probably be "welcome center exhibit." It takes up the first floor of the Old Town Hall, located off the Essex Street Pedestrian Mall, and comprises a series of large banners hanging from the ceiling covered in text and interspersed with artifacts of marginal interest. It does cover the entire story of Salem, though, from its founding in 1626 by Roger Conant and friends to 1692 all the way through the city's industrial years. The back wall is decorated with Monopoly boxes to mark the city's time as Parker Brothers HQ.

The rest of the Salem museums? Not so straightforward. Those experiences more accurately fall into the category of "attraction," some of them more than others. These attractions cover the gamut from homemade exhibit to theatrical presentation to wax figure–type museum, although the figures are usually sculpted from more modern and less easily described materials such as polyresin (since "polyresin museum" is a terrible phrase, I'll probably be using "wax" in this chapter even when not accurate). More often than not, the attractions are a combination of these media.

Regardless, it is a fact of modern Salem that the narrative of the Salem Witch Trials in the city is controlled by the tourist attractions. Which, it could be argued, means that, for all intents and purposes, they control the narrative globally, minus a bunch of books with uncracked spines at the lower end of the Amazon sales rankings. But nowhere else in Salem could I find a comprehensive, detailed telling of the Salem Witch Trials.

The first of these attractions that we visited actually didn't have the word "museum" in its name. It aimed at an even loftier concept: time machine.

There are a lot of ways to tell the fascinating story of Salem. The Salem Time Machine does it as a glow-in-the-dark 3D horror story. It's located on Essex Street, close to the pedestrian mall.

"It's just a history of Salem. Wax figures and such, I'm sure. Salem loves wax museums," I told Esme as she warily eyed the haunted house façade of its shop front. "They just glow in the dark and are 3D in this one."

I honestly did think it was an innocent Day-Glo history attraction. After all, the tagline on its sign was, "3D Walk-Thru Adventure into Salem's Past." I didn't read too much into the spooky signage spiderwebbing the rest of its exterior because, well, every business in Salem looks like a haunted house this time of year. And that's because every business in Salem probably *is* a haunted house this time of year.

Every Salem attraction diversifies during October weekends. Regardless of what you are on a Tuesday at 2:00 in the afternoon, on the weekends, you'll transmogrify into a haunted house. You'll lead tours of the city that start from your front door. You'll hire a psychic to give readings in a back room. You'll put on a dramatic presentation if you have the space. And you'll have a giftshop, of course. Many of Salem's attractions rely on these 31 days to make their entire 365. The more tentacles with which to pull people off the streets, the better.

The Salem Time Machine does most of that. However, on the weekday afternoon that me and mine visited, it was a straightforward, walk-though history tour of the city. Sort of.

We slid on our 3D glasses and headed through. Over the course of ten small but psychedelic rooms, we were told the story of such hash marks on Salem's timeline as its golden age of maritime trade, the Great Salem Fire, the city's role in the underground railroad (a pitch-black hallway—I'm not sure if that was on purpose or if the lights were broken in that room), and, of course, the Salem Witch Trials. Every so often a "time machine" sound told us when to break the laws of physics and continue through a curtain to the next moment in Salem history.

Except that in this version of Salem's past, every character—be they victim, villain, or hero—was a multi-colored monster, every scene a kaleidoscopic dark carnival. The jury at the Witch Trials was made up of black, shrouded ghosts with glowing red eyes. Sea captains were vulture-ravaged skeletons. The Great Salem Fire came with its own cavorting demons. Giles Corey looked like he was rising from the grave instead of being crushed down into it. And it was all lorded over by a narrator straight out of an old-time horror movie trailer. Like if Vincent Price or Boris Karloff was your high school history teacher.

The tableaus surrounded us on all sides. There was no place to stand without a neon fiend at our backs. I could only imagine what it was like on the weekends when similarly painted actors hid among its shadow and colors and 3D effects to jump out at you.

So the Salem Time Machine was a spooky funhouse. "The story of

Salem dressed for October," according to one of its ads in the "Haunted Happenings" brochure that I didn't see until after our visit. Maybe think twice about taking your five-year-old in there. Or at least lying to her about what it is before going in. Or you can do what I did and interpret her long silence during and after as a deeply felt awe of history.

A few storefronts down from the Salem Time Machine is the Witch History Museum. Its exterior didn't have the gaudy carnival-barking quality of the Salem Time Machine. Just a plain brick façade with a small, restrained sign bearing the illustration of a witch on a broom, complete with black cat.

Entering, I found myself in the gift shop/foyer, and after I purchased my ticket, I was ushered with the rest of my group into an auditorium. On one side of the stage was a reproduction of a First Period house. On the other, four life-sized Native American figures stood or crouched, frozen in the middle of some sort of frantic ritual. The hue of their skin seemed closer to Oompa-Loompa than Native American.

Eventually a young girl in period clothes exited the house. She gave us a five-minute introduction to the trials before directing us to a door by the stage, where she introduced another woman in period clothes. We were to follow her down a flight of stairs.

I headed down to find myself in a dim basement. As my eyes adjusted, I saw a life-sized diorama of colonial girls partying in a forest. One was doing a cartwheel. The guide gave us a brief introduction to the scene and then an ominous-sounding narration track started up, complete with cackling witches on it. In this manner, the tour guide took us down a dark hallway through about fifteen scenes, alternating with the narration and handing us off here and there like a bundle of batons to other period-dressed tour guides, all coordinating to facilitate the flow of the audience while telling the spooky story of the Witch Trials in what almost felt like campfire light.

Even in those shadows, the figures—wax or whatever—looked old. Like decades old. Like to the point of disfigurement old. Almost monstrous. And in one scene there were actual monsters. A forest diorama had a witch and a black cat and a goblin and an imp on a stump. The black cat and imp turned their heads back and forth, while the narrator explained over the sounds of demons chuckling how much fear the Salem colonists had of the supernatural and what they thought lurked in the deep, mysterious forests that pressed in upon their vulnerable homes.

One particularly striking scene depicted the arrest of the Reverend George Burroughs from his home in Maine. He was being pulled from the doorway of his house in chains, putting up an almost supernaturally strong fight along the way, judging by the man collapsed in the rubble of a barrel and another flying through the air. Lightning flickered and thunder boomed. Witnesses testified against Burroughs during the trials that he demonstrated superhuman strength, could lift entire barrels with just his fingers and hoist massive guns with one hand. And because Colonial America didn't have radiation backstories nor apparently believed the Biblical story of Samson (from the book of Judges, oddly enough), the judges, juries, and accusers could only believe the strength to be Satanic.

Weirdly, the gallows scene, which should have been the climactic moment of the tour, was shown in miniature. However, the museum more than made up for that lack of grisly detail with the dioramas that followed: skeletons of the victims half-buried in a "witch pit." Cotton Mather pinching a skull with calipers while the narrator cited an apocryphal story that Mather had Burroughs's head removed and defleshed to show the deformity that marked him as demon royalty. Philip English guarding the dead body of George Corwin, the sheriff of Salem, who died a few years after the trials. The story went that English body-snatched the corpse for ransom, or at least threatened to, until he was returned the property that had been confiscated from him for being accused of being a witch.

The tour ended with a mockup of the Howard Street Cemetery, the ghost of Giles Corey hovering above it. The spooky narrator mentioned the tale of his ghost, attributing the quote to Nathaniel Hawthorne:

> Tradition was long current in Salem that at stated periods, the ghost of Giles Corey the wizard appeared on the spot where he suffered, as the precursor of some calamity that was impending over the community, which the wizard came to announce.

Later, I looked for the quote and would find it here and there attributed to Hawthorne, although never sourced to a particular work or piece of correspondence. Eventually, I found it, but it wasn't Hawthorne's. It was in an 1883 book by Samuel Adams Drake called *New England Legends and Folk-Lore*. The closest Hawthorne came to the legend was a story in *Twice-Told Tales* called "The Gray Champion," about a ghostly figure from the past appearing on the eve of great trouble. But instead of a vengeful old codger delighting in the descendants of his killers receiving their comeuppance, it was a dignified forefather emboldening the spirits of his fellow New Englanders to fight tyranny and oppression.

But enough of Hawthorne. He gets his own chapter later.

The Witch History Museum wasn't the first wax museum–type attraction I visited in Salem. That would be the Salem Wax Museum, which is an actual wax museum. Located beside the Old Burying Point, the museum advertises "50 London-made wax figures." In October, it's surrounded by the Haunted Neighborhood. A giant gargoyle perches near its entrance.

The Salem Wax Museum is basically a single open room with about a dozen wax dioramas lining the walls. Each one depicts a moment from the history of Salem. Nathaniel Hawthorne is there. Also a few ship captains. The Witch Trial victims, of course. The place lacked the creepy atmosphere of the Witch History Museum, and the depictions were also less macabre, although they naturally slipped in a few hangings. It's also

Haunted Neighborhood

the only attraction of this sort in Salem that has an upright Giles Corey. They depict him with stone bricks at his feet instead of on his chest, and he looks like he's about to build something with them.

It also has its own private Salem Witch Trials Memorial. Back in the 1980s, a sculptor by the name of Yiannis Stefanakis designed the sculpture for a city that had yet to commemorate its signature tragedy in an official way. However, in the end, funding problems and opposition from those who wanted input on the design process kiboshed the project. Stefanakis only got as far as a fourteen-foot-tall plaster model.

So the model was painted to mimic metal and installed in the Salem Wax Museum. The memorial is called *Three Sisters*, and it depicts Rebecca Nurse, Mary Easty, and Sarah Cloyce in robes and chains, bedraggled and hopeless. In the end, only Cloyce would escape the gallows. It's an extremely morose, disconcerting depiction that better fits my preferred aesthetic for a memorial. I'll stop saying that now.

Half a mile northwest of the Salem Wax Museum is the Gallows Hill Museum, on Lynde Street. One night, the kids safely at the house with the babysitter, Lindsey and I checked it out. Despite the name, it's pretty far from Gallows Hill and isn't really a museum. It's a theater. Inside its tiny lobby, we found where the museum part of its name comes from, though: two small exhibits on witches and the Witch Trials.

Finally, we were ushered into a theater of about seventy seats. The stage was backdropped by a cottage exterior and a runway extended into the middle of the audience. We grabbed seats beside the runway.

The Gallows Hill Museum has a range of programs throughout the Halloween season, including magicians and mediums and something called Tales and Ales in which the audience samples local brews while listening to ghost stories. Various spook- and history-themed tours launch from the premises as well. But we were there for what the website called its "main event": The Witchcraft and Ghost Experience.

The lights went down, and an evil witch that looked like it had sprung from one of Jim Henson's freakier phases came cackling across the stage, cursing the audience. Next, a ghost glided out above our heads. An extremely effective costume of a monster from Native American myth called the Abamacho burst onto the stage. It had glowing red eyes, massive claws, and spikes protruding from its back, and it dashed on all fours down the runway into the audience, the house lights suddenly snuffing before it got to us. Here and there, actors would come out and tell stories associated with the monsters. At one point, small glowing bubbles floated throughout the auditorium like ghost orbs.

We were being treated to a special effects show on monsters. Much like that one diorama at the Witch History Museum, the overall purpose of the Witchcraft and Ghost Experience was to illustrate the supernatural edge on which Salemites teetered every day. One moment you're milking the cow, the next, evil creatures from beyond are chasing you through the woods to milk your soul. Circle of life.

Just down Lynde Street from the theater is an odd-looking brown building that, based on its vaulted roof, central gothic window, and tower, must, I thought, have been a church at some point in its past. Except no church I'd ever seen flies orange and black witch flags out front.

Also in front of the building were some wooden pillories into which you could stick your head and hands for a photo op. A plaque on the wall behind them declared this building as the original site of the "Old Witch Gaol," the exact claim made by the plaque a few streets away at Ten Federal. A second, smaller plaque explained that the other plaque was an old one that used to adorn Ten Federal. Sometimes plaques get plaques.

But the relationship between the two sites goes deeper. I was standing in front of the Salem Witch Dungeon Museum. Once I took my head out of the pillory, of course.

I entered and found myself in the familiar situation of buying a timed ticket and wandering around a giftshop. When my time came, I was ushered into an auditorium, the old pews and organ pipes of which validated the church hypothesis. Later I would learn it was built in 1897 as a First Church of Christ Scientist. It became the museum I was there to see in 1979.

I slipped into a pew and waited for the curtains on the dais to part. Soon, a woman in period garb came out and introduced what was about to happen: a reenactment of a Witch Trial scene based on original records. As she left the stage, the curtains parted to reveal a courtroom complete with, natch, wax-ish figures. The judge was wax-ish, the jury wax-ish. The only figures on stage not wax-ish were two women, one playing the elderly accused witch Sarah Good, the other playing the young afflicted accuser Ann Putnam.

Five minutes later, our presenter was back. Just like at the Witch History Museum, we were directed to a side door beside the stage, where we were told we would enter a full-scale replica of the witch dungeon that had been beneath the Old Witch Gaol on Federal Street.

Downstairs, it felt like, well, a dungeon. Stone walls, low ceiling, cramped, dim. Truth in advertising. A bright beam of light spotlighted a thick beam of wood on the wall. According to its placard, the beam came from the original Witch Gaol.

If the reproduction of the dungeon was even ten percent accurate, then the original was a horrifying place to spend months of one's life. The conditions were cramped and dirty, and most of the accused witches were shackled to the walls to keep them from spellcasting. It was freezing in winter. The fear of execution was hanging over their heads. I'm not rewriting that sentence. I couldn't believe children were kept in a place like this, much less born in a place like this.

Throughout the dungeon were small cells. Some were so tiny they were almost coffins. Others showed related tableaus, such as the pressing of Giles Corey. The dungeon wrapped around in a U-shape and ended with a large, dramatic hanging scene. Three bodies dangled like limp puppets from a single tree, while a hooded executioner readied a fourth. Had I witnessed this exhibit before taking my gallows walk, I would have unavoidably imagined it exactly that way on Proctor's Ledge. Yiannis Stefanakis should bronze it and install it on the Common.

But there is one wax museum that rules all others in Salem. Or, polyresin museum.

If there is a postcard image that sums up Salem or, to stop dating myself, an Instagram shot, it would be on the western edge of the Salem Common. Facing the Common there is a red gothic building, triangular and tessellated, adjacent to a large, heroic statue of a Puritan man atop a boulder. You take a single photo of that—or a selfie if you're Jesus with angles—and you can pretend that you've had a book's worth of experiences in Salem.

The statue is of Roger Conant, who founded Salem in 1626 in an area called Naumkeag by the Native Americans. Today, the Native American name pops up here and there in the city: Naumkeag Antiques on Hawthorne Boulevard, Naumkeag Ordinary in Lappin Park, Naumkeag

Block on the pedestrian mall. Conant served as the settlement's first governor, and he died in his eighties, thirteen years before the Salem Witch Trials would overwhelm the identity of his settlement. I was regularly told two things about his statue, which was erected in 1913. The first is that people often mistake it for a statue of either a witch or a witch hunter. Both make sense. The flowing robes and high hat and staff-like branch he's leaning against make him seem very wizard-like. On the other hand, his stern Puritan visage could freeze witch blood with a look. The second thing I was told was that if you look at it from the right angle, it seems like he's grabbing his crotch. That . . . also makes sense once you've seen it from that angle. With his dramatically flowing cloak and defiant stance, I've always thought he looked like a Colonial superhero.

But the statue is unconnected to the dramatic gothic building beside it, a wooden sign on which labels the building the "Salem Witch Museum."

The Salem Witch Museum is the signature attraction of Salem for three reasons. First, the exterior of the Salem Witch Museum is eye-catching. In October, with the streets thronged with monsters, you'll still notice this building. The macabre, terrifying tale of the Salem Witch Trials deserves such a mysterious-looking home. Second, it boasts an extremely prominent place in the city. Its location on the Common means everybody sees it, and it also means it doesn't have to contend with any neighboring competitors, as the rest of the Common is mostly ringed with houses. Finally, and perhaps most importantly, is its age. The Salem Witch Museum has been the faithful-ish steward of the Witch Trials story for more than four decades.

The building was constructed in 1845 as the Second Church of Salem. In 1957, it became an antique automobile and Americana museum until the structure was gutted by fire in October 1969. Pictures of its smoldering bones in the newspapers of the day show something that look like the ancient ruins of a European abbey. In 1971, Thomas and Holly Mulvihill rescued it from sure demolition. Their purpose: to tell the Witch Trials story in a city where the story wasn't really being told, despite all the visitors coming to the city expressly to learn it. A quarter of a million dollars and one year later, the Salem Witch Museum opened its massive, arched front doors to a more gentle witch hysteria. Today, the museum

Roger Conant Statue and Salem Witch Museum

gets between three hundred and fifty thousand and four hundred thousand visitors annually. Most of them in October.

We entered and got the usual timed ticket, complete with its famous entrance sticker. You can't walk anywhere in Salem without seeing these colorful circles stuck to the bricks and sidewalks of the city. On the sticker, the silhouette of an old witch looks down at a cat like she's trying to remember the last time she fed it. It's litter, sure, but the streets of Salem are all the better for it somehow.

We were led inside at the appointed half hour. The room was dark. We could barely make out the seats that lined the edge of the space or the rows of chairs that filled the middle. The only empty spot on the floor was a glowing red circle that seemed mildly Satanic. A closer look at it revealed the names of the victims of the Witch Trials in concentric circles. Around me, ten feet above my head, I could make out dim, unmoving forms.

"What's that up there?" asked Esme, pointing nervously at the shadowy forms.

"I don't see anything," I lied.

"There's something up there."

"You're imagining things."

"What's up there?"

"You're going crazy, I think."

"They're wax people, aren't they?"

I didn't have to answer because the program started.

A narrator out of a black and white horror movie spoke to us in sepulchral tones. His backup singers were the terrifying moans of ghostly women. The music was a tortured theremin. I waited for a hidden projector to throw *Black Sunday* or *I Walked with a Zombie* on one of the walls.

Instead, a light illuminated a form directly behind me. I turned and saw a massive red-skinned Lucifer with black horns and glowing eyes aiming a pitchfork at my face. "He's pointing at you, Dad," whispered Esme, satisfied. This, the narrator intoned, was the being whom the Salemites feared most. The one who caused them, directly or indirectly, to execute senior citizens and imprison children. The. Devil. Made. Them. Do. It.

From there, a series of about a dozen dioramas ringing the top of the room was sequentially lit. It was the usual story. Kids acting crazy. Courtrooms of chaos. Dingy dungeons. Of course, there was Giles Corey getting paperweighted to death. Of course, there were rope necklaces. And, of course, the installations looked like they hadn't been touched since the 1970s.

After it was over, we were directed to a back room. That second part was an exhibit called "Witches–Evolving Perceptions." As we walked into the exhibit, we passed a familiar, rough wooden beam, another remnant of the Old Witch Gaol. We flowed into a well-lit room with photos on the walls and a few full-size figures. I took up a station beside a classic witch astride a broom, her black dress flowing, her hat and shoe tips pointed, her face and hands toad green.

A guide started telling us how the word "witch" has evolved over the years. She pointed to images of familiar witches from TV and movies on the wall. To a diorama of a pagan wise woman. To the *Wizard of Oz*–style green witch that I was fighting the impulse to reach out and touch. The third diorama was of a man and a woman representing the nature-loving Wiccans of today. On the wall it listed a series of famous metaphorical witchhunts, from the Army-McCarthy Hearings of the 1950s to the AIDS epidemic of the 1980s.

I played musical schedules with the people who run the museum over the summer, and October was too busy for them to give me the time I needed. I did drop by at one point during Haunted Happenings to introduce myself and assure them I was a real person with a real project and not just a few lines of code that emailed them biweekly and then rescheduled appointments. Little did I know I'd learn something during even that five-minute visit.

I walked confidently past the long line outside and up to the woman running the ticket counter. "Is Stacy around?" I asked. Stacy Tilney is the director of communications for the museum and the person with whom I'd been making mile-long email chains with.

She picked up a phone, "Can you tell Stacy she has a vendor here to see her?" She hung up.

"Wait. I'm not vendor. Why do you think I'm a vendor?"

She didn't answer. Just dropped her eyes to what I had in my arms.

It was a witch.

We brought a few of our personal Halloween decorations to Salem, and one was the 14-inch-tall papier-mâché witch I was holding. Her hair was the color of cornstalks and her skin the color of pumpkins. Her long cloak and pointed hat were midnight blue—witching-hour blue—and her face was kindly. She looked homemade and ancient, but I don't know who made her nor how old she was. I brought her solely because she had belonged to author Ray Bradbury, the great scribe of both autumn and Halloween himself, so it seemed a fitting totem to preside over my family as we watched Halloween specials and ate candy corn in Salem, or to sit on my borrowed desk as I wrote down my Salem experiences every night. I'd bought the witch at auction, and it was our first Halloween with it.

I had it with me that day to take a picture of it in Salem and chose the museum as the perfect backdrop. I held the Bradbury witch defensively against my chest. "No, no. This isn't for sale. This girl's special." And I gave the above explanation the way I should have given it to you, in under ten words.

A staff member behind me piped up. "Did you know Ray Bradbury was the descendant of one of the Salem witches?"

No—no I did not. Turns out, he was related to Mary Bradbury. She was convicted but not executed and was the one who was supposed to have killed Timothy Swan, whose Andover grave I had visited. The "related to a witch" story is one I heard a lot from a lot of people, from the tipsy guy next to me at the bar of the Witch's Brew Café to the girl in line at the Ye Old Pepper Candy Company store where I was trying to buy chocolate skulls. Colonial Salem was full of Adams and Eves, and somewhere in almost all of our family trees is a witch. Hopefully not hanging there. My Bradbury witch is now named Mary.

Finally, in November, during the time when Plimoth Plantation gets all the historical press in the state, I sat down with the people responsible for running the Salem Witch Museum.

Tilney led me to a back office to introduce me to the museum's director, Tina Jordan. As I sat down to talk to both of them, I could hear the spooky presentation of its theater of polyresin reverberating through the wall. The Salem Witch Museum is open all year round in Salem. It's always October there.

I saw a piece of collateral on the desk with the Haunted Happenings witch, the one that flies from every pole in the city in October. "I was told you guys own the Haunted Happenings logo."

"Yes, one of our T-shirt designers created it. We lease it to the city for a dollar," answered Jordan.

"Why doesn't the city create its own logo? They can throw a witch on a broomstick, right?" That said, the Haunted Happenings Witch is pretty cool. The black silhouette has a flapping cape, hair, and broom bristles that are almost tentacular in their raggedness, and a thin, curved hat like the top half of a crescent moon.

"This has been the logo since the museum started Haunted Happenings in 1982. You don't want to mess with the brand." She dug through the papers on her desk and handed me a photocopy of the brochure from the first ever Haunted Happenings. In an orange circle on the black cover was the witch, slightly altered, but the same witch nevertheless. It took me a few seconds perusing the photocopy for what she said to register.

"Wait, are you saying this museum started Haunted Happenings?"

"Yes. It was the brainchild of Susannah Stuart, who was the director of the museum back then." According to Jordan, Stuart tried to organize the festival in 1981 to extend the tourist season past Labor Day. She called it Witchival but couldn't put together the sponsors. The next year, she teamed up with the executive director of the Salem Chamber of Commerce, Joan Gormalley, and was extremely successful, even if you don't count the thirty-odd years of Haunted Happenings that followed.

Part of that was the timing. In September 1982, the infamous Chicago Tylenol murders, in which seven people in Illinois, including a twelve-year-old girl, were killed by cyanide-laced Tylenol straight from the bottle, happened. The murderers hadn't been caught by October and, in fact, never would be, and this played right into classic fears of poisoned trick-or-treat candy and razorblade apples. Towns across the country cancelled trick-or-treating as a result of that fear and instead threw cobbled-together festivals for the kids to attend instead.

Of course, Salem had the leg up. Their event wasn't reactionary and had been in the works for a while. Plus, it was already considered a spooky destination. Even better, Halloween fell on a Sunday that year. All this added up to between forty thousand and sixty thousand people visiting the city for the weekend festival. As the years progressed, its continued success encouraged Salem to expand it to a week. And then two weeks. Until it finally ended up as the month-long party it is today.

And Jordan has been there since the beginning. She grew up in Lynn, but her mother worked in a Salem restaurant called Stromberg's until she retired. (These days it's the Black Lobster. I'm not sure why, but I assume it's because even the lobsters in Salem are spooky.) "I actually remember my first time coming to the Salem Witch Museum, somewhere around fifth grade. I found it interesting, but wanted more." In that way, she was much like Marilynne Roach, whose epiphany had occurred in part as a result of this museum. But instead of writing books, Jordan got a starter job at the museum in 1980, as a sophomore at Wheaton College. Thirty years later, in 2008, she became the museum's director.

"The museum doesn't still run Haunted Happenings, does it?"

"No. When the Tercentenary happened in 1992, the event grew and changed and became more of a city initiative. Today it's handled by Destination Salem." Destination Salem is the tourism marketing organization for the city.

"Was that a conflict of interest? A museum dedicated to the tragic events of 1692 jumpstarting Haunted Happenings in the city?"

"Oh, Haunted Happenings is completely different from what happened in 1692," she said in a manner that indicated it's an argument she's had to answer many times before. "Does a tragedy in our past mean that we can't celebrate a holiday?"

"No, no, of course not. But for some reason the tragedy makes the holiday take deeper root in this city than in most places."

"That's just because of the word *witch*." Jordan than went on to say that this quirk of linguistics is the only thing that connects 1692 to the Halloween witch. The only thing that originally connected Wiccans to the city. She pretty much gave me the spiel of the museum's Evolving Perceptions exhibit. Because five letters have multiple meanings, I was witnessing the yearly spectacle that is Salem's October.

"I assume that the museum has changed since you started here in college?"

"Yes, definitely. I remember people coming out and saying, 'Is that all there is?' or pointing out errors."

Errors like the ergot poisoning theory offered in 1976 by Professor Linnda R. Caporael. She hypothesized that ergot mold on the city's grain supply caused the symptoms that the Puritans interpreted as demon oppression. There wasn't a single Witch Trials expert I talked to who didn't bristle at the fact that people still talk about the farfetched theory, and it was only second in its capacity to annoy the still-popular idea that the Witch Trial victims were burnt at the stake.

"We've done a lot to make the museum applicable to modern day. The Evolving Perceptions exhibit was created because people came and they had the idea of the witch stereotype which, you know, is on our logo and they expect that. But it gives us the opportunity to explain about the history of the term 'witch.' Our mission officially is to be the voice of the innocent victims of 1692, but I like to take it one step beyond and make it not just the innocent witchcraft victims of 1692, but the innocent victims of witch hunts to this very day."

The spectral soundtrack I was hearing through the wall swelled ominously, reminding me to ask my next question. "The figures have been here since Day One right?" Day One being more than forty years in the past.

"About half have. And that's something we have debated for a long time. My knee-jerk reaction when I became director was to change all of the figures and make them more relatable. Some people say they look horrible. But they're stylized." Here she showed me a photocopied newspaper article from 1972. It featured a photo of one of the figures. Stylized was a kind word for it even when it was brand new. "This is how Ann Putnam looked when the museum opened, very gloomy. And she's one of the figures we've updated. I know we face a conflict. Sometimes the museum is referred to as cheesy. Some of the figures look a little depressing. But we're a time capsule of what we were in 1972. They don't make museums like ours anymore. People come back to us who visited as children and are very nostalgic about it."

"There must be a lot of good reasons to upgrade, though. You've done half of them, you said. How come you haven't done them all?"

"It's hugely expensive to make extensive changes to the current museum format, and we were looking to do more than change the figures. We did at one point get the budget to improve the main exhibit. But while we were researching it, the front of the building, our best friend and worst enemy, started to shear off. So instead of allocating the $1.5 million to the exhibit, we repaired the front of the building."

"Tell me about the competitive landscape here. Salem is a town of figure-based museums now. Is there more than enough to go around in October or can it get cutthroat?" I guess nooseneck would've been a better term. Also, I refrained from using the term Wax City.

"We have a combo ticket with the Witch House and the Rebecca Nurse Homestead. What we say is that visitors should learn the history here and then go walk in the footsteps of the participants, to the home of a judge and the home of a victim. The Witch Dungeon took a different angle. I love the trial they present and also the dungeon. I see that as a way of complementing what we do. We're all working together to bring visitors to Salem."

It was here that Stacy Tilney joined in. Tilney was from Michigan but had moved to Salem in 2008. She started doing tours here, but her background in sales and marketing helped her find a niche as the PR liaison for the museum.

"People confuse us with other museums," Tilney said. "And they do that a lot. "

"But that gives you an out, right? If somebody says, 'The museum was a little cheesy,' you can say, 'Oh, they're not talking about us, they're talking about a different museum.'"

"We'll take cheesy, but it's when it goes way beyond that we have to say, no that's not us," said Tilney.

"I feel very strongly that part of what differentiates us is that Biff has invested in the community as a whole," said Jordan. Biff Michaud is the long-time owner of the Salem Witch Museum, having bought the place form the Mulvihill family in 1980. Michaud came from a travel industry family whose bus tour business dates back to the early twentieth century. "Sometimes he gets accused of capitalizing on the hysteria. People see the long lines in October. But they don't see us open in January when there are more staff here than visitors. We're involved in making Salem a better place."

"Cheesy" is a great word that Jordan beat me to. It has various meanings: tacky, unsubtle, inauthentic, unsophisticated . . . of or like cheese. For Salem's detractors, cheesy, in all of its definitions minus that last one, is what the Salem witch tourism industry is, a blight on a city with genuine appeal and a multifaceted history.

And the Witch Trials attractions of Salem are, in general, cheesy. But that doesn't mean they're not compelling.

I imagine the alternative. That these attractions were slick, cutting-edge presentations of the Salem Witch Trials. That they used 5K HD screens and virtual reality headsets and smartphone-based augmented reality. That would be pretty awesome. I assume you'd need more than a crowded October to support that, but it would be pretty awesome, nevertheless. But I see something lost in that, too. *Slick* seems a weird way to tell the Witch Trials story. The reality of the story is visceral, and any telling of it also needs to be visceral. It needs to be uncomfortable. It needs to look you right in the eyeballs. And old fashioned wax-ish museums and amateur dramas seem to do that well. I admit that I'm a bit biased on this point. I often find charm in the cheesy.

But something else would get lost in a cleaner telling of the Salem Witch Trials tale, one that foregoes spooky narration and Halloween sound effects and costumed monsters. And that is that the story of the Salem Witch Trials is a horror story.

I don't mean that metaphorically, although it is true. The Salem Witch

Trials was a massive tragedy committed by real people against real people. The tragic deaths of twenty innocent people are a horror of human history. But I also mean it in the genre way.

The Puritans in Salem, like so many people of their day and ours, believed that their souls were threatened by powerful supernatural forces. That there was an invisible and cosmic war in the air around them. Every breath took in armies of the ethereal and every exhalation unleashed new angels and demons. That monsters were nightly at their windows. That story belongs in the horror genre.

Keep in mind, there were more monsters in the story of the Salem Witch Trials than just the perceived witches. There were ghosts—dead relatives returning from the grave. There were demons. Satan doesn't go anywhere without his entourage. There were succubi and incubi. Tituba described a three-foot-tall hairy creature she called an imp. There were were-creatures, people who could change into animals. The Black Sabbath celebrants were drinking blood like vampires and eating a flesh-like bread like cannibals. Many ministers thought the apocalypse was to happen soon, and that the chaos around the trials was the first cracking sounds of the breaking of the Seven Seals. There were more perceived monsters in this real-life episode of human history than in a marathon of Universal Studios monster movies.

Were I to have pulled the Salem Witch Trials from my own head and turned them into a novel, the story would have ended up on a Barnes & Noble shelf right between Clive Barker and H. P. Lovecraft, assuming the stocker was bad at the alphabet. The Salem Witch Trials is a horror story, in every sense of the term.

I mean, sure, those Salemites had plenty of real, terrestrial fears scratching at their psyches in addition to the spectral. The dangerous vengeance of the natives whose land they usurped, the uncertainty produced by the loss of the colony's charter—meaning that the King of England could take away their land—the deadly diseases for which they had no earthly explanation, the economic friction between Salem Village and Salem Town. The colonists had a lot to fear in their lives. But starvation, disease, winter, war—these terrors could only threaten to end the short travail of living. Their earthly lives were temporary. What happened next was all that mattered. So at the top of that hierarchy of fears was a dark man with a high-crowned hat that hid a set of horns who could ruin their lives by destroying their afterlives.

In a way, the Salem Witch Museum's figure of Lucifer is the most relevant figure in the entire story. Far more than John Hathorne or William Stoughton. Or the Putnams. Or the Parrises. Far more than Cotton Mather. Or the twenty victims. Or the teenage girls wiggling across the meetinghouse floors.

However, in this the second decade of the twenty-first century, how Salem is telling the Witch Trials story is irrelevant. It's whether the full story is being told at all. Salem has a duty to this story. If the waxy attractions weren't telling it—if they slunk away ashamed of being cheesy in a world of phone apps and Elie Weisel unveiling discreet monuments—nobody in the city would be. There would be pieces scattered about the city, but nowhere you could send a visitor to learn about the trials in the city where they happened.

And that's why you can't marginalize the "cheesy" attractions of Salem. Most of them have been around for decades, steadfastly telling the story, out-surviving other attractions, inspiring people to learn more about the trials and, as we've seen with authors like Roach and Hill, write great books about them.

And if that means that the Salem Witch Trials story will always be a waxen one in the imaginations of most tourists, then so be it. But that still leaves the question: If not the attractions, who should control the narrative of the Salem Witch Trials in Salem?

5

THE ART OF SELLING SALEM

What the Birds Know, Patrick Dougherty

"Witch tourism is on the decline." The statement was spoken to me with both certainty and not a small amount of anticipation.

It was a gutsy statement. Witch tourism has been a part of Salem almost from the time the last noose was taken down. In 1766, future US President John Adams himself even checked it out. If you want it define witch tourism more narrowly, as a commercial enterprise, it still goes pretty far back, to at least the late nineteenth century. Around that time businesses started using the phrase "Witch City" in their names and the first witch souvenirs were produced.

I was having lunch at the Village Tavern on the Essex Street Pedestrian Mall. My companion, who had made the statement, represented one of the more intriguing elements of Salem, an ill-fitting but marvelously shaped piece of the city.

It didn't take long wandering the streets of downtown Salem for me to feel the presence of this element. It appeared everywhere I went. On the Essex Street Pedestrian Mall. By the Witch Trials Memorial. Walking past many of the city's historic homes. It was always in the corner of my eye, its name everywhere on buildings and signs. Still, it's an easy thing to overlook in a city festooned in orange and black, where witches on broomsticks fly in a cloud of storefront signs and banners above one's head.

But, mostly, that's because the presence recedes in October because it has nothing to do with witches. On purpose. In fact, it's almost more anti-witch than the Puritans of 1692. This omnipresent presence is the Peabody Essex Museum, also known as PEM. "You know how I know you're not a local?" a tour guide would later say to me over cocktails at the Hawthorne Hotel. "Because you just called it PEM."

PEM's most obvious manifestation is its tall, sophisticated, glass-fronted entrance at 161 Essex Street, which towers prominently over gaudy neighbors selling Harry Potter merchandise, Tarot readings, and Witch City T-shirts. Less obvious are its offices across the street. Or the commercial properties it rents to some of those aforementioned shops. Or the small parks and gardens here and there. Or the two dozen historic homes it manages throughout the city, such as the Ropes Mansion and the Crowninshield-Bentley House. In many ways, Salem is more PEM City than Witch City.

PEM is an upscale museum of international art and culture. Its pieces come from all over the world and are arranged in spacious, spartan galleries that span three floors. Again, not the type of place you'd expect to visit after buying a smudge stick from a Witch shop or getting your face painted like a skull. Actually, they won't let you in if you have that on your face. The museum has a "no costumes" policy, which is a much stricter version of the "no masks" policy prevalent in many of the downtown retail establishments in Salem.

The galleries pretty much represent the entire globe, with modern American, Native American, African, Indian, and Oceanic art. And what's on display there is only a tiny portion of the 1.8 million items in its collection. But the museum, overall, has a decidedly Asian feel, with large collections of Japanese and Chinese works, as if there were a portal in one of the back rooms straight to the other side of the world where curators toss items back and forth.

And that includes what might be its signature piece: a two-hundred-year-old Chinese house called Yin Yu Tang. Built sometime after 1800 in the village of Huang Cun, about 250 miles southwest of Shanghai, the house has been inhabited by eight generations of the Huang family. In the 1990s, the family sold it to PEM. It was disassembled and moved—through that back room portal I assume—and then rebuilt as part of the museum, where it opened to visitors in 2003.

You can see the rear of Yin Yu Tang from the Witch Trials Memorial, where the tiled roof and exotic exterior ornamentation make it seem like the building phased into its location among the surrounding buildings after a physics experiment gone awry. It also sits across the street from a First Period home called the Pickman House, also owned by PEM, offering a fascinating juxtaposition of history and place and time.

It felt strange walking around inside an exotic artifact. The layout of the house was like an apartment complex, with sixteen bedrooms and two reception halls along two floors surrounding a central courtyard. The house was also filled with artifacts, about 60 percent of which came with the house and belonged to its former residents. It was an experience you should literally have to cross the world to have, and here it was in a suburb of Boston.

After we finished with Yin Yu Tang, we wended our way through the rest of the PEM galleries. As we looked at American ship models and Chinese jars and Polynesian idols, I kept my eyes peeled for any semblance of witchery. I saw not one broom straw. Not one Witch Trials victim quote. Not even a single Halloween decoration. I could have been strolling through any art museum in any city in any month.

However, beneath the placid, white-walled ambiance of the museum is a roiling story that goes back to the eighteenth century. And, yes, there be witches in it.

PEM is the oldest continually operating museum in America. It was started in 1799 by the East India Marine Society, a group of wealthy seamen and merchants who gathered to raise money for the widows and orphans of their fellow sailors lost at sea. They also threw parties with that kitty and bragged about the mermaids they'd bagged. Membership requirements in the society included sailing around one of the world's devil horns, either South America's Cape Horn or Africa's Cape of Good Hope. And you had to bring cool stuff back with you for the society's collection. In 1825, to house it all, they built the East India Marine Hall, the opening ceremonies of which were attended by John Quincy Adams at the start of his presidential term. The large gray building still stands today, adjacent to the PEM entrance.

The East India Marine Hall is open to anyone who purchases admission to the PEM. The top floor is the most interesting, with a banquet hall lined with ship mastheads and portraits of captains and a couple of small *Wunderkammer* filled with items brought back by members of the East India Marine Society—like a bedraggled penguin with a foot-long neck, put together blindly by a taxidermist in a country that had yet to get the National Geographic Channel.

A couple of name changes later, it became the Peabody Museum of Salem. Meanwhile, in 1848, the Essex Institute was formed out of the Essex Historical Society and the Essex County Natural Historic Society. While the Peabody was salty and exotic, the Essex Institute was dusty and historic, its collection comprised of historical buildings, records, and artifacts, as well as natural history items from the region. It was also the steward of the surviving trial records of the Witch Trials and the artifacts related to them.

In 1992, the two institutions mergerd, becoming the Peabody Essex Museum, or PEM. Its new director was a man named Dan Monroe. He had some serious ideas for the place, starting with a ten-year plan that would completely transform the museum.

And out of the massive collections of these two history museums came, somehow, a world-class art museum. The sixteenth largest in the country, in fact.

Certain groups of locals didn't like the idea. Historians didn't like the decreased emphasis on local history, nor the fact that the museum's archive access policies became much more restrictive. People who had grown up in Salem missed the strange charm of the quirky museums that had shown them odd wonders like shrunken heads when they were children. Some in this working-class town didn't like what seemed to be pretentiousness on the part of the museum. Many felt like the museum had taken itself out of the community. The tourist industry didn't want a major and central swathe of the downtown not bread-and-buttered with witches. The city itself fought with them over facility expansions and taxes. It got so bad that PEM threatened to leave the city. In designing the building that came out of the decade-long project, they had a back-up design for Boston in their back pockets, just in case things went, well, south.

So it was with some surprise, based on the type of book I was writing, that someone from the museum agreed to talk to me. His name is Jay Finney, and he is the Chief Marketing Officer for PEM. He's the one with whom I was eating lunch at the Village Tavern and discussing the demise of witch tourism.

Finney is from New Jersey, although he has Massachusetts years in his timeline. He spent his childhood at a boarding school in Andover, itself a runner-up for the title of Witch City. Still, he would take the long way round to return to the state as an adult. After nabbing degrees in archeology and art history at the University of Pennsylvania, he headed west and worked in advertising and corporate marketing in Los Angeles. As this eventually landed him marketing gigs at art museums in San Francisco, it provided him with a more direct approach to history and the arts than his actual degrees had. He came to PEM in 2002, just before the ten-year expansion finished, to try to figure out how to market this new, strange thing that locals do not call PEM.

"I've wanted to work in museums since I was four. My temple was the American Museum of Natural History in New York." Finney told me that when he was eight, his grandmother arranged for him to meet a curator named Hobart Van Duesen, whose office was made up of glass cases of animals three stories high with metal catwalks and spiral staircases. "It was like out of Jules Verne. And that was it for me."

"And now you're in Salem. With witches."

"I don't even know where to start for you with the Unholy Wars—at least that's what I call them—between what Salem was and what it's trying to be."

"Let's start with the merger. How does local history museum plus science and nature museum equal high-end art institution?"

"We took it back to the vision of the museum's founders. They were

America's first global entrepreneurs, the first Americans to encounter cultures in Japan and India and Africa and all kinds of points east and west. They were bringing stuff back that was legitimate art from these cultures, and so they created America's first privately financed public museum to display it. They wanted to educate Salemites that it's a big world out there, that we're part of a global society and economy. That's what we do now. We don't talk about Salem, we talk about the world."

"But you got some resistance for that."

"Some people lament that we went from this wonderful history museum of Salem to an 'art museum'," Finney said, pronouncing the phrase with faux-hauteur. "But being a history museum wasn't a path to sustainability for us. The crowd that loves the way the museum used to be, they aren't giving money. The people that give money are the ones interested in interacting with global societies and expanding world views and understanding of all these places. But that other crowd, they're a minority today. Most people will say PEM has been the best thing that's ever happened to the town."

Finny then went on to explain that when Monroe developed the plan for the merged museums, part of that was a $25 million capital campaign to expand the footprint to display more of the collections. The museum not only hit the funding goal, it exceeded the goal, eventually raising more than $200 million. "They kept coming up with new ways to view the collection and to get it out of storage and become a real museum with modern facilities. The money followed the ideas," he explained.

Finney pointed out the museum's strong Asian collection, which was deemphasized for political reasons during World War II. At that point, the emphasis went to the safer, more politically acceptable maritime collection. "So it became known for ships, and when grandpa came to town, that's where you took him. But it was a fraction of the collection and not at all what it could be. So we had to change everyone's perception of the place from being a sleepy little maritime history museum with marginal facilities into a model of a very modern, major museum."

That model includes one of the largest suites of temporary exhibition space on the East Coast, with cutting-edge environmental controls and all the other features that enable them to take work from top museums. But it took a lot more than having the facilities. They had to let other museums know through major outreach initiatives and by putting together their own traveling exhibits. "Now we are a player. We are seen as a real art museum and nobody asks anymore, 'Why is that show at PEM?' But it took a lot from a marketing and curatorial standpoint."

Finney didn't know it at the time, but this was a point he didn't have to sell to me. In the single month I lived in Salem, PEM brought in amazing work from two of my favorite contemporary artists.

The first was a Patrick Dougherty installation. I've chased Dougherty installations all over New England, so having one just down the street from where I was staying in Salem was a fantastic experience.

Dougherty is a North Carolina–based artist who weaves large, hollow structures out of thousands of dried saplings over a period of weeks with the help of local volunteers. The end result is a rustic configuration that looks like a large bird got bored with making nest shapes. They're the size of small houses, and are made up of multiple rooms that visitors can walk through until the sculptures decay over time and are mulched. For the Salem piece, *What the Birds Know,* the rustic shapes looked like a row of cottages from a Dr. Seuss book if Dr. Seuss lost all of his crayons except for the brown one, all tilted and rounded and ready for creatures with nonsense names to take up residence.

I've never caught a Dougherty sculpture in such an urban environment before. I've seen them in cities, but always on a common or in a park or on some stretch of open grass. This one was in the small front yard of the Crowninshield-Bentley house, mere feet away from the busy streets of Salem, at the intersection of Hawthorne Boulevard and Essex Street. During the Halloween month, Dougherty's handiwork was haunted by hordes of monsters and thronged by crowds of tourists, which was another way I'd never experienced his work.

And I think having Dougherty's wickerwork in Witch City jibes beyond art appreciation. I could imagine a fairy tale witch living inside *What the Birds Know,* sucking on the bones of children as clouds of deep purple waft from her cauldron and through the tops of the structures. Admittedly, my imagination was helped by the many costumed witches who flowed by the installation every day in October.

The second installation was one I'd wanted to see for a long time. PEM brought Theo Jansen's Strandbeests to Salem for the autumn season, housing them in one of the temporary exhibit spaces that the museum transformation produced. Jansen is out of the Netherlands and creates creatures out of PVC pipe, plastic bottles, and canvas. That's a bad description. Makes it seem like kitsch on a craft show table. Let's try again.

Jansen creates large, skeletal, multi-legged creatures that get as big as elephants and seem more alive than any girl painted by a Dutch Master or any Ron Mueck sculpture. These complex moving structures are equipped with sails that power a system of intricate movements that make the Strandbeests walk across the ground. And they do so in a way that seems organic instead of mechanistic. They have no faces, no skin, no recognizable biological shape, nothing for us to react to but their alien movement. And yet the hundreds of thousands of years of evolved instinct riddling our brains insists that they are indeed alive. You really need to stop reading my inadequate descriptions and hit up YouTube.

If you do that, you'll probably see one of Jansen's Erector Set–like lattices of moving plastic taking off rapidly down a beach under its own power while Jansen chases it from behind like a dog owner with a frayed leash in his hand. He's often quoted as wanting to create herds of these creatures and let them loose into the world. That's the day that the world gets much better.

On my visit to PEM, the poor Yin Yu Tang was shown up by a whole room of these creatures. A few massive ones that had broken and become still life were on display. Others, though, were smaller, like the size of a grand piano, and visitors were encouraged to push them around, since there was no wind to animate them. Of course, I did that, and found that with only a tiny amount of force, these things would take off, seemingly of their own volition. My time pushing Jansen's Strandbeests will never get knocked out of my top art experiences.

Back at the Village Tavern, I was curious about the latest expansion plans for the museum, which involved a successful and staggering $650 million fundraising campaign. "Seems like you guys are still aggressively enlarging the facility. Is that because you've not quite arrived at where you want to be?"

"We actually haven't grown in size since 2003. Most of the growth was in the exhibition program. We fitted out the galleries, reinstalled the permanent collection, created the temporary exhibition spaces, and developed our own traveling exhibits. It also took us a few years to figure out how to run the facility. We were like Gremlin drivers getting into a Maserati: 'Whoa, what does this button do?' So we haven't grown in our footprint. Now we will."

"So you're doing all this, and meanwhile, twenty-five miles away, is Boston's Museum of Fine Arts, which would seem like overwhelming competition."

"Ours is a very unusual museum. It's the sixteenth-largest art museum in North America and the only museum in the top fifty that is not in a major downtown metro where you're close to a million-plus visitors. We would be the biggest museum in most big cities. If we were in Boston, we'd probably triple our attendance, even with the MFA there. It just means we have to be more creative. Our brand is surprise and delight. It's about creating a different experience than what you'll see anywhere else, including the MFA."

Finney admitted that, despite the unique aspects of the collection, there are practical barriers to increasing the amount of vistors they get every year past a certain point. "Salem is known all over the world for one thing, and it's not arts and culture."

"What about that? What about leveraging the Witch Trials?"

"I'd lose my job." Finney's boss, Dan Monroe, was notoriously against anything witchy brushing against the museum. That included exhibits, that included marketing, that included the museum's own Witch Trials collection.

"But as a hypothetical, that wouldn't impact attendance?"

"The people that come for that, the October crowd, they don't go to art museums. There could be twenty thousand people walking past our entrance and maybe fifty will come in." That had been my own experience. We visited the museum on a weekend morning in October. It wasn't empty, but it was sparsely attended, which is maybe exactly the right amount of patronage for our timing. Still, it was certainly out of proportion to the crowd already streaming past outside on the pedestrian mall. And I didn't see a single jack-o'-lantern T-shirt being worn inside. I'd forgotten to wear mine.

"Sure, they're here for a certain thing that PEM doesn't offer, but

PEM could, right? You have the documents and artifacts from the Witch Trials." I wouldn't let the point go. Talking museum branding and economic models was fun, but this was the real reason I wanted to talk to a PEM representative. I'm not sure what all PEM held from the witch trials in its dark basements. The trial records, sure, but I'd also heard stories of George Jacob's crutches and John Proctor's sundial and pins that had magically pierced the flesh of the afflicted. I'd even heard rumors of a rough piece of coffin that might have been from the Gallows Hill burial site. At the very least, I'm sure they had an Old Witch Gaol beam.

"Yes, we have the only authentic items from the Witch Trials in the city. However, we are a museum of art and culture, not a museum of social history. And any connection whatsoever to the witch trials is a complete non-starter for our director. But the truth is, tourists would rather spend twice as much as the museum admission to do the schlocky things in Salem instead." The average yearly attendance at PEM is about two hundred and fifty thousand, lower than the four hundred thousand or so people drawn to the Salem Witch Museum. Finney continued, "Keep in mind, too, that there is a huge difference between people who are interested in witches and people who are interested in witch history. And during October, it's the former, not the latter. And so we lower our heads and wait for it to blow over. Our model is the visitor experience, what happens in the galleries. That's why our brand is really important."

"It's fascinating to hear you talk about brand, because the city you're in, it has its own brand, and it has exactly what every marketer prays for every night before going to bed, an obvious differentiator. I mean, witches, nobody has that reputation."

"It has a place. If you stick historic homes and sailboats on the cover of Salem's tourist brochures, what's different between us and Rockport or Gloucester? That funky part is what makes this place so cool, and that helps the city. October is what it is, but throughout the rest of the year, you also have this offbeat, Greenwich Village–type vibe in addition to the classic New England one. And the coexistence of those two things is what makes this place special."

"So why fight against it again?"

"Well, we fight against the overemphasis on witches. Because at the same time, a lot of businesses in Salem do terrible at Halloween. Like the nice restaurants. Those price points are too high for a crowd of mostly T-shirt buyers. There's nothing wrong with that demographic, but they don't stay long and don't spend much. Cultural tourists are older, stay longer, and spend more money. And that's a much better reputation for the city. So a lot of people just want Halloween to go away or at least get toned down."

Finney then explained that, despite the city's international reputation, it almost didn't matter to PEM. Only 18 percent of museum attendance is from tourism, so its best bet is to play the "local market game," in which they focus on visitors from Boston and areas west of Boston. "If I can get them here once, it's infinitely easier to get them here again. Just don't come in October," he said.

That's when he dropped the big one on me. "I think witch tourism is on the decline and has been for several years. There's been no investment in the witch tourism infrastructure. The witch museums haven't touched their figures in decades, no one has put any money into any of that stuff. It just basically happens that they get all their revenue in one month. With the advent of social media and Yelp, it's much harder to play that game. And also Halloween has become a big, big business in other places. PEM's attendance meanwhile is the best it's ever been, and this year was our best yet. Salem is almost there and is moving away from the witch thing."

"You think October in Salem will one day not be, I don't know, October in Salem?"

"No, October, fine, that's your brand, no point in raising your hand and saying, 'art and culture, art and culture.' My kids love it here during October. But there are eleven other months in the year and Salem has really come a long way, and that has taken some of the teeth out of the witch crowd."

"I still wonder about the potential of the Witch Trial artifacts. You could sub-brand them. Stick them in one of your historic homes that nobody associates with you and have the witch museum to end all witch museums. There is a specific historic narrative that people are looking for when they come here, during any month really, and if the place with the actual artifacts isn't controlling that narrative, others are going to fill that void. In this case, the type of tourism that you say is bad for the PEM brand."

"It's just a non-starter with us. We're not about aggrandizing the myth of Salem, which for a tiny moment was really amazing. We're about connecting with a global society, and that's more true to our founding fathers." He then said that the only reason it's an issue is that in 1992, the Witch Trials Tercentenary happened and Halloween was growing in general, and that all merged and became huge. "But now it's in a kind of decay, and most of the articles you see in the press are, 'Hey, there's more to Salem than witches, and it's cooler than we thought.' So make sure your book doesn't take us backwards."

Much of what Finney said made sense to me. The moves made by PEM were practical ones, fueled by concerns about viability. They were looking for a way to use what they had to prosper as a museum despite geographical limitations. But, honestly, it wouldn't matter if the reasoning made zero sense. The one PEM argument you cannot argue with is its success.

PEM's operating budget has risen from $3.4 million before the merger to $30 million today. Its endowment rose from $23 million to more than $300 million. Even though its current attendance is below that of the Salem Witch Museum, it still ballooned from eighty thousand a year to two hundred and fifty thousand. And when you factor in its traveling exhibitions, which it never had before, that gives them face time with half a million more people across the country. And when it finishes its current expansions, it may actually improve its already impressive ranking of sixteenth largest art museum in the country.

Later, I found a 2013 *Wall Street Journal* article depicting PEM's endowment-first strategy as revolutionary, if perhaps not reproducible outside of New England, which is something Finney himself had echoed to me. That made me wonder if the difference is the witches, if they galvanize a certain, well-off segment of Salem, making them more willing to invest in anything that will flatten the conical hats of the city. If that's the case, then it certainly isn't a reproducible strategy. Except maybe in Transylvania. I brought the idea up to Finney over email. His response? "I can assure you that hardly any of our donors care a whit about the Witch City reference."

And I'm sure he's right. But I do love the idea of friction between PEM and its surroundings, even if most of that friction is in the past. It's too reminiscent of the political and economic friction that started the Witch

Trials in the first place—between the working-class, parochial farmers of Salem Village and the rich, globetrotting entrepreneurs of Salem Town. In this case, it's the schlocky T-shirt demographic vs. the millionaire museum donors. Class is just never out.

But all that aside, I still can't shake the discomfort with the fact that the Witch Trials artifacts aren't on public view. Poor George Jacob's crutches are sitting lonely in an *Indiana Jones* warehouse somewhere, Proctor's sundial may never again see the light of day, and the trial transcripts are only available if your driver's license has an ivory tower on it. For the record, I did ask to see them, but I was turned down for lack of legitimate academic motivation. Which is true. I don't need to tell you that what's in your hands is not even close to a scholarly work. Still, usually my inroads into museum basements are for public relations reasons, and Finney made it clear over the course of our conversation that there are certain publics the museum doesn't want relations with. No offense intended by him, if you're reading this, of course.

So that's valid, if seemingly a tad insecure. I mean, Boston's Museum of Fine Arts has a stellar Egyptology collection on permanent view. But they are not in the least afraid of being pigeonholed into being a "mummy museum." Of course, the MFA doesn't have the years of baggage that PEM has to carry.

But that baggage will be impossible to shrug off as long as they hold the Witch Trial artifacts in its basement. As long as they have them, the museum will be inextricably connected to them, even if it doesn't want to be. PEM is their official protector, and it could be argued that because of that role, it has a duty to them, especially in city where most of the traces of the Witch Trials have been allowed to vanish and in a country where every schoolchild learns about the trials.

Also, in the end, I, personally, just want to see Witch Trials stuff.

Now, other marketing organizations in the city are more secure about their cauldrons and brooms. In fact, they rely on them. And, as I said at the beginning of the chapter, the city has had more than a century of practice at it.

I was looking forward to talking to Kate Fox. As the head of Destination Salem, she's responsible for the destination marketing efforts for the entire city.

I made my way to the organization's headquarters on Washington Street. It was directly across from where the old Salem courthouse had stood. Fox ushered me into her office, which had hanging on a wall one of the five-foot-tall orange and green vinyl Haunted Happenings banners with the duly licensed Salem Witch Museum witch on it that festoons the city. She was taking time out from fulfilling the avalanche of international media request she receives every year during October to speak with me. Her most recent press requests, she told me, were from Mexico, Australia, and Dubai.

Fox grew up in Rye, New York, where she attended the same school where Margaret Hamilton—the actress who played the green-skinned Wicked Witch of the West in *The Wizard of Oz*—taught kindergarten in the early 1930s. Fox moved to Massachusetts in 1998 and started working for Destination Salem that October. She stayed in the strange, strange world of Witch City marketing until 2002, when she took a break for a few years. In 2007, she returned.

"Why'd you come back?"

"I love Salem. It's such a unique place. Nobody else is having conversations about zombies and witches and how that impacts the costume dog show while being surrounded by amazing maritime and architectural heritages. It's just such a unique, dynamic destination full of a bizarre mix of people."

"You're pitching to me, I think. Is your background in destination marketing?"

"No, I'm an English Major with a Religious Studies minor." Oddly enough, that meant she studied Nathaniel Hawthorne for her major and pagan traditions for her minor. Little could she have known she would end up in the one city where both of those would come in handy. And there goes my best opportunity for having a chapter in this book that doesn't mention the native author.

"Tell me what it's like being in charge of marketing a city with such a massive and bizarre international reputation."

"I always ask people when they travel abroad, 'How long do you tell people you're from Salem?' Because no matter where you go in the world, people respond with, 'Oh, are you a witch?' At some point people get tired of that and just say they're from Boston. It happens with domestic travel as well, but it's more remarkable to think you can go anywhere on the planet and that will happen. People know Salem."

I asked how they approach the busy season, when the town gets some two hundred and fifty thousand visitors over the course of October, not counting Halloween itself. She explained that they divide the month into thirty-one days and one night: Haunted Happenings and Halloween. Once they hit Halloween, at about 4 p.m. on the 31st, it's no longer a marketing effort. Instead it's a safety effort. "People are going to come that evening whether I want them to or not. If it's nice weather on a Saturday night, we're going to have seventy-five thousand people on the streets of Salem. And they're not here to be tourists, they're not here to spend money, they're just here to be here." That's a big, single-day chunk for a city that welcomes about a million visitors over the entire year.

Many of those visitors come to Salem by bus, but at one point during the month I saw a large cruise ship docked in the harbor. I was eating at a restaurant called Victoria Station on Pickering Wharf, and there it was, massive and white in the distance. A city docked by a city. It looked like it had been Photoshopped into the harbor or had suddenly appeared direct from the Bermuda Triangle.

Salem has always marketed to cruise ships docking in Boston, but last year was the first year it was able to take on one of the massive crafts at its doorstep. To do that, it just had to spend $800,000 to repurpose an old 800-foot coal dock from the nearby power plant, which was in the process of being demolished for a natural gas plant. Its last smokestack towered in Salem's sky during my October stay.

In September and October, two different cruise ships docked at Salem, the United States–based, 450-passenger *Seabourn Quest*, and the 1,300-passenger *Balmoral* out of England. They only stay for about one day, tops, but with the dock only half a mile or so from downtown, it's enough of a window to get people off the ship and into the city. "It's huge that they can dock here, so I think we'll see exponential growth in cruise ships," Fox told me.

Of course, we're talking about September and October. The story I'd always heard is that throughout the rest of the year, Salem is pretty empty. But my experience visiting over the summer and spring didn't reflect that at all. So I asked her if it was an old anecdote.

"It's just the smaller attractions that close from November to April. But January in Salem is hard to market, for sure."

"That's a lot of New England, though, right? Unless you're a major city or a ski town."

"Right. But the Peabody Essex Museum does tremendous programming year-round. And it can be frustrating for me when they have a great evening event in January or February with extended hours, and people come to see it, but can't find anything else to do because the retail is shuttered. I hope that we evolve to the point where that's not an issue."

"How do you interface with an organization like PEM, since it has its own marketing group?"

"I think its marketing budget is bigger than my annual budget. But we do collaborate. They helped us with our rebranding. Somebody from PEM is always on the board. They have tremendous staff resources and a great perspective on marketing and communications, and they're constantly bringing in new assets for the city to make us marketable."

"But obviously they have a discomfort with the Witch part of Witch City."

"Yes, they don't want anything to do with the witch." She said "the witch" like it was a giant mountain on the edge of town.

"How long ago was the rebranding?" Salem's current tagline is "Still Making History." Before that, it was "A Bewitching Seaport." But more interesting than removing "witch" from the tagline was its new logo: a triangular shape that could be interpreted as either a witch hat or a sailboat depending on, I guess, one's biases. It's a Rorschach test for a person's feelings about Salem.

"That was in 2010." She said that during the process one of the concepts their agency came up with was "We Can't Make This Stuff Up," which stuck as the unofficial tagline behind the scenes. "We had a live news broadcast in September on the Common, and all these locals were gathered around watching it. All of a sudden Nosferatu shows up in full costume. Something happens on an almost daily basis where we scratch our heads and say, 'We can't make this stuff up." But 'Still Making History' is so true and so applicable to Salem."

"But you've had a few wars in that history, right?" She didn't come right out and say it to me, but I caught the implication that her decision to leave Destination Salem in 2002 had to do with some political infighting about marketing the city. "Like you have PEM, who doesn't like the witch story, and then you have all the Witch Trials attractions that rely on it, so you're in this constant flux betwee the two poles."

She laughed. "I'm supported by my advertisers. I love all my children equally."

"Oh, you're all in this together, definitely. I would love to see your board meetings sometime, art museum staff and Witch shop owners and attraction managers."

"It has been antagonistic in the past. When Destination Salem was started in 1998, there was no witch. We were interested in cultural tourism. The National Trust for Historic Preservation published several publications about cultural heritage tourists and how they stay longer and spend more and that's what we wanted. But that was the wrong path. I'm glad there was a correction and that when I came back in 2007, we were able to market everything we have." By that time the city had a lot more to market, as well—more tours, more restaurants, more boutique shopping, and everything that PEM was doing. "So by saying we were going to incorporate the witch, it no longer had to be 90 percent of the story. Still, when Salem tried to get rid of the witch, the city got international press about it. We also got a tremendous amount of press when we launched 'Still Making History' and the witch hat logo."

"But you're okay with this summing it all up?" I point to the Haunted Happenings logo on the banner hanging in her office.

"In October, yes, because that's Halloween, and we're a Halloween destination. Unless you read *USA Today*."

Thanks to Twitter, I knew what she was talking about. *USA Today* had been running a reader poll to determine what city was the best Halloween destination, and the Destination Salem Twitter account had been trying to rally its voters. "You guys didn't win that?"

"We came in third. Derry, Ireland, was first and Anoka, Minnesota, was second."

That was a haunting reminder of what Finney has said about Halloween becoming big everywhere, but this smacked more of a stuffed ballot box. Ireland was where Halloween started, of course, and Derry, it's been said, throws one of the biggest Halloween parties in Europe. About

twenty-five thousand people show up for it. Anoka is famous for putting on the first city-sponsored Halloween celebration back in 1920 and bills itself as "The Halloween Capitol of the World." They get about forty thousand on Halloween. Neither achieves Salem's numbers, nor has either location really woven the spooky into the fabric of its city—month-long and year-round—like Salem has.

"Is Haunted Happenings a more family-friendly event than it has been in the past?"

"We've worked really hard on that. Which is why this year's cover of the Haunted Happenings brochure got a lot of pushback."

She handed me one, although at this point in the month I had about half a dozen already. She pointed to Lucifer on the cover.

"I thought it was a good picture and the colors worked, but I got some flack that it wasn't family-friendly. Last year we had a cover that was almost too family-friendly." She picked one of those out of a file and handed it to me. It was an inoffensive child's sketch of a group of people in costume. "We've been family-friendly for a really long time, but this year we wanted to be a little edgier because there is so much to do after dark. In the past, we needed to pull back on the twenty-one-and-over crowd, especially for Halloween night. It was getting unsafe and there was a lot of vandalism, so we wanted to seem almost too boring for that type of crowd. These days it's less of an issue."

It was one more way that Salem found itself in a constant balancing act. But, honestly, it really sounded to me that by 2015 they had found that balance, or at least they had come the closest they've ever been to it. Even the balancing act I had grown the most interested in, PEM vs. The Witch. Inside the Haunted Happenings brochure that Fox handed me, on a page advertising a haunted house called Chambers of Terror and the *Golden Girls: The Lost Halloween Episode* theater show, was a PEM advertisement for the Strandbeest exhibition. In a typeface straight out of a 1950s monster movie trailer, it read, "Release the Beest!"

As I left, Fox gifted me the large Haunted Happenings banner in her office, which now adorns a wall in my study and has helped me stay in the Halloween spirit as I continued putting this book together over the holidays and snow days that followed October. As I walked back home, the banner rolled up tightly under my arm, I looked at the Haunted Happenings banners unfurled across the city. Unlike mine, each one of them had a small sponsorship sign attached to its lower edge. And on the one dangling from the bottom of the banner beside the Salem Witch Museum were the words, "Sponsored by Peabody Essex Museum."

6

WITCHES VS. PIRATES

Friendship of Salem

I was walking down Derby Street for the thousandth time on this October adventure. Maybe I was heading to the Haunted Neighborhood to breathe some machine fog and eat some fried Oreos in the graveyard. Maybe I was just trying to avoid the attraction pamphleteers in flowing black costumes a couple of streets over on the Essex Street Pedestrian Mall. Maybe I was looking for one of the few Halloween-themed cocktails that I hadn't yet tried. Regardless, by this time my eyes had mostly adjusted to all the witches and weirdness around town. Then I got to it. That one thing on Derby Street that seems out of place in this place where there is almost no out of place.

It's just a mural on the side of a brick building. A simple one. A couple of men climbing ropes. There's a similar one on the other side of the building. The men look like sailors. I almost want to call them . . . pirates. That can't be, right, can it? Pirates? In Salem? But the two blokes with tricorn hats and eye patches cajoling passersby in front of the building made the observation indisputable, even without the name above their heads: New England Pirate Museum.

Witch City has a pirate museum.

The Wizard of Oz taught us that witches hate water, but Salem is completely sodden. Or at least, it was. You can't walk anywhere without crossing a street named after a sea captain, and most often a family of them, like Derby Street itself. Their graves dot the Old Burying Point, their titles often abbreviated on the stone to "Capt." with the "t" in superscript. Many of the historic mansions in town were built by these prosperous ocean merchants. The city may have had nine months of witches, but it also had half a century or more of sailors. That's why the stylized witch's hat that is Salem's current logo is designed to also potentially look like a tall ship, depending on whether your Halloween costume features an eye patch or a warty nose.

To better sound these briny depths, we're going back two months and trading the gray and white skies of the New England autumn for the blue and yellow skies of the previous New England summer.

It was August 2, and I was still on Derby Street, further east this time, a few blocks shy of The House of the Seven Gables. Behind me loomed the big, blocky, and historic Custom House, the massive golden eagle on its roof glinting in the sun. In front of me was an expanse of green leading to Salem Harbor. The expanse is usually bare except for a scattering of people. Today it was covered in white tents. For a festival.

Salem has other festivals besides Haunted Happenings. Like its Jazz and Soul Festival. And its Literature Festival. And its Film Festival. And Holiday Happenings. "We have at least one festival every month," Kate Fox had told me. Certainly none of them have the duration or success or energy or economic impact of Haunted Happenings, but they are parties nonetheless. This one happened to be the 27th annual Salem Maritime Festival.

Almost as soon as the people of Salem established the city, they left it. These adventurers sailed everywhere on the planet, exploring harbors at all ends of the earth. The city motto is still "To the farthest port of the rich East." Across the world, Salem was often synonymous with America. There's even a rumor of a Chinese map that labels the entire North American continent as Salem. Salemites would run into each other in China and the islands of the East Indies almost as often as on the streets of their own city. They were trading everything—ceramics, furniture, textiles, silk, figs, teas—but spices were really their game. The city had almost a monopoly on pepper. Yup, Pepper City. Today the city seal is a figure dressed in Sumatran garb to represent the land from which they got all that sneeze powder.

As a result, by the end of the eighteenth century, Salem was the wealthiest city per capita in the country.

Its fleet particularly came in handy in battle. During the Revolutionary War, it sent out 158 privateers—civilian reserve forces activated during wartime—from its harbor, more than any other port in the country. Salem did the same during the War of 1812, launching about a sixth of the country's ships for the war effort.

And then history banished them from sea and told them to grow some legs.

In 1807, President Thomas Jefferson placed an embargo on all US exports to protest the European powers seizing US ships during the

Salem Custom House

Napoleonic Wars. This act shut down all US ports and cut Salem off from its lucrative trade routes. This was followed closely by the War of 1812, which beat up the Salem fleet pretty bad. But the biggest assault on Salem's seaworthiness came from their neighbors to the south. Boston and New York were growing and overtook Salem with bigger, deeper harbors and better internal infrastructure. The sea dried up for Salem before the midway point of the nineteenth century, so the city turned to what many towns in America were turning to after the Industrial Revolution: manufacturing. That's how the leather industry started, and it's why Parker Brothers was around. Of course, that way of life eventually went the way of most US manufacturing, forcing Salem to re-invent itself yet again, this time as the tourist destination we know today.

But time hasn't scraped off all of the city's barnacles. And the Salem Maritime National Historic Site, the center of all things salty in Salem, is there to make sure that never happens.

The Salem Maritime National Historic Site was granted its status by the National Park Service in 1938. In fact, it was the first national historic site ever established.

Today, the site is a conglomeration of about twelve structures, a tall ship, and nine acres of Salem waterfront. Derby Street cuts right through it all. In this part of town, you have as much of a chance of running into Smokey the Bear hats as you do witch hats. Still, despite its location and size, you could drive directly through it and not know that you had just buzzed a site of national significance.

But on the day of the festival, there was no mistaking it. In the tents, people showed off knot-tying skills that had nothing to do with nooses and intricate model ships that looked sea-worthy. On the open spaces of the green, people in period costumes ran cannon drills. Old sea shanties were being played on concertinas and violins on a small stage, the backdrop of which looked like the ribs of a ship hull. Researchers were showing passersby marine biology specimens in plastic tubs of cold water. I saw a few pirate costumes. Interspersed throughout it all, people in colonial attire or Park Service uniforms directed visitors to all the various activities underway.

I knew exactly what I wanted to see: the triple-masted, black and yellow tall ship docked beside the green, placid and lonely, as though waiting for all of its friends to come back. Maybe that's why it's called the *Friendship of Salem*.

The sailing ship was built in 1998 and was modeled after another Salem-based ship called the *Friendship* that was built 200 years earlier. The first *Friendship* was made for trade and sailed all over the world, to Europe, to China and the East Indies, to South America and Russia. She was seized and sold by the British in 1812. Her captain and crew were unaware of the war that had started a couple of months earlier.

I walked up the metal gangway to the deck. The second I set foot on its planks, one of the crew approached me and said, "This is a working ship. So be careful where you step and don't be a jackass about everything." Half of that was a direct quote and the other half was a paraphrase. In fact, the *Friendship* is sea-worthy. Most of the year, you'll find it docked at the maritime site, but every once in a while it stretches its canvas and heads to open water.

The deck was black, but most everything on it was painted green, including the ship's wheel, which was lashed into immobility. The hull length of the ship is 116 feet, and it gains another 55 feet with the yellow booms at the ends that match the masts. At the prow is a wooden figurehead of a woman in a long blue and white dress holding flowers. As I meandered, I watched one of the crew ascend the 106 feet to the top of the highest mast to adjust the US flag flapping there. The ship has about 55 miles of spidery rigging and 23 sails that cover 9,409 square feet. Below deck, it felt like a windowless wilderness cabin, all unpainted wood and stuffed with bunk beds and barrels and ladders.

The *Friendship* was the second ship I had visited that day. The other was a bit more modern and was in port just for the festival. Metal-gray, compact, the US Coast Guard patrol boat looked like a tank. Like it was built to ram things instead of float. One of the crewmembers told me that the boat can face off with waves the size of buildings and completely roll over and right itself. "It's not something we want to do, but the ship can take it."

Clambering through this ship, the interior was full of buttons and lights and display screens, a far cry from the piles of rope and wooden barrels of its neighbor. It's weird to think that these two ships tackle the exact same seas.

But those two ships were as far as my sea legs took me. I was a landlubber for the rest of the festival. The dozen buildings that form the architectural holdings of the park line Derby Street, but not all are open to the public. Some house park offices. Most you can only enter on scheduled tours. During the festival, the public buildings were open for anybody to enter.

Before I visited any of them, though, I walked a half a mile out on Derby Wharf, one of the last remaining of the more than fifty wharves that once lined Salem Harbor, on past the *Friendship* and to the squat light station at the tip of the wharf. It's about twenty feet tall and topped by a black cupola, and it has guided ships into the harbor since 1871. Back then the mini-lighthouse used an oil lamp. Today, it's a solar-powered red light. But the real reason to walk out that far on the wharf is to look back at the coast. From that vantage, I could pick out The House of the Seven Gables, Pickering Wharf, the large colorful historical homes that make up the park, the smoke stack of the power plant. Most prominent on the coastline, though, was the Custom House.

Erected in 1819 for the US Customs Service, the building is an august-looking structure. Its main two floors form a brick rectangle topped by four chimneys, a white cupola, and the aforementioned golden eagle. Eight white pillars frame the front door and hold up a terrace on the second floor. A large, wide, block staircase leads up to the front door. The Custom House represents the red tape that marks the finish line for the ships of Salem's past. It declared in no uncertain terms to those water-weary souls entering the harbor, "Don't forget to pay your taxes."

Inside, the rooms of the Custom House are set up to show the less-than-glamorous life of a customs inspector, which, apparently, involves lots of logging and inspecting cargo and weighing barrels and keeping records and stamping documents.

But, thanks to author Nathaniel Hawthorne, we don't have to imagine the life. I know. This guy again. But Hawthorne worked at this Custom House for nearly three years. *The Scarlet Letter* uses the Custom House as a jumping-off point, as the narrator finds there the tattered letter and the records that tell the story of Hester Prynne. Before doing so, he describes working at the building, which is a decrepit, empty shell that matches the rotting warehouses and wharves of the neighborhood. The Custom

House is staffed by a skeleton crew of boring, bumbling clerks as dusty and cobwebbed as the offices they work in, most appointed only because of family connections. There's not much to do there, because no ships come into Salem's haunted house-like harbor that often anymore. So not so much red tape as gray. But the people of Salem didn't like the picture it painted of a prominent part of their city. In one of his later prefaces to the novel, Hawthorne discusses the fierce reception of the introduction: "It could hardly have been more violent, indeed, had [I] burned down the Custom-House, and quenched its last smoking ember in the blood of a certain venerable personage." But Salem got over it. Today, one of the rooms in the Custom House is dedicated to him, a surprise literary exhibit in a building dedicated to bureaucracy up into the 1930s. We'll come back to it during the Hawthorne chapter.

On the second floor, I walked up to the central window for a great view of the harbor and the Maritime Festival. Almost completely filling one of the rooms on this floor is a massive, golden eagle. This is the original eagle, carved in 1826 and hanging over Hawthorne's head during his tenure at the Custom House, that adorned the building. However, during his time, it would have had its original paint job, brown and white like a real bald eagle. It was gilded later in the century. The eagle made it to the new millennium before being taken down, repaired, conserved, and retired inside the house. Today, the eagle glinting from the building's facade is a fiberglass replica.

Most of the Custom House's neighbors are part of the park. Adjacent to it is the Hawkes House, a three-story, yellow Federal–style mansion that was completed in 1800 and named after its original owner, Benjamin Hawkes, who ran a shipyard. Beside it is a brick, three-story mansion dating to 1762 called the Derby House. It was the home of Elias Hasket Derby and Elizabeth Crowninshield—both of those surnames represented rich and powerful ocean merchant families of Salem. Next to that house was a tiny, two-story building, faded blue and trimmed in brown. A sign above the door declared it the "West India Goods Store." After the festival, I found myself inside this building to talk to Emily Murphy, the park historian.

Murphy is originally from Pennsylvania, but she bounced around the upper East Coast pursuing degrees in American Studies. One of the places she matriculated was St. John's College in Annapolis, Maryland, a strange school that graduates strange people. It's one of my alma maters.

When Murphy moved to Salem, she parlayed her previous experience as a ranger at Independence Hall in Philadelphia and called up the Maritime National Historic Site, "Hey, I've got the funny hat. Do you guys have any jobs?" Today, she's full time, with an office in the old shop. "Every day people knock on my door thinking it's an actual store."

"So why the sign out front?"

"Well, until four or five years ago, it was a store. Actually, this building really encapsulates the history of the park and the maritime history." She then told me that the store was built around 1800 by Captain Henry Prince, who bought the Derby mansion next door. "Captain Prince is an example of one of the Salem merchants who didn't make it, unlike the Derbys and the Crowninshields and the Grays and the Forresters and all the Salem merchants who became millionaires."

Prince built the West India Goods Store as a warehouse. But when Salem's maritime economy tanked, he went bankrupt. When the Park Service took over the property, they turned it into a gift shop that sold goods that would have been available in Salem around 1800: coffee, tea, spices, textiles, books. Eventually, they turned the building into office space.

"So what do you actually do here? I'm assuming you're not just sitting around, waiting to explain to anybody who knocks on the door what this building used to be?"

"I'm the curator, archivist, librarian, and historian for the site. What I really do is resource management, which at the National Park Service is a catch-all term that covers museum curatorship, historic preservation, regulatory compliance, and the record archives."

Since this was the first National Historic Site to be designated after the passing of the Historic Sites Act of 1935, the park's records cover the gamut of preservation movements, from the federal government's involvement to the Colonial Revival movement to New England's own historic preservation activities. "All the major players of historic preservation here are represented in this park," she said.

"Is it weird to have this big site that people can walk through on the way to the grocery store and not even realize they're on a National Historic Site?"

"When I was working at the site's orientation center, I had vehement arguments with locals who swore there wasn't a National Historic Site here while they were growing up. And they didn't look 65 years old. In the early days there wasn't as much signage and we didn't have the *Friendship*, and a lot of it is open space, but even these days it wouldn't surprise me if there were people who don't realize that there is actually a National Park here in Salem."

Murphy explained that the park's identity issue has less to do with signage and more to do with the broad scope of its government-mandated purpose. "It's not an easy park to interpret because our enabling legislation says that we're here to educate people about the maritime history of New England and the United States. How broad can you get? There are days I wish I had a Minute Man Park: One day, April 19, 1775, that's it." As a result, the site has buildings interpreted to various centuries or, sometimes, to multiple centuries, like the Narbonne House.

I visited the Narbonne House during the Salem Maritime Festival. It's a two-story gray building behind the buildings on Derby Street. To get to it from the wharf area, I took a brick path between the Hawkes House and the Derby House until it ended at the house, which abuts Essex Street. When I moved to Essex Street, I would pass it every day, and, because of my conversation with Murphy, every time I thought about Sarah Narbonne.

The house was built in 1675 and is named for a woman who lived there in the nineteenth century. Like, all of the nineteenth century. Sarah Narbonne was born in the house in 1794, lived there her entire life, and then died there in 1895 at the age of 101. She saw more than a fourth of the city's entire history from the windows of that house.

Inside, it was mostly empty of furniture. Some of the walls had wallpaper and others were stripped to the building material. That way, visitors and researchers could see the different ways the house had changed over the centuries. Some of the rooms had display cases of artifacts in them. Archeologists had dug up some one hundred and fifty thousand items from the house's backyard. These artifacts dated to every century and included items of international origin. In those cases, I saw pottery and dishware, brushes and children's toys, all cracked or broken, all stuff that the original owners would have considered trash but which we, of course, encase in glass and stare at. One shattered, eyeless doll face will stick with me for life.

Back in the West India Goods Store, I wanted to know how tourists are supposed to "do" the site, considering that there are so many structures and that it's all mixed in with the city.

"The buildings are generally only open by tour. That's partially resource protection, as we have some structural issues in some of the houses. We usually do the Custom House and the *Friendship* on a single tour. It's all free, of course, you just have to sign up for them at the visitor's center." During the summer, she said, they often have both the Custom House and *Friendship* open and staffed so people can just walk in.

Because federal taxes pay for the site, I was interested in her take on what it's like to have a property like this in a city with a tourism-based economy, especially one that has traditionally been built around a single month on the calendar.

She told me that when she moved here in 2001, the city was still very much dependent on October. "They could not keep people in the shops on Essex Street." However, over the course of the last ten years, she watched the city move from a one-month-a-year city to a twelve-month-a-year city. "October is not nearly as important as it used to be. When I first moved here, people came for the witches and were surprised to find maritime history, too. And now we're seeing a much larger percentage of people coming in just for the maritime history or the art and architecture or the Peabody Essex Museum. So that has really changed."

The Salem Maritime Historic Park protects some amazing maritime sites, but the most intriguing maritime site in the city falls outside its purview. Long one of Salem's many secrets, it's only been within the past decade or so that the existence of this site has become more common knowledge, though it is still difficult to access. To find it, I had to go to a hotel.

The Hawthorne Hotel sits is on the Common, across the street from the start of the Essex Street Pedestrian Mall and within sight of the Salem Witch Museum. Basically, it's centrally located. It's where you want to stay during Haunted Happenings . . . if you can find a vacancy.

The ninety-three-room boutique hotel was built in 1925. It is said to have hosted a stream of notables over the course of its life, including Bette

Davis, Johnny Cash, and Bill Clinton. And it has thrown some serious Halloween parties.

The lobby is ornate and vintage, with large patterned chairs and couches, gilded mirrors, and inset bookshelves. It's like visiting the home of a rich grandmother. During October, a giant pumpkin serves as the centerpiece. Its bar, Tavern on the Green, opens off the lobby, as does Nathaniel's, its restaurant.

I was with Esme, in a group small enough to fit into one of the hotel's old-fashioned elevators. The staff member hit the button for the highest of the hotel's six floors. We exited the elevator and walked down a hall to a set of stairs, where we ascended yet again, somehow. At the top of those stairs, the staff member opened another door.

And we found ourselves in an old ship's cabin.

It was all dark, polished wood, the ceiling concave and ribbed with beams like we were beneath a deck. On the walls were antique devices and portraits of local seafarers. One was flipped around to face the wall. In the middle of it all, the foot of a mast descended from the ceiling like a rounded pillar, taking a bite out of a central table on its way to the floor. The room was elegant, not at all like the rough cabin of the *Friendship*. A side door was open, out of which we could see the rooftops of Salem.

The ship's cabin is the headquarters of the Salem Marine Society. Started in 1766, more than thirty years before the East India Marine Society, its purpose was similar: to take care of widows and orphans of the sea (it's motto is "Where virtue reins, the unfortunate find relief") and throw some killer parties. But while the East India Marine Society focused on traveling the globe and bringing back pieces of the world, the Salem Marine Society focused on advancing the science of ocean navigation. The biggest portrait in the cabin was of society member Nathaniel Bowditch, the Salem native who is known as the founder of modern maritime navigation. His home is preserved on North Street, right behind the Witch House. Membership in the society was also less strict. Instead of having to navigate the horns of the earth, you just had to be a sea captain.

It was installed atop the Hawthorne as part of the original architecture. The Society owned the land where the Hawthorne now stands. As part of the sale, they were to give the society a clubhouse on its roof free of charge.

The staff member showed us a curved wooden ballot box. Inside were white circles and black squares, the yeas and nays of the society's voting system. And then he told us the story of the backwards portrait.

Society member Matthew Fontaine Maury was a Virginia-born seafarer. During the Civil War, he sided with the Confederacy, so the society turned his portrait upside down and hung it backwards. In 2008, a new portrait of him was installed as an act of reconciliation and to make it easier to tell the story, but the original still faces the wall.

Eventually we all went out on the "deck," the roof of the hotel, and took in the harbor and the streets and ogled a real-life, real-time map of Salem, a rare view in a city with few high-rises downtown. For most of its existence, the society headquarters was a secret. The roof barnacle is invisible from street level, and access was only given to members.

Later, I would talk to the master of the Salem Marine Society. Surprisingly, 250 years after its establishment, the society is still active. It even outlasted the East India Marine Society. But the Salem Marine Society has changed. And a big piece of evidence of that change is its current master, Joanie Ingraham.

Ingraham is a retired mariner. She was born in Beverly, but her ances-

Salem Marine Society Headquarters

tors are from Salem. She proudly told me she's descended from Joseph Peabody, who was one of the more successful of the Salem merchants.

"When I was a child, we'd go to the Peabody Essex Museum, and just inside was a portrait of Peabody on the left and William Gray, a merchant and ship owner, on the right." Captain Peabody wasn't the Peabody of the Peabody Essex Museum—that would be philanthropist George Peabody. "My father would have us go in and bow to the east. I didn't understand the family tradition until I was older, that being his descendent gave me some advantages."

Her father was also master of the Salem Marine Society, as was her brother. Over the years, the marine society changed its membership laws, which is one of the reasons it has survived. But even then it took a while for it to allow women members. Ingraham was the first.

"There are two ways to get in: in your own right, as a professional mariner, or as a legacy, which means you're descended from one. I could have gotten in either way, but I was proposed in my own right."

"How did you become a mariner?"

"When I was seventeen, I had a summer job taking care of people's boats. I later taught sailing. I've just been in the water all my life. Early on, I almost had enough hours to get my Coast Guard license, and the man who ran the club encouraged me to get it so that he could give me a real job. I got it at the age of twenty. At the time, in the early seventies, it was a big deal."

In October 2015, Ingraham became the first female master of the society, a position she will hold for three years, a period which just happens to include the society's 250th anniversary. "We're going to throw a big party."

The society has about thirty active members and meets four times a year. "We still hold pretty much to the original purpose of the society. We offer relief to members in need, provide educational scholarships, support maintenance to navigational aids, and donate to the Maritime Department of the Peabody Essex Museum in support of the legacy of the old East India Marine Society." The Salem Marine Society distributes about $50,000 a year from its endowment.

Its educational donations go to the two academies of New England Maritime and Salem-based youth sailing programs. As for the navigational aids, they've restored signal towers and lighthouses all over the region. "The Salem Marine Society was responsible for the first lighthouse on Baker's Island in Salem Harbor. If you come in on the wrong side of Baker's, you're in deep trouble."

One of the perks of membership is access to the ship's cabin at any time. In recent years, they've opened it to the public in a limited fashion. During certain heritage events, you can take a quick guided tour. That's how Esme and I got in. I asked Ingraham about the shift, and she told me that one of the owners of the hotel started objecting to the Society's not paying any rent, so he took them to court. "The judge said, 'Sorry, you'll have to take this back to England, because I have no jurisdiction here. Your incorporation laws predate 1776.' He suggested an amicable agreement, and part of that was letting the hotel brag about it on their website and place photos of it in the lobby. And we pay one dollar a year."

"Does the society like being more visible?"

"Thirty years ago it was a secret society, but as times change, people want to be able to say 'I'm a member' and 'we do good works.' They don't want to be anonymous donors anymore. And the society needs to be a part of Salem history."

Ingraham wasn't the only member of the Salem Marine Society I talked to. I also sat down with an honorary member who was also the head of the maritime department at PEM. Of course, my interest in his perspective didn't have anything to do with the society. It was because he was the curator of a fascinating maritime collection.

I'm a big fan of curators. I always imagine them with a cloud of artifacts behind them wherever they go. In Dan Finamore's case, all the items in his contrail have floated on an ocean or have been inspired by it. Finamore is the Russell W. Knight Curator of Maritime Art and History. He lives in Salem but grew up in New York. "I'm not related to any of the old Salem sea captains," he told me with mock-regret in his office at PEM.

His first visit to Salem was in his twenties. He was in college and looking into all the wet archeology fields. He came to the city to see the collection of that "charming nineteenth century institution" that was the Peabody Museum of Salem before the merger. He hit it off with the staff and got a job there at age twenty-eight. Since he worked for PEM in both the pre-merger and post-merger days, he had a unique perspective on the direction of the museum.

"Back then, we had a tiny staff and a tiny budget, and everybody pitched in on every project. There was great camaraderie, but not many people came through the door. I'm incredibly grateful that we have grown to become the institution that we are today. I would probably have left if we hadn't changed. But I'm really glad I got that window into it."

"Why would you have left?"

"Well, today I'll do an exhibition and I might get eighty thousand people come to it. That's extremely satisfying. Also, I got paid such a miniscule amount back then I couldn't possibly have survived on it for long. For many years, the staff took a vow of poverty or just didn't need their salaries."

He told me that the levels of maritime history that a researcher can do in Salem pretty much can't be done anywhere else in the country—say, New York or Boston. Nobody bothered to save very basic records in other cities. "Salem was fully convinced that what they were doing was worthy of documenting and preserving."

Of course, the other part of that is that Salem's maritime heritage fossilized, while maritime industry in Boston and New York continue to this day.

"I understand that the museum management thinks that the maritime story sticks too much to the museum," I said. I had heard that from Finney. "Yet you're in charge of making maritime exhibits and events. Do you have to balance that with the people in your office who say, 'Let's not be too maritime'?"

"Every day. But I think about it in terms of what's best for the museum in the long-term and what's best for the maritime field. As far as the museum, all of us have to strike a balance between emotion and nostalgia and intellect and strategy. We have to be a viable operation financially, strategically. Our message has to be relevant to people today and in the future. And to do that we need to define our audience ambitiously, as more than just who it used to be."

The "what's best for the maritime world" part of his answer was a little more complicated. "Almost everything in my department is art. It's paintings, it's prints, it's drawings, it's illustrated journals, it's scrimshaw, it's ship models. But it was all exhibited for many years as illustrating a historical storyline. I would argue that both the art and the history are equally important, but the worst thing that can happen is for people who don't understand the history to walk into the museum and feel on the outside of it." He told me that in addition to that concern, the world of people who know the history is getting smaller. "The old guy from the financial district of Boston who lined his office with portraits of his ancestor's ships, he's dying off. So, on one hand you might say the museum is diversifying and paying less attention to its maritime heritage, but what I'm doing is making maritime relevant to a wider audience and the audience of today and tomorrow in addition to the audience of yesterday. It's a balance."

"So how do you navigate art and history in the museum?"

"How we interpret our collections is a constant conversation. Right now, if I were to walk you across the street to the museum, I could show you two official maritime galleries. But, the more we walked through the museum, I could say, 'Look, there's some maritime over here in the American Decorative Arts section and over here in the Asian Arts section and, oh wait a second, all of this stuff was brought to New England on ships.' There have been times when, partially to be poetic and partially just for fun, I have argued that everything in the museum is maritime."

"That must drive your bosses crazy."

"It can be entertaining. But it's just one perspective. Somebody else can come in, say, the curator of Asian art, and say the same thing. And she would be kind of right, too. It's actually still way under-studied as far as American history goes. We have the myth of the American West, over land, but it's unbelievable how they ignore what was happening in nineteenth-century America when the real money and real investment was looking out from the shores overseas to land that was not America."

"That's the irony of the Witch Trials, right? A big reason why 1692 happened was because you had two groups, one that wanted to work the land they had and were having a hard time financially and the other that took off in boats to get trade rolling and were doing quite well."

"So I can claim the Witch Trials as maritime history. Great."

"I'd actually love to hear your perspective on that part of Salem—the witches, Halloween."

"The museum has a love/hate relationship with Halloween, but we're invested in it more than we like to admit because if you are in Salem, you are a part of that scene, whether you like it or not. It's just the way it is. And if you carry yourself as if you're somehow above it, you're deluding yourself. I mean I walk down the street on Halloween, and I see thousands of people for whom it actually, seriously connects with them on an emotional level. It's clearly important to them."

"Do you find that at all infringing on what you need to do here at the museum?"

"It chases away other types of tourism in October. Part of what bothers me most is that if you're trying to hold a conference or a meeting, everybody will say, 'You can't do it in October.' A lot of that is practical, hotel room vacancies and traffic problems, but I wonder if it's also because we're embarrassed that people will come and see us in this state. So there's that element that somehow October is off limits for regular business. That kind of bugs me."

There was one question I'd been saving for Finamore. It has almost nothing to do with this book, but I needed to ask it. I tried to be subtle, but it was an appalling attempt. "Is there a maritime artifact that PEM is known for, that people always ask about? I might have one in my head, but . . . "

"I know which one you have in your head."

"OK."

"First let me answer that the maritime world is worlds within worlds. It's independent circles and they don't always overlap, so I deal with this all the time. There is the nineteenth-century merchant history crowd, there is the art collector crowd, there is the history of science crowd, there is the naval history crowd, there is the yachting crowd, there is the ocean liner crowd. Their interests are actually quite disparate. Each one of those worlds has its iconic object. That makes my job harder."

"Because they're always wanting to see a certain thing on display, a certain thing that only you have, and their only chance to see it would be for you to have it on display, right?"

"The choice to exhibit something is the choice to not exhibit something else. And so I also have an equally large array of items in storage that I love and think we need to get out, that people need to know about. And so part of my motivation to change up what's expected in the galleries is to surprise people and introduce them to a whole new realm of great things." He paused. "So the reason we don't have Blackbeard's skull on display?"

"You nailed me." That's right. PEM is supposed to have Blackbeard's skull in its basement. Blackbeard was beheaded off Ocracoke Island in North Carolina. His head was then transported, affixed to a ship's bow, to Hampton, Virginia, where it was stuck on a pike as a warning to other pirates and in celebration of the end of one of the most infamous figures of his time. After that, nobody knows what happened to it. But storytellers can't let a thing like Blackbeard's head go off into obscurity. Legend has it that the skull was plated in silver and turned into a drinking vessel for this or that secret society.

PEM's silver skull came from the collection of Edward Rowe Snow, a famous author of New England coastal history. He wrote dozens of books on the topic, many of them about pirates. How he got his hands on the most infamous maritime artifact of all time is unknown. Some say he grabbed it from a local biology lab and painted the thing silver. Whatever its provenance, PEM has a silver skull connected to a pirate legend that they have to contend with when people like me bring it up.

"I think in some ways it's an iconic object for the folklore of the sea because Snow was incredibly successful at telling stories," said Finamore. "Some of them were true, some were imbued with truth, and some of them were total fabrications, but he's hugely important in terms of the lore of New England and the elevation of that to something related to cultural identity."

Of course, the official position of PEM is that they do not own the skull of Blackbeard. "Whether people are misled to believe it's really Blackbeard's or else it's just a gruesome thing, neither one of those options accomplishes our end goal. But when we exhibit it, we exhibit it very carefully." You and I probably have the best chance of seeing the skull when PEM loans it to other museums, like it has done with maritime institutions in South Carolina and Virginia. The south, it seems, is a far enough distance away for the artifact to not reflect too much on PEM.

"How often do you go to the basement to see items like that?"

"Never often enough. It gets harder and harder when you have your long-term plans and your paperwork and that kind of stuff, but I try to work it into a regular routine, just to look at things. I was very lucky early in my career to spend tons of time in the basement. I really got to know the collection extremely well."

And that's how I turned an interview with a respectable curator from a respectable museum with a respectable collection into a tawdry tale of pirates. There's no going back from that, so we might as well stay here. I eventually made it into the New England Pirate Museum.

It turned out to be, natch, a wax-ish museum. One with atmospherically lit tableaus and worn-out figures and a college-aged guide dressed unenthusiastically as a pirate.

The museum had that mildly creepy tone that I dug at the other Salem museums, but in the dimness, the life-sized dioramas seemed more immersive than any I'd encountered so far. We found ourselves in a colonial seaport. Aboard a ship, watching pirates behead victims. Below decks, watching them drink and count their hauls. On islands, witnessing them bury treasure. At a pirate execution. Salem was really acclimatizing me to the feeling of standing at the feet of a gallows.

All the jolliest of Rogers with connections to New England were there, often in areas not too far away from Salem. The New England coastline is only so long. Like in nearby Lynn, home of the Blue Anchor Tavern, where pirate captain Jack Quelch was arrested, and Dungeon Rock, site of the cave where pirate Thomas Veale lived until he was buried in a cave-in.

New England's only female pirate, Rachel Wall, was there. She has the added resume fodder of being the last woman hanged in Massachusetts. Captain Kidd was there, too, as a result of his partnership with Richard Coote, the governor of the Massachusetts Bay Colony after William Phips, the governor during the Witch Trials. Rumor has it Kidd hid treasure near Boston. Black Sam Bellamy and the *Whydah*, whose treasure and ship wreckage today sit in a tiny museum at the tip of Cape Cod after being discovered in 1984 off that peninsula.

Blackbeard was there, of course. No mention of his rumored skull mug a few blocks away at PEM. Instead, the museum told the story of the treasure he's supposed to have buried on Lunging Island off the coast of New Hampshire.

Cotton Mather even got a placard in the museum. He was as into saving the souls of pirates as he was into hanging witches. He published *An*

Account of the Behaviours and Last Dying Speeches of the Six Pirates in 1704 and spent his career trying to convert them on death row.

The museum exit was an eighty-foot cavern with pirate skeletons strewn on the floor and rubber bats dangling above our heads. At the end of it, a seated, masked figure jump-scared the people in front of us. Because Salem in October. It spared us due to Esme and Hazel, I assume.

The New England Pirate Museum is an attraction focused on villainy, but it is somehow much easier to stomach than an attraction focused on the different kind of villainy that was the Salem Witch Trials. You never hear anybody criticizing Salem for capitalizing on victims of piracy. And they had two dozen pirate costumes marching in the Grand Parade. Plus, there are pirate museums lining the East Coast. Perhaps it's the anonymity of the victims, the over-there-ness of the crimes. Or the caricatures into which pirates have been turned by culture. Maybe it's that there is no uncomfortable religious aspect to piracy, as there is with the Witch Trials. Or that most of the pirates met an appropriate end instead of going on about their lives like nothing wrong had happened.

Regardless, as with any town that touches the sea, even pirates are part of the Salem story.

As you can tell, I squeezed an entire book into this chapter. I flattened the *Argo* between the Symplegades. Salem's got a fishy past. It's so maritime that it should be an island. The earliest settlers heading east to water instead of west to land. The golden sailing age that minted the country's first millionaires. The decrepit docks of Hawthorne's day. The exclusive marine societies that lasted centuries. The maritime tourist attractions, historic sites, and art exhibits.

But honestly, as fascinating and as deep as Salem's maritime history is, it doesn't make the city all that unique from a tourist perspective. It's on the North Shore, after all. Its neighbors are Ipswich and Gloucester and Marblehead and Rockport and a bunch of towns nobody outside of a Red Sox hat has ever heard of. And while those towns were built by fishermen, not merchants and explorers like in Salem, it's all so many ship wheels on signs and lobster claws on menus to tourists. Had Salem needed to rely on this part of its past to make its present fortune and reputation, it may very well have sunk years ago, Atlantis-ing into anonymity or low-boiling interest, if not economic ruin.

But then you take that secret ingredient. You mix some witch into the water, and magic happens. Suddenly you are a city that stands out not just from the surrounding towns, but from the entire coastline of the country. You're of international interest. And the two go together quite well, like sea and hag. You can have a Witch Museum and a Pirate Museum. A Witch Memorial and a National Maritime Historic Site. A Witch House and a Derby House. You can have a witch logo and a boat logo. You can carve Ursula the Sea Witch into a figurehead and mount in onto the front of the *Friendship* if you want to.

Besides, thanks to the economic rift between Salem Village and Salem Town, salt water was one of the main ingredients that made the witch in the first place.

7

GRAVE MAGISTRATES AND JUDGES NOT

Tomb of William Stoughton

At some point, I got it into my head that I wanted to track down as many graves of the Witch Trial judges as I could find over the course of this project. I had a few reasons for this, none of which involve advancing the story of this book one single paragraph. The first, as I've said before, is that I only need the flimsiest of pretexts to visit an old New England graveyard. Like, my elbow itches. Or I'm out of bread. Second, I find it helpful when writing about people long dead to stand near what's left of them. To see physical evidence that these people whose names I easily peck into glowing software were real people with real lives dealing with real challenges in a real moment in time. Third, because the judges are pretty much the only ones with surviving gravestones.

The victims were chucked into the crevices of Gallows Hill or were buried anonymously on family land. The one surviving exception, the grave of George Jacobs, may or may not contain his actual remains. Most of the willing participants, the accused and the confessors and the jurors and the audience, were historically anonymous aside from this one event. After their fifteen minutes, they went on with their lives, and when those lives ended, their final resting places weren't recorded or preserved. The closest we get is a hump of Putnams and scattered gravestones across Essex County. But the judges were VIPs, notable personages, the one percent of a much smaller pie chart, wealthy merchants and politicians and military men of high standing before they sat their august behinds on the bench. Afterwards, they continued to be so, moving higher in politics and business and society and easily fitting all twenty of their Witch Trials skeletons onto hangers in their walk-in closets.

There were ten magistrates involved in the trials: William Stoughton, John Richards, Nathaniel Saltonstall, Wait Still Winthrop, Bartholomew Gedney, Samuel Sewall, John Hathorne, Jonathan Corwin, Peter Sergeant, and John Foster. Nine were on the bench originally, and one joined shortly after the trials started. All of these men were members of the Governor's Council and were appointed to the court by Governor William Phips. They were also all interrelated through marriage and business, and more than half attended Harvard. These men were the authorities in the trials, give or take a few ministers on the other side of the bench.

As a result, they might be the closest thing we have to villains in the Witch Trials story. And that, of course, makes them compelling. Although the Witch Trials crimes are one of the few instances in history where the victims became more well-known by name than the villains.

That is, if the judges really are the villains. The Salem Witch Trials are shades of gray overlaid so many times that black patches may only seem to appear here and there. To call anybody a villain in that tragedy is to ignore many factors: humanity, culture, religion, history, law, and environment. Still, it's tempting and psychologically comforting to have bad guys in the story. So if one had to assign the full blast of blame, it seems right to skip over the afflicted and the accusers and the jurors and the supporters and the capitalizers, and head straight to the magistrates, those judges who had the most influence, the most power, and the final say over whether an accused returned home or wound up at the end of a rope. In fact, this is how the Salem Witch Trials eventually did end, with magistrates telling everybody to stop being silly, go home, and concentrate on working out the finer points of lobster bakes.

But the thing is, these men tried their best. They were zealots, sure. They were arrogant, sure. But they weren't uninformed or inexperienced, nor did they take their duty lightly. This wasn't a matter of, "Witches, you say? Get a rope." They consulted experts, even if those experts were vague and confusing. They read the literature, even if the literature was vague and confusing. There were decades of judicial precedent in New England and centuries more from back in the homeland, even if it was all vague and confusing. They discussed it. They debated it. And they were up against some pretty amazing performances and testimony and confessions and, most daunting, an extremely impenetrable God.

That said, it's not like there were no voices of reason crying out in that wilderness. Twenty people refused to confess to being something they were not. Parties both inside and outside the proceedings were immediately appalled. But when everybody awoke from the nightmare, few of the magistrates showed any remorse or took any real blame.

So let's go dance on some graves. Stick with me. I promise the chapter gets interesting by the end.

On the northwest edge of Essex County is the city of Haverhill, Massachusetts. It's the birthplace of Hannah Duston and her axe, John Greenleaf Whittier and his quill, and Rob Zombie and his microphone. It is also the final resting place of Nathaniel Saltonstall.

Saltonstall was born in Ipswich and would go on to achieve the rank of colonel in the local militia, as well as hold public office. He was fifty-three when he was appointed to the Court of Oyer and Terminer.

Saltonstall is a big reason why it's difficult to give the other Witch Trials judges a pass. He resigned out of dissatisfaction with the proceedings days before the first execution, that of Bridget Bishop. In his mind, scary stories and contorted children were one thing, but killing somebody over them was another. It took nineteen more victims for the rest of Massachusetts to start coming to the conclusions he did before the first rope was strung. He died in 1707 in Haverhill and was buried in Pentucket Cemetery.

Pentucket Cemetery was established in 1668. It's located on Water Street and is tiny enough that it's easy to find Saltonstall's grave. As you enter the short stone gateway, it's on the right-hand side, close to the edge of the graveyard. The white rectangular column is five or six feet tall. Inscribed on one side is the surname of the family.

Next, we head about thirty-five miles south to Boston. If you follow the red stripe of that city's Freedom Trail, you'll cross the three oldest cemeteries in the city, all dating back to the seventeenth century. Each has some of the stones and bones that we're looking for.

First up is the Granary Burying Ground on Tremont Street, a few steps from the start of the Freedom Trail at Boston Common. It was founded in 1660, and of the three historic cemeteries, it gets the bronze medal for age. However, it gets the gold as far as famous interments. Paul Revere's here. As is Sam Adams. Ben Franklin's parents have the biggest monument in the yard, even bigger than John Hancock's a few sections away. All the victims of the Boston Massacre share a headstone here. In the warm months, the graveyard gives Salem's Old Burying Point a run for its pennies as far as how thronged with people it is, although nobody's in costume at the Granary. Well, maybe a colonial reenactor or two. The cemetery also has one, possibly two, of the Salem judges.

Peter Sergeant is one of the least-spoken names in the story of the Witch Trials. This English-born Bostonian was a wealthy merchant who was forty-five when he was entrusted with fighting witches and demons while wearing a black robe. One of his four wives was a Corwin, another a Phips. He died in 1714. I couldn't find his grave, nor any real direction anywhere other than a few sources testifying that he was in the Granary Burying Ground. And that's possible. Less than half of the five thousand burials in that cemetery retain their markers and, like most historic cemeteries, the stones have been moved into orderly rows regardless of where the bodies are for convenience and access.

Samuel Sewall is the exact opposite of Sergeant and leaves much more of a trail behind him. Another English-born Bostonian, Sewall was forty, the youngest of the judges. His brother Stephen was the court clerk. His most notable act regarding the trials came years later when he issued a remorseful public apology, spurred by the death of his two-year-old daughter, which he thought may have been a punishment from God for his Salem sins. He died in 1730 in a land that had already both changed in some ways and remained very much the same in others since the days of the Witch Trials.

Sewall's stone is on the tourist map for the cemetery. His death decoration is a rectangular tomb across the path from Paul Revere's well-visited monument at the back of the cemetery.

The next cemetery on the trek is King's Chapel Cemetery. It's a few steps up Tremont and is the oldest cemetery in Boston, dating to 1630, only four years after Salem itself was founded. Graveyards are usually the sidecar to their neighboring churches, but in this case the church wasn't built until 1688.

But there lies Wait Still Winthrop, or Wait to his friends. Winthrop was from Boston, and he was also the grandson of John Winthrop, one of the founders of the Massachusetts Bay Colony and the area's first governor. Winthrop was fifty-one when he adjudicated the Witch Trials. He would go on to become Chief Justice of Massachusetts, a dubitable superhero name for a Witch Trials judge. He died in 1717.

King's Chapel Cemetery is small, and the Winthrop tomb is on the left side of the cemetery as you enter. A path leads directly to it. On the surface of the rectangle of stone is the Winthrop family seal with about a dozen Winthrops and wives listed below it. Governor John Winthrop reigns at the top of the list, and Wait is four names down.

While I was at King's Chapel, I also checked out a grave on the opposite side of the cemetery, close to the church wall. Here was the tiny, tilted headstone of Elizabeth Pain, bearing a shield decorated with stripes and lions. Nathaniel Hawthorne, who I can't escape even outside of Salem, is supposed to have been inspired by this tombstone in writing *The Scarlet Letter.* The novel ends with the gravestone of Hester Prynne in King's Chapel Cemetery. Her stone bears a shield with an A on it. Many see enough of an A in the lines of Pain's shield to call it out.

Our last cemetery in Boston is the second oldest in the city. And it took a little more walking to get to. Copp's Hill Burying Ground is on Hull Street, about a mile away from King's Chapel. The cemetery was established in 1659 and is atop a hill close to where the Freedom Trail crosses the Charlestown Bridge on its way to Bunker Hill.

John Richards was an English-born Dorchester resident who died in Boston and may, may, may be buried among the thousands of others interred on Copp's Hill. He, like Peter Sergeant, is another judge who seems to have only wrinkled a history page in 1692. He died two years later. He was the usual type: a military man, a merchant, a politician. He was sixty-seven when he was appointed to the court.

But I didn't walk all that way just to tell you about the possible gravesite of one of the more minor judges. I came here because it's the site of the Mather tomb. At the back of the cemetery, closer to the Charter Street side, is a low red-brick rectangle with its own historical plaque. Increase and his son are, after all, New England celebrities.

The two Mathers were major ministers in a family full of them. Increase was the head of the North Square Church and the President of Harvard, a divinity school back then. Cotton was less successful as a religious official but prolific as a writer, composing hundreds of books and pamphlets. Both men had roles in the Witch Trials, advising the judges, visiting the proceedings, and writing about the matter. Increase took a more cautious view of the whole thing but still waffled between zeal and caution with the trials, as most ministers did.

Cotton, though, at twenty-nine, was a religious rabblerouser. He became the Witch Trials' biggest cheerleader even years after, when most saw the events of Salem as a stain on the New England map. Before the trials, he had already warred with demons and witches in his backyard in Boston when the children of a local family called the Goodwins were diagnosed as bewitched. The doctors of New England were probably the real cause of all the witchcraft hysterias. A woman named Ann Glover was accused, condemned, and hanged as the witch responsible for the strange tribulations of the children. She was the last person hanged for witchcraft in Boston, years before the Salem Witch Trials even started.

Cotton was basically a Puritan Ghostbuster, and the Witch Trials were a great opportunity for him to enlarge his status in the field.

Cotton, by his own pen, can easily be positioned as worse than the judges themselves, especially because of his characterization of the trials and methods in his 1693 work *Wonders of the Invisible World*. And then of course there's his whole making sure George Burroughs hanged even after the convicted minister moved the crowd with a perfect rendition of the Lord's Prayer (some historians doubt the complete veracity of that account).

But Cotton's part cowers in the shadow of an even bigger bad: The chief justice of the Witch Trials, William Stoughton.

Stoughton was sixty years old and the Lieutenant Governor of the Massachusetts colony when he was appointed chief justice of the Court of Oyer and Terminer. Basically, he was in charge of the Salem Witch Trials. He was the guy who made the jurors rethink their not guilty verdict for Rebecca Nurse. He was the guy who, during the Superior Court of Judicature—the one that put an end to the whole shameful deal—got angry that people were being acquitted instead of executed and stormed out of the proceedings. He also never apologized for his role, nor showed any guilt, although he lived almost a decade beyond the trials.

After everybody involved in the trials went their awkward, separate ways, Stoughton prospered. He even went on to become the acting governor of the Massachusetts colony the year before his death in 1701. Stoughton, Massachusetts, is named after him.

But he didn't die in Stoughton. He dusted in the Boston's Dorchester neighborhood, where he grew up. He was buried in the North Burying Ground, which dates back to 1634. The cemetery sits at the busy intersection of Columbia Road and Stoughton Street (natch) and is locked at all times, unless you call ahead to the staff of Mount Auburn Cemetery in Cambridge, who administer the North Burying Ground.

I'd always wanted to see Stoughton's tomb, even before this project. It wasn't so much his involvement in the Witch Trials, though, or at least not solely because it. It was because of his skulls.

I've never seen a villain's tomb that matched the villain it marked. I mean, I've been to some infamous graves—the plaque that marks the dirty decay of Boston Strangler Albert DeSalvo, for instance, and the white military stone in Colorado that memorializes the cannibal Alferd Packer. But those graves, like most, are boring. I've also been to creepy, evil-looking graves, but those always seem to be of regular people whose stones have been transmogrified by age or are the innocent products of an older aesthetic. But Stoughton's comes the closest to any I've yet seen.

I called in advance and arranged to have the gates opened. The North Burying Ground is a relatively small cemetery, but it is large enough to ramble in. Stoughton's tomb isn't far from the entrance, although it's hidden beneath a massive tree and covered in creepers (as any good villain's grave should be).

The tomb was rectangular, like a chest, about three feet wide, six feet long, and four feet tall. In a previous century, his tomb had a 170-word Latin epitaph adapted from the tomb of French scientist and philosopher Blaise Pascal. It basically beatified the man: "Devout in Religion, Renowned for Virtue, Famous for Erudition, Acute in Judgement, Equally illustrious by Kindred and Spirit, A lover of Equity," etc., etc. Not "Guy Who Steered the Witch Trials Wrong." So not exactly a villain's epitaph. But I've never seen an epitaph I could trust anyway.

Today, it doesn't bear any epitaph. The top is smooth and unmarked. The only words are on one of the longer sides of the tomb and are basically a label:

STOUGHTON MONUMENT
REPAIRED BY
HARVARD COLLEGE
MDCCCXXVIII.

Stoughton was a Harvard graduate and he left it plenty of cash. He has a hall named after him there to this day.

The opposite side of the memorial was blank. One of the shorter sides bears the Stoughton crest, complete with a knight's helm. And on the opposite side from that . . . was a pair of skulls.

Now, I'm not talking the usual (and amazing) memento mori engravings that you can see in any cemetery in New England. I'm talking two large, realistic, beautiful, bulbous skulls that protrude from the vertical plane of the tomb and are backed by crossed bones and topped by a bat-winged hourglass. So perfect. Instantly one of my favorite graves in all New England. I mean, I could see it as a prop in a story about an ancient, evil sorcerer inadvertently raised from the dead by some curious boy who recently moved to town and didn't believe the legends and was just trying to impress a girl.

I'm going to insert the next judge right here just because not only could I not find his grave, I didn't even look for it: Boston merchant John Foster. After all the books and articles that I read over the course of my year-long research, I didn't even know he was a Witch Trials judge until days before my deadline. Turns out, he wasn't originally chosen to be on the Court of Oyer and Terminer. But when Saltonstall left out of good conscience, they needed a bad one to fill his spot. So he was brought off the bench to the bench.

"So why'd the guy before me leave?"

"He thinks we're killing innocent people and history will revile us for it. Are you okay with that?"

"Sure."

I don't know if you've been counting, but we're down to three judges. And they bring us back to Salem.

The first is the original owner of Salem's Witch House. Jonathan Corwin was a fifty-two-year-old merchant and poliction. He was related to three of the judges and was the uncle of twenty-six-year-old George Corwin, the town sheriff. Jonathan Corwin was there from word one of Tituba's spooky stories, assisting Hathorne at the preliminary questioning in Salem Village.

Corwin spent the rest of his days as a Massachusetts judge. He died in 1718 and was buried in Salem's Broad Street Cemetery.

He didn't have to walk far to get buried. A few blocks south of the Witch House, Broad Street Cemetery is an undulating strip of land that dates back to 1655, the second oldest cemetery in Salem. The Corwin marker is a stubby, discolored obelisk, the names adorning it barely readable. Both he and his nephew are among the Corwins moldering there.

We visited the cemetery deep into October, and nobody was around save the dead. I'm assuming that's because they were all at Salem's favorite cemetery, which is also our next and final destination for this chapter.

Established in 1637, the Old Burying Point, also called the Charter Street Cemetery, is the oldest stretch of planted death in Salem. Every Salem story overlaps at the Old Burying Point. The Witch Trials will lead you here, as will the maritime story, the literary story, and even the city's Halloween story. All of Salem's past and present can be found on this little hilltop graveyard with its delicate, skull-decorated stones.

Within its confines are buried a *Mayflower* passenger, a Massachusetts governor, enough ship captains for an armada, and our last two Witch Trial judges, Bartholomew Gedney and John Hathorne.

Gedney was a local guy, born and raised in Salem. His father helped found the city. He was fifty-two during the Witch Trials and had all the titles his fellow judges had, with one additional resume bullet: He was a physician. This gave him a little bit of a leg up, as physicians could diagnose enchantment back then. He didn't survive the end of the 1690s.

Hathorne was another local boy with another founding father. He's usually the one who gets the twirly moustache and black cape in the popular perceptions of the Witch Trials. His infamy surpassed that of his fellow judges, including William Stoughton, for a few reasons, not all of which are his fault. First, the records for the preliminary hearings survived, so the lines of questioning he used are recorded for an aghast posterity. That includes extremely leading questions, word games, suppositions of guilt. Basically, his questions boiled down to, "Just say you're a witch already." Almost 250 years later, Stephen Vincent Benet tapped Hathorne as the judge that the Devil chose in his story *The Devil and Daniel Webster.* It's some bad PR for the Devil to want you as his judge. Then, two decades later, Arthur Miller cast him unflatteringly in *The Crucible.* Most interestingly, Hathorne's great-great grandson became one of America's most famous writers, one who just happened to obsess about the sins of the past in his work. Right. This guy again. Nathaniel Hawthorne. We'll talk about that extra *w* later.

John Hathorne died in 1717 after earning the rank of colonel and a seat on the Massachusetts Superior Court.

Grave of John Hathorne

Finding Gedney's and Hathorne's graves is easy. A bronze map near the Charter Street entrance points out the notable graves in the cemetery. In October, though, you just have to follow the crowds.

Both graves are steps away from the bronze map. Gedney's is another rectangular tomb. On its dark, deteriorating surface is a light-colored diamond-shaped stone inset at one end, with a list of dead Gedneys below it. On one of my visits during the month of October, there were about three hundred pennies in thirteen ordered rows across the diamond-shaped stone. I don't know why they were there, nor do I know who carries pennies around these days. I was told later, concerning the coins in the cemetery, "It's drinking money for the homeless. Pretty smart, putting the dead to work for you like that."

Hathorne's marker is an individual gravestone, crumbling enough that it has been encased in a sheet of concrete to preserve it—which also make it seem like it's being forced to stay upright and witness all the visitors who come to see it. Like most of the stones in that cemetery, it's topped by a winged skull. Although, in this case, it's easy to read the lipless grin as sheepish.

That's it for tromping over the remains of the Salem Witch Trial judges, but let's stay at the Old Burying Point for a little while longer. This graveyard is one of the spots we frequented the most during our stay in Salem. And it's probably the second most crowded area in the entire city during Haunted Happenings.

To understand the Old Burying Point, it's less important to know what's inside its walls than what's outside them. Few graveyards find themselves in such an odd neighborhood. Let's start at the main entrance on Charter Street.

This side is where the Witch Trials Memorial is installed and where the Pickman house is, across the street from the rear of Yin Yu Tang. When I was walking around inside Yin Yu Tang, I could see the cemetery through one of its windows. It was a strange experience to be looking out the window of an eighteenth-century Chinese house at a seventeenth-century colonial graveyard full of people in twenty-first-century Halloween costumes. Salem, guys.

But the east side of the graveyard is just as weird. It's bordered by two buildings. The first is by far the spookiest looking place in Salem, the ideal graveyard neighbor. Large, white, rotten, and overgrown, the three-story house dates back to the 17th century. It's known, perfectly, as the Grimshawe House. The Grimshawe House is privately owned but not lived in. It's my favorite building in Salem. And . . . it's a Hawthorne site. So we'll come back to it.

From there, the land outside the graveyard slopes down so that the graveyard is at the level of the upper story of the second building, Murphy's, a pub and restaurant. It wasn't until we were eating there with some friends one day that I realized that, as a result, the windowless stone wall our table was up against was separating us from all the dead in the cemetery. That the gravestones were above us and that we were probably at eye and plate level with the historic residents of the Old Burying Point. They should paint a mural on the wall that looks like a cross-section of the cemetery. Outside, during October, the restaurant did erect a fake cemetery as a Halloween decoration . . . on the other side of the wall from the real cemetery. Salem, guys.

The south side of the graveyard looms higher than the roof of a tourist bus above Derby Street. Standing at the stone wall and looking down in October will give you a view of, well, all the tourist buses parked there. Across the road, during the latter half of October, a carnival spins and

Old Burying Point and Carnival

roars and screams and flashes, offering a unique opportunity to fit headstones and a Ferris wheel into the same camera frame. Beside that is a movie monster museum. Salem, guys.

And then we get to Liberty Street, where you can find the other cemetery entrance. Liberty Street is an alley that connects Derby Street to Charter Street. I've told you that in October it's the home of the Haunted Neighborhood. But I never gave you the full and overwhelming description of this month-long Halloween block party.

If you hit the Haunted Neighborhood on a weekend near the end of October, you won't be able to walk through it without rubbing your shoulders and elbows smooth on fellow crowd members or getting fake blood from somebody's costume on your clothes. Barkers on ladders yell out entrance times for attractions, and loudspeakers blare radio hits. Screaming visitors run out of a side door while somebody with a convenience store mask and a bladeless hedge trimmer chases after them as far as its cord will reach. Fake fog washes the alley. Statues of wizards and witches are set up for photo ops. The attraction list includes the Salem Wax Museum, the Witch Village, Frankenstein's Castle. You can buy tickets to candle-lit walking tours or watch Witches cast a spell circle. A small group of booths selling carnival food fill the area with the smell of sugar and fat.

Old Burying Point

The Haunted Neighborhood is, most likely, the place people have in mind when they call Haunted Happenings, or Salem in general, tacky or cheesy or schlocky or a tourist trap. And that's fair. If two-bit haunted houses and funnel cake and tourist crowds aren't your deal, that's understandable. However, the opinion gets over-inflated to the level of reputation merely because of the placement of the Haunted Neighborhood.

I mean, it's conjoined to both an historic graveyard full of the historic dead and a solemn memorial to a tragedy. There's nobody really to fault for that. But it does mean that the party fog creeps into the graveyard. That people gaze at ancient epitaphs while balancing a plastic tub of nachos in one palm and slurping soda through a straw. That people are wearing costumes that in any other graveyard in the country would be considered sacrilegious or disrespectful, skeletons wandering above the real skeletons, animated corpses above the nonanimated ones, Grim Reapers that incorporate the entire cemetery into their costumes just by being there.

So it's no surprise that some people can't tell if the cemetery is real or made for tourists. I heard it myself one of the times I was hanging out in the graveyard (no costume, maybe nachos). A woman asked her husband as they trepidatiously entered the Liberty Street gate, "Is this a real cemetery?" She sounded like she had just crossed through Alice's looking glass.

And nothing is more telling than the signs that greet you at each entrance. The Charter Street entrance features a historical sign that lists the notable dead. The Liberty Street entrance reads:

Place of Respect
No Admittance After Dusk (6PM)
Stay on Paths
Please Keep Off Stones and Tombs
Walls and Trees
No Stone Rubbing Allowed
Report Suspicious Activity

One evening, I stuck around to see who closed the place up at night. At 6:01, a skinny man with long gray hair and a yellow reflective vest roared into the cemetery, yelling at the masses lingering that it was time to go, that the cemetery was closed, can't they read the sign. He even had to fight with one of the tour guides there who was trundling about thirty people through a gate. They argued over the meaning of the sign for a few minutes, since dusk and 6 p.m. were not yet aligning at that time of year.

Finally, everybody left, and as he locked up the Liberty Street entrance, I greeted him.

"Are you the cemetery caretaker?"

"I'm security," he said fumbling with the lock.

I explained that I was writing a book about the city. "Can I interview you some time?"

"Uh, I don't know much about the history. You should talk to one of the tour guides."

That happened a lot to me. Everybody assumed I wanted a history lesson instead of a personal perspective. I explained further.

"Oh, okay. I don't know if I have anything interesting to say, but sure."

We made arrangements to meet during his shift on another day, and as we parted he made his way toward the middle of the graveyard, "I have to go make sure there aren't any assholes hiding behind any of the tombstones."

On the day we talked, the cemetery was packed. I don't know how the dead got any sleep that day. The cemetery was acting more like the Salem Common than the actual Salem Common. Fortunately, the cemetery security guard was wearing his bright yellow vest. He showed me a name tag clipped to it that identified him as Richard St. Amour. He lived in Salem but was originally from Stoughton.

"Do you do this year round?"

"No, I work for the city as an engineer. I just do this in October for extra cash. Nobody needs to do this job the rest of the year."

"What's the weirdest thing you've seen happen here?"

"Oh, I don't know." He thought for a bit. "I mean, people do all kinds of weird things here, try to have picnics on the tombs and stuff like that."

The guy was obviously overloaded by all the weirdness he'd seen in his time as cemetery security, so I helped him out. "I heard somebody tried to dig up a grave here last year."

"Oh yeah, this grave over here actually." He took me a few steps over to a stone with a bald patch of dirt at its base. The stone looked like a replacement stone, dark and crisply edged, its epitaph clear and deeply inscribed. There weren't many words in the epitaph. It named Nathaniel Silsbee (or Silfbee, to be exact) and Martha Silsbee and stated that Nathaniel had died on January 2, 1769. There was no date of death for the gloriously immortal Martha.

St. Amour didn't tell me too much beyond which stone it happened at. Later, I'd look up the details. It happened on October 13, 2014. The first line of the article read, "A Beverly man was arrested Monday after he was found digging up dirt at a gravesite while tourists looked on." It was 3:30 in the afternoon. The article included a picture of his handiwork, which merely went down about an inch and cleared only an 18 by 36-inch patch that matched up with the bald spot I saw. The cleared dirt revealed what was probably an older, cracked tombstone, perhaps buried there when it was replaced by the one marking the grave today.

According to the article, the witnesses thought it was part of a performance and didn't interfere. Salem, guys. It wasn't until security noticed the crowd that the twenty-six-year-old was stopped and arrested. My head returned to Kate Fox's tagline, "You can't make this stuff up."

"He had mental problems," St. Amour said.

"I assume that's the weirdest people get in here?"

"Probably. But they get more annoying. People ask me questions a five-year-old wouldn't ask."

"Like what?"

"Like, 'Where are the witches' heads?' That question doesn't even make sense. They were hanged. Then they ask me which of these trees is the hanging tree." I looked around and among the trees in the cemetery were two great big oaks, each with stout limbs extending horizontally for about 20 feet. Either one could have been the perfect hanging tree for eight firebrands of hell. "None of these trees were around in the 1600s."

Twice, St. Amour had to stop the conversation to pull adults out of the trees who were trying to get their pictures taken. "People have no respect. These are real graves." We watched as one girl dressed head to toe in black lay down on her back, her head at the foot of a tombstone, while her two friends took photos. "At least she's not hurting anything. If they're not hurting anything, I let it go."

"You have to be a mean guy, huh?"

"I tell my wife, when I come here, 'I'm off to be an asshole.' I'm not an asshole. I'm a nice guy. But I have to be one here. Next weekend, I'll have a couple of cops with me." Next weekend was Halloween weekend.

The whole thing sounds disgraceful, and at times it definitely is. But there is a big part of me that thinks more parties should be thrown in cemeteries. Not the damaging, irresponsibly drunken kind, but the "we're alive while recognizing life is short" drunken kind. But even if one finds it completely enraging to see how the dead and the memorialized seem to be treated in this spot during October, you have to admit that when you think about it from the perspective of it all happening around the graves of two Witch Trial judges, it's kind of satisfying. I wish all the judges were buried here. If you could go back in time and show them all the photos on your phone of the weirdness that has been spawned as a result of their judgements and what's happening in the twenty-first century above their bones, you'd probably save twenty lives. Or maybe just end your own at the gallows.

But here's something about those judges that further complicates the story. You know who was in the second court, the Superior Court of Judicature, Court of Assizes, etc., etc. that sent everybody home? William Stoughton, Wait Still Winthrop, John Richards, Samuel Sewall, and Thomas Danforth. That's right. Four out of five of the judges were from the Court of Oyer and Terminer. The same men who sent twenty people to their death freed another 150 or so afterward. William Stoughton certainly wasn't happy about that, but we don't have a record of any of the others being displeased with the happy ending.

The big reason for sending everybody home was that spectral evidence wasn't allowed anymore. Again, another reason the Witch Trial judges weren't completely the bad guys. They were following the rules of the court. Except Stoughton. He's still a bad guy.

Had they thrown out spectral evidence in the Court of Oyer and Terminer, the Salem Witch Trial judges would be heroes of history instead of villains. Maybe they'd get statues alongside Roger Conant. Or, more than likely, we would never have heard of the Witch Trials, Salem would be an anonymous Boston suburb, and most of us wouldn't have a good metaphor for when innocent people are targeted. Maybe Salem should still erect statues to them.

As to the only new guy on the bench, Thomas Danforth, he was a sixty-nine-year-old English-born resident of Cambridge and deputy governor. He went to Salem and witnessed some of the preliminary questioning and ultimately didn't like what he was seeing. So his presence in that second court shouldn't be under-emphasized. However, for some reason, Arthur Miller made him the bad judge of *The Crucible*. Danforth died in 1699. I don't know where he's buried.

8

A WALK ON THE WEIRD SIDE

Humans are not that varied as a species. Short people and tall people are only a few feet apart. Wide people and thin people are even less so. We're colored with a narrow, bland rainbow of flesh tones and topped by an even thinner, blander rainbow of hair color. Gender has little variety. We're disgustingly symmetrical. And the rare exceptions outside that range we call disfigured, as if the figure itself was anything to aspire to. Our bodies are so bland we cover them—in clothing just as uninspired. It's no wonder we had to overachieve in the technology arena. We are the most boring-looking creature evolution ever forgot to shove into the fossil record and forget.

Except on Salem's Essex Street Pedestrian Mall. And this chapter is an ode to it.

For most of the year, the Essex Street Pedestrian Mall is a simple, short section of Essex Street, a retail strip about two-tenths of a mile on a road that runs roughly east-west for most of its length. It has always been the main street of Salem, from the packed dirt of colonial times to the asphalt of later centuries. Ever since 1976, though, the Essex Street Pedestrian Mall has been paved with cobblestones and closed to all vehicular traffic, except for the occasional tourist trolley or rumbling delivery truck.

But on October weekends, the mall erupts.

Then, on the Essex Street Pedestrian Mall, you will find every shade of flesh in every pattern and texture. Where color is not adornment enough, skin is covered in furs or feathers or scales. Sometimes it's completely forgone for pure white bone and skull. Horns of all sizes and shapes poke from heads and shoulders and backs. Clown mouths, ogre mouths, vampire teeth, beast fangs, and tusks all glint in lurid smiles. Eyes shine iridescent in a chameleon horde of colors and in a variety of sizes and numbers. Bodies sport extra arms and legs, wings, fins, tails, tentacles. If nightmare or nature birthed it, it walks the cobblestones of the Essex Street Pedestrian Mall in October. Mos Eisley Cantina has nothing on this fantastic strip of Salem. I am not updating that reference.

The pedestrian mall is also a crossroads of time, with pirates and medieval knights shouldering up to hot dog stands as well as cowboys and aliens trying on matching "I got stoned in Salem" T-shirts. Robots and presidents buying each other drinks poured into souvenir coffin-shaped bottles. Spacemen and cavemen posing together for photos. Time travel was invented at some point, but time travelers seem to only want to go to modern-day Salem.

The pedestrian mall is also a film festival, with costume-worthy characters from every movie tripping over its cobblestones. Eighties slasher villains wander around reminiscing about their gory days. Superheroes and *Star Wars* characters pose heroically in the streets. Every weirdo Tim Burton ever created is there somewhere—Beetlejuice is mugging for the camera in East India Square, Jack Skeleton is taking refuge in the doorway of Crow Haven Corner, and Edward Scissorhands is trying to figure out how to eat a candy apple. Frankenstein's monster is by far the most popular Universal Horror monster in Salem, and Harry Potter is the most popular movie series. You can hear parents pointing and shouting

enthusiastically to their kids, "That's the guy from *Labyrinth*," and then you can imagine their children going home and eventually watching the movie for the first time and screaming, "That's the guy from Salem." Either way, David Bowie weeps lightning bolt-shaped tears from the most recently discovered planet.

And, of course, the top of the crowd is prickly with witch hats.

On weekends in late October, you could crowd-surf the entire length of the pedestrian mall without fear of falling. On weeknights, you could have the place to yourself. You can tell how lively the entire city is on any given day by what is happening on this street. I walked it in all manner of conditions: lonely foggy mornings, rainy wet afternoons, chilly days and nights, and at sunset, when the sky went pink and yellow and impossible. When I had something to do, it was usually on the pedestrian mall. When I had nothing to, I still usually found myself on the pedestrian mall.

The strip is always lined by retail and restaurants, Witch shops and tourist attractions and historic buildings, but in October they're all open and they've all sprouted an extra layer of retail in front of them, like a second row of shark teeth. That inner row is made of white tents that line both sides of the street, each one a little island of wares, carnival foods, crafts, jewelry, T-shirts and witch hats, caricaturists and spirit photographers and face painters. Four-fifths of the city's name is "Sale," after all. It's here that you try on twenty witch hats in search of the perfect one to wear during your visit.

Let me guide you through this endlessly fascinating strip of Salem. We'll start on the east, where it intersects with Hawthorne Boulevard.

We're in front of the southwest corner of the Hawthorne Hotel. Across the street is the seasonal start of the Essex Street Pedestrian Mall, which extends for another tenth of a mile on weekends in October to contain all the monsters and magic. Wooden sawhorses at the entrance block any cars tempted to turn into the melee. Somebody reaches between the shocks of corn that decorate the traffic-light poles to hit the crosswalk button. It turns green. Crowds on both sides of the street converge in the middle of the road like attacking armies.

On the north side of the pedestrian mall is the Crowninshield-Bentley House, a big yellow block of a house built in the late 1720s by John Crowninshield. This year, its small front yard is dominated by Patrick Dougherty's art installation, *What the Birds Know*. Tourists pack its chambers and masked creatures pop up in the circular windows to get their pictures taken in that strange architecture of woven saplings so out of place in the urban landscape.

Beside it is the Gardner-Pingree House, another PEM property and the site of one of the most infamous murders of the nineteenth century, one that is said to have inspired Edgar Allan Poe's *The Tell-Tale Heart* and, of course, some of Nathaniel Hawthorne's work. The three-story brick mansion was built in 1804 for John Gardner. Later, in 1814, it was sold to Captain Joseph White, who didn't know that he was buying his own future crime scene.

The eighty-two-year-old was murdered in bed in that house in 1830, his skull fractured by, it would later be learned, a custom-made cudgel, and his chest porous with dagger holes. Nothing was stolen. As the investigation progressed, it uncovered a conspiracy based around a will, a murder for hire, blackmail, and a prominent Salem family. The trial was just as dramatic, with a prison suicide and hangings and none other than Daniel Webster leading the prosecution. The cudgel still survives and is supposed to be in PEM's collection. They'll probably never exhibit it, of course.

Across the street from these two historic houses is the Olde Main

Street Pub, a tavern that's easy to miss because its immediate neighbor is a three-story, ominous-looking black building. Crow Haven Corner is the oldest operating and most prominent Witch shop in Salem. It was started by Salem's most important Witch, Laurie Cabot. Inside, you can get your fortune read or buy a book of magic or pick up a spell at its "spell bar," which is exactly what it sounds like.

On the far side of Crow Haven Corner is a low strip of shops with two different Harry Potter–themed stores. Remember Salem offers merchandise based on the books and movies. Wynott's Wands is a reproduction of the wand store from the stories and is full of handmade wands for the right wizard-in-training. Its sign reads, "Makers of Fine Wands Since 1692."

Harry Potter has a legitimate claim on Salem. The city was referenced in the Harry Potter series, and Rowling has refashioned and incorporated the Witch Trials into her latest spin-off movies and stories about wizarding in America. *Harry Potter* costumes are everywhere in Salem. I saw Snape, Voldemort, and Sirius Black waving wands around, plus lots of Hogwarts attendees, all from Gryffindor. More relevant than all that, though, is how J.K. Rowling has altered the witchcraft conversation in Salem with her invention of the word "muggle," meaning someone who lacks magical ability. In more than one conversation I had, that term was used to draw the line between those who had believed in Witch magic and those who didn't.

The next building on that side of the street is a three-story condo building. I can't imagine what it's like to live on the Essex Street Pedestrian Mall during October, but there's a bunch of people who do. In addition to these residences, pretty much every building on the strip is topped with condos and apartments. I'm assuming everybody there swings their couches to face the windows in October instead of the TV.

Darting back across the asphalt to the other side of the street, we come up against the red-brick Phillips Library, which holds all of PEM's special collections. The library is made up of two connected buildings: the Essex Institute building, which still has the outdated name carved into its lintel, and Plummer Hall, which was originally built to house the Salem Athenaeum. Today, the Athenaeum is farther down Essex, past the end of the pedestrian mall. Phillips Library holds the original Witch Trial documents . . . away from the public.

Back across the street is a Mexican taqueria, a Witch shop called New England Magic ("A Shop and School of Witchcraft and Wizardry") and the Salem Time Machine that I've already encouraged you to visit/warned you about. Beside that store is a brick path that cuts south to Charter Street, ending near the Charter Street Cemetery.

On the other side of Essex is a small park owned by PEM, formed by the intersection of Essex Street and New Liberty Street. On New Liberty is a parking garage as well as the Salem Visitor Center inside the remnants of the old Salem Armory. The large castle-like building once took up most of the land where the park is now before it was burned by an arsonist in 1982. Its empty, fire-scoured shell was later torn down by PEM.

At this intersection, the asphalt changes to cobblestone, and the Essex Street Pedestrian Mall proper starts. And it starts with what is so far the theme of this walking tour: PEM. On the south side is the entrance to the museum itself, and on the north side are the museum offices where I was introduced to Jay Finney and Dan Finamore. Farther down is the East India Marine Hall on one side and East India Square on the other.

Most of the small East India Square is taken up by a fountain. Built in 1976, it's called "Salem's Gateway to the Far East." A tall Asian-inspired arch rises out of the fountain and pours water into a basin that, depending on its level, outlines the shape of Salem in either pre–twentieth century or contemporary times, after areas of its shoreline filled in. A placard in front of the fountain illustrates both outlines of Salem, which has, honestly, always struck me as witch-shaped. The Bridge Street Neck peninsula, on the west side of Collins Cove, form her head and pointy hat. The east side, Salem Neck, is her broom. And if the Salem Willows and Winter Island make the tip too bulbous for a broom, that's because her black cat is resting there. Behind her, across the North River, flaps North Salem like a billowing cape.

Also on the square is the entrance to the Museum Place Mall, a single-level section of indoor shops. There's a bathroom in there if you need it.

From here, it's a gauntlet of shops, from Witch shops like Omen ("Psychic Parlor and Witch Emporium") and The Coven's Cottage ("A Family-Owned Witchcraft Shop") to the Witch Mansion haunted house and gift shops like the Trolley Depot.

Beside the Trolley Depot is Central Street, which comes from the south and dead-ends at the pedestrian mall. The relatively mundane street seems intrusive, giving us a glimpse of the less interesting world outside of the pedestrian mall. Fortunately, it doesn't grab our attention for long. Because at that intersection, in front of the Trolley Depot, is the King of the Essex Street Pedestrian Mall.

His face is blue and emaciated, his head hairless. His eyes are yellow, and his teeth bestial. His blue claws stick through the sleeves of his black robes, and he wears a red amulet around his neck. More often than not, he is biting passersby. His name is Steve the Vampire.

Steve is one of the many street performers who can be found on the Essex Street Pedestrian Mall in October. Some are musicians, but most are costumed characters. Some mix the two, like the sax player in a demonic clown mask. At our place on Essex Street, I would see the creepy saxophonist walking past our window on the way to the pedestrian mall, his mask already in place and ready for work. Esme made us tip him every time we passed, and he'd always blow a few notes in her direction. There was a group dressed up as the Addams Family, a Minion, Jack Sparrow. A group of three Ghostbusters with an extra proton pack for eager participants to strap on. A Frankenstein's monster seated on a chair wrapped in lights. When kids were brave enough to get their picture taken with him,

Steve the Vampire

he would rummage in a small black sack and give them a spider ring or a set of plastic vampire teeth like some kind of Halloween Santa Claus. There was a Chewbacca and a Michael Myers, each of whom had seen much better days. On the best days, you couldn't tell the visitors from the performers because of all the costumes.

If you want to know what it's like to be a superstar on a red carpet, wear a great costume on the pedestrian mall. You'll be stopped every step to get your picture taken. The best spectacle on the entire strip is monsters taking photos of other monsters.

One of the organizations in the city throws a children's costume parade. Most of its route wends through this street. We enrolled Esme in it, and she wore a peacock-inspired dress and eye mask that was almost her daily uniform in Salem. As the string of adorably and sometimes terrifyingly costumed children marched down the strip, a parade of about a dozen evil clowns passed them from the opposite direction. That's Salem.

But even in the middle of all of that, Steve the Vampire sticks out. That's why photos of him regularly show up in the Haunted Happenings brochures and the newspapers anytime somebody needs to illustrate the weirdness of Salem in one photo. I've watched Esme grow up in his claws, as we take her photo with him almost every year.

The thing about Steve, besides his great costume, was how he handled his audience. He knew all the best poses, whether he had one person or eight around him. He would make sure kids were comfortable, telling them in muffled words through his long, jagged teeth appliance, "You know that this is pretend, honey, right?" He wordlessly communicated his tip system by waving a long-nailed blue hand at his tip box, a three-foot-tall coffin with a slot atop it. He would dramatically turn his back or block his face with his claws when too many people took photos without tipping him. When times were slow, he would creep up on unsuspecting tourists or grab a quick smoke around the corner on Central Street. At one point I saw him making change from his coffin for a local retailer. "You're awesome!" she yelled as she ran back to her store.

To get an interview with this vampire, I dropped a tip and my number in his coffin and gave him a quick explanation about the book. Eventually he called me up and we met at the Village Tavern. He was not in make-up. Non-vampire Steve was lean, graying, and getting close to fifty.

As we sat down, I asked him whether he wanted me to put his full name in the book.

"Steve's fine. I like to keep a little bit of mystery."

Steve the Vampire was born in Salem but grew up in Peabody. He eventually hit the road as a carney, where he performed a range of roles, from assembling and operating the Ferris Wheel to manning food stands to running games. In 2009, he returned to Salem. The next year, Steve the Vampire was born.

"How did you become a vampire?"

"I was looking for a way to make extra money. I was out here playing my harmonica in 2009 and I did okay. But I looked down the street and saw this woman who did the bronze witch." I remembered her from previous years myself. She painted her face and hands bronze to match the color of her witch hat and dress, which dropped in a long waterfall to the ground over the stilts that she wore. She looked exactly like the witch statue I've always thought Salem needed. "I saw the money she was making, and I thought I could really have fun with that."

"How'd you come up with the character?"

That character is Mr. Barlow from, appropriately enough, the 1979 *Salem's Lot* television miniseries based on the Stephen King book. "I wanted something that scared me when I was a kid. I love horror movies. It was the first vampire I ever saw on film where the moment you looked at him, you knew he was dead. It wasn't just some normal-looking guy with a couple of pointy teeth, you know what I mean?" He also likes the throwback nature of the character and seeing people remember the movie when he explains who he is. He said about one in twenty recognize the character right away, whereas most people think he's Nosferatu. When Kate Fox told me the story of the Nosferatu jumping into the news shoot on the Common, she was talking about Steve. I also once heard an eight-year-old girl call him Voldemort, but that's probably a different issue.

"I've noticed that over the years, your costume has gotten more sophisticated."

"The first year I was dealing with what money I had, and then the next year, I took all the money that I got and I put it into the character. I got my coffin, a new costume, and I started having my face painted professionally."

"And now you wear high-end masks?"

"Yes, and I have a new mask this season. The mask that I had previously was as close as it's going to get to the original character, but it's not good enough for me. So I'm going in the other direction. More withered, more corpse-like, nice sunken eyeballs." He told me the name of the mask and the company he gets it from. I looked it up later to learn that it was actually a mummy mask that he was having repurposed into a vampire by painting it blue and adding pointed ears. And it was a good bit of cash. Steve takes his alter ego seriously.

Unlike many of the street performers, Steve is a local, so he also plies his trade in the spring and summer, as well. He has to wear an ice vest under his robe in the summertime.

"What's it like being a vampire in the offseason?"

"The first time, I thought I was going to come down here and all I was going to hear was, 'It's April! Go back home!' But surprisingly, I didn't. Every now and then somebody gives me a hard time, but it's always a local. People get mad if they see that you're having more fun than they are. But not all the locals are like that. I've got tons of little local fans, ones that are shorter than my coffin. They call me Mr. Vampire."

He told me the story of "Miss Caroline," a five-year-old girl who took a picture with him and then left with her mother. Fifteen minutes later, she returned with a picture she had drawn of him. "That's framed and at my house. When I run into the jerks, I take a deep breath and realize those aren't the people I'm out here for. It's people like Miss Caroline."

"What kind of hoops do you have to jump through to get your performer's license?"

"It's not a rough deal. You go down to the city licensing department and fill out an application. They run a background check on you, and if you pass that, you go to the next licensing meeting and give a brief explanation of what you're planning to do. 'I'm downtown, I'm a vampire, I bite people.' They haven't said no yet."

"Do you come out here on Halloween night or do you avoid that scene?"

"I do come out here, but to tell the truth, by that time, I am so done with taking pictures for the year. I love it, but October's a very long month. So Halloween Night, I just want to walk around and see things."

"So you take off the costume."

"No, I'm in costume, in my Barlow suit because it's the only one I can afford. I just don't want to take pictures. Unless you got a decent costume."

He then told me something that surprised me, but which I would hear again. That there aren't enough Halloween costumes on Halloween. "Too many people come down just to look. If I were mayor, I would have a roadblock on every major road, and if the people that drive up don't live in Salem or aren't in costume, I'd send them home. There are tons of people here on Halloween, but the sad thing is that only like three or four out of ten are dressed."

Back in 2014, Steve got some publicity when he faced off—in full Barlow makeup—with a street preacher. It was filmed by a passerby and put on YouTube. Actually, it happened a couple of times with different preachers. But this particular preacher's name was Stephen Brock. Right. Steve the Vampire vs. Steve the Preacher.

I asked Steve the Vampire about him.

He groaned, "Oh, that guy. Those preachers are the most horrible people. I spend a lot of time making sure kids aren't completely terrified of me. And I'd just finished talking to a little girl and showing her it was all pretend, and she got her picture taken with me. That guy pointed at them and said,"—here Steve adopted a southern accent—"'You just took a picture with the spawn of Satan, and you're going to burn.' Look, a kid that age only has the vaguest concept of God, the Devil, but they know what burning is, so yeah, all the footage came shortly after that. But I've had words with him before. We still have the same kind of preaching we had three hundred years ago."

Brock was also my first experience with a Salem street preacher. He had a bullhorn and was preaching his lungs out, holding up a Bible and declaiming in a sing-song preacher cadence about this or that sin. It seemed extremely performative. He would roll up on his toes, his Bible held in the air, and close his eyes for entire sentences. I don't remember his exact words. What struck me more was the crowd's reaction to him. They were taking photos and video. Keep in mind we were on a strip of retail where everywhere you looked was something interesting: Steve in his vampire get-up, an eight-foot-tall drag queen named Duchess Gigi in a bright orange witch suit, a mime giving directions to a white dog whose fur was painted with black spiders. In all of that, Stephen Brock was the oddity.

Brock has lived in Salem for about six years. He runs a storefront church on Bridge Street called True Gospel Baptist Church. That would be right in the head of the witch that is Salem on the map. He's an Independent Baptist preacher who grew up in "the mountains of North Carolina."

I tried to pull an in-person interview with Brock, but couldn't. He did, however, offer to answer some questions over email.

JWO: Why choose Salem as your mission field?

SB: This is the area the Lord laid on our hearts to go to reach whosoever with the glorious gospel of Christ for salvation of their eternal souls.

JWO: Has Salem changed during your time in the city?

SB: The city of Salem is still in spiritual darkness and continues to grow in paganism. The pagan religion strives to make Salem a mecca for witchcraft in America. The city takes pride in this movement that brings millions of dollars to the city throughout the year and especially during Haunted Happenings and the witch's Festival of the Dead in October. "For the love of money is the root of all evil." 1 Timothy 6:10.

JWO: Why do you street preach?

SB: Street preaching, or as the Bible says public speaking, is not the only way we evangelize. Outside of street preaching, we also do door-to-door evangelism. We have knocked on almost thirty-nine thousand homes in six years in Salem and surrounding cities. The reason why we do street preaching is because it is 100% biblical. From the prophets of the Old Testament to Jesus Christ, Our Saviour, the Begotten Son of God, to John the Baptist and the New Testament church in the book of Acts, street preaching has been done as a means of evangelization. Jesus Christ in all four of the gospels of Matthew, Mark, Luke, and John commanded the New Testament church to go out into all the world and preach ("preach" means to herald and cry out) the gospel to every creature (Mark 16:15) preaching repentance and remission of sin in

His name (Luke 24:47). So to be a biblical, New Testament church, we obey His commands.

JWO: Do you feel Salem is unique in its need for evangelization compared to other cities?

SB: Yes, it is unique due to the way it embraces and commercializes witchcraft and paganism more than most other cities.

JWO: How do you view the witch culture of Salem? Do you see it as just one sin on a list of sins or do you see it as particularly nefarious?

SB: I see it as sin just as adultery, drunkenness, homosexuality, fornication, rebelliousness, blasphemy, etc. are all sins before a Holy God, which is why we preach against all these sins and not just against witchcraft when we preach on the streets.

JWO: Antagonism seems like part of the definition of street preaching. It's very aggressive, direct, and it addresses people in a space where they're not used to being addressed. Do you find that beneficial to evangelism?

SB: It is not meant by us to be aggressive, however, when we preach the "light shineth in darkness; and the darkness comprehended it not." (John 1:5)

JWO: What does it feel like to be giving your all at the top of your lungs in a public space? Especially when the crowd is not being receptive or perhaps even argumentative?

SB: I know when I am preaching out in the streets it is pleasing God and doing His will as He commands us to "cry aloud and spare not" (Isaiah 58:1). I know that the Word of God never goes void and the Word of the Lord endureth forever. When we are preaching, we are bearing precious seeds of the Gospel to the hearts and souls of the people, reaching many people at once.

JWO: Are you against Halloween in general?

SB: Yes.

JWO: How do you feel street preaching when twenty feet away from you is a guy dressed as a vampire giving a performance to the same audience you're addressing? I guess, more succinctly, how does it feel to share audiences with a performer like that?

SB: I don't think about it. It does not faze me. I just focus on what I am doing, preaching with compassion to people on the streets as I face this all the time, and I guess I have gotten used to it.

Not all of Salem's hopeful saviors are as bombastic as the street preachers. One older bespectacled gentlemen I saw multiple times over the month wordlessly handed out Gospel tracts with both hands to passersby. He was calm, rarely made eye contact, and I never saw him get into a conversation, much less a confrontation. But his vest. His glorious vest. Clashing with his placid demeanor was an orange safety vest on which was pinned on both his front and back signs with cartoon illustrations of people burning in fire captioned with, "Rejecting Jesus is choosing Hell!" and "Your future without Christ: Everlasting torment in the lake of fire."

Past Steve the Vampire's station is the Witch History Museum. And the rest of the strip is more stores and restaurants. A dentist. A bank. A toy store. Perhaps the strangest place on the entire pedestrian mall is the large CVS, hunkered there and failing miserably at fitting in with all the oddity. On the south side of the street, beside a book shop called Wicked Good Books, is Derby Square, site of the Old Town Hall, the bottom floor of which is the Salem Museum. I did eventually make it to the top floor. But it took a trial.

During one of my pedestrian mall rambles, I saw a commotion near a standalone green clock with the name of a defunct department on its face. In front of the clock, two men in period dress were yelling at the crowd around them. I pressed closer. They were loudly discussing rumors of witchcraft in the village and were looking for a woman named Bridget Bishop. As soon as the name was mentioned, someone in the crowd, an older woman in a leather jacket and smoking a cigarette yelled out, "Here she is!" and pushed a period-clad woman into the circle that had formed around the other men. Bridget Bishop looked distraught and confused. Meanwhile, the Essex Street Pedestrian Mall continued to be the Essex Street Pedestrian Mall around us.

Bishop was arrested by the two men, who took her down the pedestrian mall, one of them waving a large, noisy bell in the air as they walked. We followed them to the Old Town House, where those of us with

tickets—a plastic button in a small mesh bag—handed them to a woman with a basket and then headed up the stairs just inside the main entrance.

There, on the top floor, was an open space with rows of folding chairs on two sides. We were about to be treated to "Cry Innocent: The People Versus Bridget Bishop," an interactive dramatization of a preliminary Witch Trials hearing. We the audience were the jury. Five actors played a dozen different parts, switching between them with slight changes in costume and voice, usually while we were distracted by other actors elsewhere on the floor.

Throughout the performance, we were encouraged to get involved, to ask questions of the accused and the accusers, to read statements that were handed to us. "And remember," one of the actors told us at the beginning of the performance, sweeping her hand in the direction of five empty chairs on a dais, each one with a cloak on the back and the familiar names of the afflicted girls written on small chalk boards in the seats, "While this is going on, these girls are screaming and writhing and making chaos of the proceedings."

At the end of the performance, we voted on whether Bishop should be sent to trial for witchcraft or freed. Unlike history, my group set her free. I voted against her. Figured the honorable judges in Salem Town could suss out the truth.

At the end of the Essex Street Pedestrian Mall is a restaurant called Rockafellas in the Daniel Low building. It originally belonged to a jeweler who made some of the first known Witch City souveniers in the late nineteenth century, silver spoons with witches on them. There's also a fountain with an interesting literary story, which I'll save for the Hawthorne chapter, because I need this guy to stop cutting in line.

The pedestrian mall ends here at Washington Street, although Essex Street itself continues for another mile. Across Washington Street are Lappin Park and the bronze statue of Elizabeth Montgomery on her broom.

In my experience, walking this street multiple times every day for thirty-one days, Halloween can seem less like a holiday here, less like a season, less like a theme. On the Essex Street Pedestrian Mall in October, Halloween feels like a place.

And on Halloween itself, the Essex Street Pedestrian Mall is what I've just described multiplied by a thousand.

9

FICTITIOUS WITCHES

Salem Pioneer Village 1630

It's nighttime, and the roofs of a small, rustic town glow in the full moon. Close by, through a copse of bare-limbed trees, is a cemetery. Lightning flashes, and as the accompanying thunder dies, the distinctive crunch of metal biting dirt reveals the presence of an old grave digger. "A storm be bad luck on Halloween," he says to nobody in particular, pausing briefly between shovelfuls of dirt to look at the sky. Not too far away is a tall tombstone. The epitaph reads, "Melissa Wilcox (1733-1778). Witch." Lightning crashes again, and a cloud of green smoke bursts behind the tombstone, accompanied by a wicked cackling. The green smoke quickly disperses to reveal a young-looking woman in purple robes and a matching pointy hat, her hair a wild green and vampire fangs in her mouth.

She holds her hands in front of her, fingers arched like claws, and continues cackling. The grave digger throws down his shovel and runs to town, screaming, "She's back! She's back!" At the first door that opens to him, he says, "She's risen from her grave on Halloween, like she swore she would when they burned her at the stake two hundred years ago." The sleepy man who answered the door testily demands to know whom he's talking about. "Melissa Wilcox. The Witch of Salem." Cut to a gaudily painted van bouncing on the road, the phrase *The Mystery Machine* emblazoned on its side panel. "There's the sign," says a girl in an orange sweater and thick black-framed glasses in the front seat, "Old Salem."

Yup, the Scooby Gang has been to Salem. Multiple times throughout its many incarnations. I even saw them in Salem once myself during this project, as it makes for a great group costume. The secret is for whoever plays Shaggy to carry a stuffed Scooby Doo, the closer to life-sized, er, cartoon-sized, the better.

Salem lurks ubiquitously in the cobwebbed and creepy corners of pop culture. When the stories aren't directly about Salem witches, then they use Salem as a touchstone. Sometimes that means having a character who is descended from a Salem witch, such as Bonnie Bennet from *The Vampire Diaries*. Sometimes that means creating a coven of witches displaced from Salem, as in the third season of *American Horror Story*. And sometimes that means using a Salem analog, say, Whitewood or Westbridge or Blithe Hollow, fictional Massachusetts towns in witch stories such as the 1960 film *Horror Hotel* with Christopher Lee or the late-'90s/early-'00s series *Sabrina the Teenage Witch* or the 2012 stop-motion animated film *ParaNorman*.

It's almost as if we can only suspend our disbelief for an American witch story if that story traces its witches through Salem. It's like Dracula, Transylvania, and vampires, except that the Salem Witch Trials is an historical event and *Dracula* is a literary one.

If it seems that I'm focusing solely on television and films as opposed to other forms of storytelling, there's a reason. Well, two. The first is my own unbalanced media consumption habits, but more importantly, it's because another way to see Salem is through the lenses of those productions that have filmed there.

Despite Salem's rich visual landscape, few witch productions of either the historical or fantastical sort have filmed in the city itself. Even the current-day series *Salem* films elsewhere, in Shreveport, Louisiana—a land of swamp witches, not Old World ones. In April 2015, when I was still panicking over my living arrangements in Salem, the movie *Joy*, starring Jennifer Lawrence and Robert DeNiro, about the woman who invented the self-wringing Miracle Mop, filmed scenes at the Hawthorne Hotel. But since that's the story of a girl and her mop instead of a girl and her broom, it's not the kind of film I'm looking for to frame some of my experiences in Salem.

There are two types of Salem witch movies: the historical ones, which attempt to dramatize the real-life events of 1692, and the fantastical ones, which attempt to, well, *really* dramatize them.

Only one real major historical movie was filmed in Salem, and that was a three-part PBS series called *Three Sovereigns for Sarah*. The 1985 miniseries told the story of the Witch Trials from the perspective of accused witch and trial survivor Sarah Cloyce, whose sisters Mary Easty and Rebecca Nurse found themselves levitating above Gallows Hill. Vanessa Redgrave starred as Cloyce.

The three-hour story was filmed all over eastern Massachusetts, including Saugus, Topsfield, Ipswich, Sandwich, and Hamilton—basically anywhere they found suitable seventeenth-century houses. There were two Salem sites. The first is the John Ward House at the intersection of Brown Street and Howard Street in Salem, half a block directly behind Roger Conant's bronze back. The second is Pickering Wharf, where the Old Witch Gaol scenes were filmed on a stage in a warehouse back when there were warehouses on Pickering Wharf. But a critical part of the production was filmed in ex-Salem—good old Danvers.

And that means Richard Trask is jumping back into our story.

Trask calls *Three Sovereigns for Sarah* "the first serious treatment on film of the 1692 witchcraft crisis." But he's a little biased. He was a historical consultant for the project, along with Stephen Nissenbaum. Nissenbaum was the co-author with Paul Boyer of one of the landmark explorations of the Salem Witch Trials, the 1974 book *Salem Possessed*. Trask got involved when the screenwriter and eventual producer, Victor Pisano, came to the Danvers Archival Center to do some research. Pisano chose Sarah Cloyce, who survived the Witch Trials, to be his main character. Cloyce is remembered for storming out of the church in protest when the Reverend Parris implied in one of his sermons that her sister Rebecca was a devil.

"We had a lot more power on the production than historians usually have on commercial things," Trask told me. "We didn't understand it at the time, but that was very unusual." The production even based some of the props on the shards that Trask and team had dug up from the parsonage site.

Trask and Nissenbaum took their jobs seriously. At one point, the director hired Alexander Scourby to play a chief magistrate. "Scourby had a wonderful voice, but he also had a beard," said Trask. Trask isn't an anti-beardite, but apparently they weren't very common in late seventeenth-century New England, at least among the upper levels of society. But Scourby's beard had become his trademark, and the New Yorker wasn't going to shave it off for some New England witches. "You have to understand," Trask told me when I wasn't appalled myself at the idea of facial hair on a judge, "having a judge in a 1690s courtroom with a beard would be like having a judge today with a pink mohawk." He and Nissenbaum felt so strongly about the historical accuracy of the shoot, that they approached Pisano and told him that if Scourby didn't go face-naked, they'd have to remove their names from the credits because all their fellow historians would laugh at them.

According to Trask, the filmmakers actually broke contract with Scourby, although how much of that was the beard and how much was his ailing health (he died three months before the production aired), is unknown. In his place, the beautifully clean-shaven Patrick McGoohan of *Secret Agent* and *The Prisoner* fame donned the white wig instead.

As part of his contract, Trask was required to be on hand during filming. He took some vacation days and found himself hanging out both behind the camera and in front of it as an extra. He and his family even had Vanessa Redgrave over to their First Period home for dinner. "It was a magical time, it really was."

Now, the real reason I'm spending so much page-space on a thirty-year-old PBS special, instead of skipping right to Disney's *Hocus Pocus*, is because of what that special left behind.

The filmmakers shot the meetinghouse scenes at the Rebecca Nurse Homestead in a meetinghouse custom-built for the production. The same meetinghouse we entered on our own visit. Trask was instrumental in its design.

"They wanted to find a meetinghouse somewhere in New England. And I told them that there isn't one. But we spent two days going through New England to find sites." Finding seventeenth-century sites in New England isn't difficult, but finding one that isn't hemmed in on all sides by twentieth-century sites was pretty hard, especially in those pre-Internet days. So they decided to build one and gave Trask the job of designing it. "I did a ton of research, and it was pretty accurate. The building inspector wanted it overbuilt for safety reasons, but the ceiling, which was an open ceiling with a truss-post system, was just right for the period. Of course, they never used one frame of film on it."

I would hazard to say that the meetinghouse has done more to fire the imaginations of people envisioning the Salem Witch Trials than *Three Sovereigns for Sarah*, which was popular in its day. I mean, you can, today, walk into a building that mimics the exact space where all the hearings started, right in the town where they were held. That's potent.

Now, let's get back to spooky.

One of the things on our must-do list while we were in Salem in October was to watch the 1993 Disney movie *Hocus Pocus*. You probably already know why, but let's go through it together.

Hocus Pocus came out on July 16, 1993, but I've only known it as an always-existing thing, one that's ever-present on one or another of Disney's cable channels during October. Each Halloween season, I end up seeing the entire movie three times, just all out of order and in twenty-minute segments, usually while I'm doing something else.

Hocus Pocus is about the Sanderson sisters, three witches who are hanged in old Salem for sucking the essences from children to maintain their youth. The trio are then resurrected on Halloween in modern Salem when a virgin named Max lights a candle with a black flame in the abandoned museum that used to be the Sanderson sisters' cottage—a Salem Witch Museum, so to speak. Their Satanic shenanigans can only be stopped by Max, his little sister Dani, their friend Allison, and an immortal talking black cat.

The witches are played by Bette Midler, Sarah Jessica Parker, and Kathy Najimy in, if not exactly career-defining roles, roles that will probably outlast anything they've ever done. There are entire generations of people who know *Hocus Pocus,* but have no idea about wind, wings, sex, city, hair, or spray.

The movie certainly gets you in the Halloween spirit. I mean, witches, costume parties, a zombie, a talking black cat, graveyards, trick-or-treating . . . all backed by Disney's budget in the same year that the company released *The Nightmare Before Christmas.*

Even better, this grand romp across a fictional Salem was actually filmed all over the real Salem. No other movie has ever taken such delightful advantage of the mythology and geography of Salem before.

These days, I'm old enough to sympathize more with the witches than the kids in *Hocus Pocus.* So, with the weight of so many Halloweens firmly depressing me, we watched the movie in our Essex Street pad and then stepped outside to visit some filming sites. Actually, revisit, as I've been to most of them over the years. I guess I'm that big a fan of the movie.

The movie starts out in Ye Olde Salem during the Witch Trials. You've gotta execute the witches to get cursed by them, after all. To recreate a 1600s-era Salem, they used, well, a recreated 1600s-era Salem. Salem Pioneer Village 1630 is what it's called, and it's a reenactment village located in Salem's Forest River Park, which is a waterfront park about a mile and a half from the pedestrian mall and near Salem State University. Technically, they used an amalgamation of that and Plimoth Plantation. The movie opens with a broom's view fly-over of the village, which is played by Plimoth Plantation. But once we're firmly on the ground, we're in the Salem Pioneer Village.

The living museum that is Salem Pioneer Village 1630 was built in 1930 after the 300th anniversary of the city's founding. However, until recently, the collection of about a half dozen structures hasn't really been used much as an attraction. Instead, it has rotted on the beach while various groups tried their hands at managing it. Today, it's run by the Witch House, and colonial life is starting to stir there again.

When I talked to Elizabeth Peterson at the Witch House, we discussed this site, too.

"It was very popular when it was built," she told me. "It is the first ever living museum in America. President Calvin Coolidge visited it and so did Bette Davis. But at some point interest in it dropped off. I've not yet discovered when or why."

This was the second year that it has been managed by the Witch House. "The budget's low, so we can't fully staff the village, but I would love to see it being a fully functioning living museum again," said Peterson.

But what they're doing with it currently is fantastic. Lindsey and I visited the village one night for an event called The Dark of the Night. We were part of a group of about fifteen people, and we followed our guide down a dirt path lined by tea lights until we arrived at the fire. We could see an orange glow through the windows of the houses and the silhouettes of people sitting inside. We kept ourselves close to the flames until it was our turn. Sitting at the fire, we couldn't tell we were near the harbor or the park or the parking lot. The village seemed isolated in the night, black where the orange flames didn't reach.

In the first house, a young man dressed in period clothes sat in front of a cold fireplace. In his hands were sheets of paper. We sat down in chairs around him in the orange light, the dark pressing in from outside, as he half-read, half-told us the story of a ghost ship out in Salem Harbor. This is exactly the type of stuff I want to do around Halloween.

But even better is when you can do it in the house of a character from a Halloween movie.

When the first story ended, we were led across the grass to another building, where another storyteller sat. This one made no eye contact. We couldn't even see his face under the wide brim of his hat, which was turned down toward the book on his lap. He told us a story about a cornfield ghost. The fact that I even remember that was a testament to the story, since I was distracted by the idea that we were sitting and listening to a ghost story in the house of Thackery Binx, the character in *Hocus Pocus* who saves his sister in seventeenth-century Salem from the witches, but is in turn cursed to live forever as a black cat.

After that, we had one more house and one more ghost story before we were led through the pitch black back to the gate. On the way, the guide mentioned that he would be doing tours the next morning. We immediately decided to return for a daylight view of the place.

The next day, it was still cold, the sky gray with what looked like snow clouds. We were in a group of about a dozen waiting to get inside. Across the harbor, we could clearly hear the terrifying roar of motorcycles downtown. We were missing the Halloween Witch Ride. Every October, two thousand bikers, some in costume, some with motorcycles decked out for the holiday, fill the streets of Salem with engine noise and leather.

Eventually, our tour guide peeked his head through the gate. He was wearing a long black cloak that covered his body. He was shifting on his feet and shaking to try to keep warm. "Ah," he said at three college-aged kids in the group, "My trespassers have returned." Apparently, he had caught them trying to climb the fence to get into the village. He had told them to come back for a legal tour. Turns out, they were *Hocus Pocus* fans. Turns out, everyone in the group was.

Even in the daytime, the village still felt as secluded as it had seemed the previous night. Trees blocked most of the fence and all of the parking lot. You could just see the harbor in the distance, and a little swamp separated us from the front gate. One of the group pointed excitedly to a spot above us. Perched on the chimney of one of the buildings was a hawk, yanking violently with its beak at a squirrel it had just caught.

Most of the buildings were about the size of large sheds, except for one two-story building for the leader of the colony. The buildings looked like they needed a lot of restoration work. These rustic houses had been through almost a century of New England winters and long periods of abandonment. Still, standing there among them in the cold forest, it felt like we were far, far in the past.

The guide told us about Salem in the pre-witch days of its early founding. As we walked from building to building, I kept looking at Thackery Binx's house at the end of the row. It was small, a fence of sticks outlining a tiny front yard in front of it. We were handed to another tour guide, the same one who had told us the ghost ship story the night before, and he continued the tour.

He led us toward the Binx house but then veered right, toward a blacksmith's hut. As he told us what it was like to do tortuous things to hot metal in the colonial days, I could hear the whispers. The same ones I heard at other *Hocus Pocus* sites in Salem: "*Hocus Pocus*." After we were done with the blacksmith hut, the guide tried to lead us away from it and the Binx house, but nobody moved. As he walked off, unaware that none were following (or, perhaps, completely aware, but resigned to it) everybody in the tour started taking photos of the Binx place. We walked inside, checked it out. We all knew exactly why we were at the house of Thackery Binx. Except for one girl who asked, "Jar Jar Binks?"

I brought it up to Peterson later. "People always want to see it for that reason, and that's nice. Last year, a little black cat showed up and stayed with us the whole season. When I shook my keys, he would run to me. We named him Thackery."

Our original guide didn't get it. He had talked about it with us the night before when we were huddled around the fire. "I don't understand it. Twelve seconds of a twenty-year old movie was filmed here, and people want to break in." In addition to it being inadvertently prophetic, the statement also sounded very close to, "It's all just a bunch of hocus pocus."

As we walked back, I got a text from a friend back in Nashua saying that it was snowing. I looked up at the sky. It still looked like snow in Salem, although no flakes ended up falling that day. I would never have made it through a single winter in the 1630s.

"We're doing a lot of work to bring the Pioneer Village back to life," Peterson told me. "It's transportive and immersive, and the 1630 story isn't being told as much as the 1692 story. We have a responsibility to that period, as well."

And that responsibility, she told me, isn't just for the history of it. It's also for the context that it gives to the Witch Trials. "How they lived is an important part of why superstition ran rampant, how everything was viewed as an omen or a portent." She told me about a game the colonials played called Coffins or Purses. When an ember popped from the fire, they would follow it to see what shape it took. A coffin-shaped ember meant death, and a purse-shaped one meant wealth. And the Pioneer Village is a great tool in Peterson's purpose of trying to communicate the seventeenth-century mindset. "With it, we want to try to give people that sense of how apprehensive day-to-day life was, how immediate death was, how dark the night was. We forget just how scary it was just getting through the night."

I can totally see that. Just a few hours in the dark in a rustic cabin and a couple of ghost stories, and it got me.

One of the main sites for *Hocus Pocus* was the house of Max and Dani, the brother and sister who were freshly transplanted from Los Angeles to the weirdness of Salem. It was only a block away from Forest River Park. It's at the end of Ocean Avenue and is easy to find since it has that unique cupola on its roof and is adjacent to a small beach. On our way to the Dark of the Night event, we stopped there to find a dozen or more people standing in the street taking pictures of it. Paper jack-o'-lanterns on its doors smiled for the cameras. It really needs one of those white, house-shaped historical placards you find on most of the houses in Salem: The *Hocus Pocus* House.

Most of the characters in the movie were kids, and since the story took place in October, that means school. In the movie, the school they attended was Jacob Baily High School. In real life, it's the old Phillips Elementary School building, which stopped being a school about a year or so before the movie filmed there.

The tall, red brick building looms on the south edge of Salem Common. It's full of condos these days, but it still bears the name of its previous incarnation on the distinctive central tower that in the movie exudes the glowing green ashes of the temporarily incinerated witches, fresh from the kiln.

At one point in my Salem life I was crossing the Common after dark.

Max and Dani's House from *Hocus Pocus*

On the western edge, I could see the Salem Witch Museum, eerily lit. At night its central window glows a dramatic red, and exterior lights throw alternating colors of blue and green and red on the brick facade, creating an almost *Suspiria*-like backdrop for Conant's silhouette. But there, on the Common itself, were hundreds of people bundled in blankets and sitting in camp chairs facing a large stone gazebo. Stretched across it was a white sheet on which were a familiar trio of witch sisters. Every Saturday in October, Salem plays movies on the Common. That night the feature presentation was *Hocus Pocus*, and I assume everybody gathered around was fully aware that they were sitting on the same grass where some of the scenes were filmed. There are perfect Halloween moments everywhere in Salem in October.

Allison's house in the movie is a prominent Salem site, the Ropes Mansion. The big white house, with its black shutters and massive fence posts, is on Essex Street next to the tall, gray, castle-like edifice that is the First Church in Salem, Unitarian. The church building dates back to 1836, and the congregation itself dates back to the city's founding. Old-time religion means something a bit different there at the First Church. And if you're sensing the pattern that everything interesting in Salem seems to be on Essex Street, you're pretty close to right.

The Ropes Mansion was built in the early eighteenth century and is named for the family who lived there for almost 150 years. It's currently operated by PEM (I've already pointed out that pattern).

When we stayed on Chestnut Street, we were right around the corner from the mansion. I was excited to see the inside of it, to see if it matched up with the movie. The house had reopened to the public a few months earlier after the completion of a renovation project. Unfortunately, it looked nothing like the interior of Allison's house. But it was a fantastic house. Because it was in the same family for so long, much of their stuff survived and is on display.

It was also pretty crowded for a site that was a good five-minute walk from the end of the pedestrian mall. Looking around, the crowd seemed much younger than the people I assume visit an innocuous historic house when there's so much else to do in Salem in October. But they were avid, listening with patience to the spiels of the staff who welcomed them and then not asking any questions in return. Instead, they wandered off and took lots of photos on their phones. This time I didn't hear the whisper,

"*Hocus Pocus*," but most of the people around me definitely had black flames in their eyes. I could only assume that they were hitting the socials with an "I'm at Allison's house from *Hocus Pocus*." Witch emoji, jack-o'-lantern emoji, excited face emoji. That's what my post looked like, anyway.

Another prominent site is the Old Town Hall, on the second floor of which was thrown the Halloween party where Bette Midler sings Screamin' Jay Hawkins's "I Put a Spell on You." It was also where I had sat and self-consciously participated in Cry Innocent. The side of the exterior that faces Essex Street was also used, steps away from where people dressed in Sanderson sisters costumes regularly parade down the strip. Here at the Old Town Hall, the phrase "*Hocus Pocus*" regularly wafted on the air, and every tour guide pointed it out.

And that's it, although it's also plenty. If you head next door to Marblehead to see Wilmot Redd's memorial, that graveyard was also used in the film for the scene in which Max gets his shoes stolen.

The latest witch movie to employ the atmosphere and geography of Salem is Rob Zombie's *The Lords of Salem*, which came out in 2012. You're going to want to put the kids to bed for this one.

Zombie was the lead singer of the horror movie–inspired rock act White Zombie, and then he went solo with an even more horror movie–inspired rock act, and then he finally said, screw it, I need to direct horror movies. He was born nearby in Haverhill, so it seems natural that his fifth movie would be about the Salem witches. However, according to him, he only got the idea to write the movie when he returned to Massachusetts for the wedding of a friend. He picked up a book from the hotel giftshop. "I . . . found this book called like *Hunting Witches* or something, just a skinny little book, and I just got it to read because I had nothing else to do, and that's what kicked it off," he said in an interview online. I think he was talking about Francis Hill's book, *Hunting for Witches*. Remind me to tell her that next time I see her.

The Lords of Salem is basically a remake of *Hocus Pocus*, just with geriatric nudity, lots of F-bombs, and a grungy cast that looked like it rarely showered during filming. It has feral seventeenth-century Salem witches and a curse that manifests itself in modern-day Salem, although instead of a black flame candle, it manifests itself through an ancient piece of music that finds its way to a local DJ, played by Zombie's wife, Cheryl Moon Zombie.

The movie zagged from Zombie's usual violent horror stories, throwing back instead to the trippy horror movies of the '60s and '70s. As a result, the movie gets pretty surreal at times.

When Zombie was filming his horror movie in the winter of 2011 in Salem, I followed the reports avidly. I didn't drive over and try to sneak onto set, though. I just liked that it was happening, that one of the spookiest dudes in the movie biz was filming spooky stuff in one of the spookiest cities in the country.

The Essex Street Pedestrian Mall, as Salem's signature space, was featured in the movie multiple times. Even the *Bewitched* statue made a cameo. The second floor of the Old Town Hall found itself transformed into a set again, this time as a theater, with a much more intense and disturbing party than it had previously hosted with *Hocus Pocus*.

About two blocks away from Derby Square is another filming location, the Engine House. This small, fire-station–themed pizza place is located on Lafayette Street, across the street from the actual Salem fire station. It's only featured briefly in a collage of scenes in which women react to hearing the mysterious tune over the radio.

I bring it up more to show how even a trip to a pizza joint in Salem in October is a haunted house experience. Outside the small corner restaurant, a giant pumpkin creature towered over anybody who dared get close enough to read its menu. Inside there was a life-sized Grim Reaper and a Headless Horseman. I got pizza there a few times during my stay. But I'll love the place forever for inspiring this conversation I had with Esme:

"Is that skeleton with the thing in his hand . . ." she began.

"It's a scythe," I corrected her.

"Is that skeleton with the scythe in his hand a dead farmer?"

Another briefly featured site can be found at the Salem Willows. Salem Willows is a beach park about a mile from the downtown area, located at the tip of the broom of this witch-shaped city. It's the closest thing Salem has to a boardwalk. Its attractions are closed by October, but you can still hit the park area. On the beach there is a long dock, and it was at the end of that dock that Jeff Daniel Phillips takes a phone call. Sorry. Anticlimactic paragraph ending.

We also visited Greenlawn Cemetery, which is in North Salem, the cape of the witch, about a mile from the pedestrian mall. Established in 1807 and covering one hundred acres, it's a fine enough cemetery as far as they go, but since Sheri Moon and some faceless thing leading a goat walked there, it adds to its spooky cred. The two main sites in the cemetery that were used in the movie were the bridge that arches over the cemetery pond, and the chapel.

But honestly, all you really need to see in Salem from the movie is the house.

Most of *The Lords of Salem* takes place at a creepy-looking apartment building carved out of an old house. It's three-stories tall, blocky, and white, with a distinctive brown trim and green shutters. Anywhere else, the house would stick out even if it wasn't the location of a movie shoot, but on Essex Street, it's about par for the course. Only about a block from the Ropes Mansion, the house sits at the intersection of Essex Street and Hamilton Street. It's here where three mysterious witches lived, played by Meg Foster, Patricia Quinn, and Dee Wallace—the Sanderson sisters of the movie.

The house was built in 1850, but only the exterior was used for filming. Based on the interior images I saw on a real estate website, it's more grand than gloomy. It also has a strange mural with trees and exotic buildings that covers the wall of the stairwell and continues to the hall on the second floor.

Lords of Salem House

This house is officially the *Lords of Salem* house to me now, and it's just one more bit of macabre interest in a town already bristling with it.

But of all the TV and movie witches in the world, only one has a bronze statue in Salem: Samantha Stephens from the 1960s sitcom *Bewitched*.

I've mentioned this statue a few times so far in passing because it's impossible not to pass it. For many, it'll be the first site they see in Salem. It's at the most prominent corner of Lappin Park, directly across from the west end of the Essex Street Pedestrian Mall.

Bewitched was a sitcom about a witch and her muggle husband who wanted to live normal, non-magical lives for some really, really unknown reason, but kept finding that mundane dream of a boring life regularly interrupted by other witches and their zany spells. The core cast included Elizabeth Montgomery as Samantha Stephens, Dick York and then later Dick Sargent as Darrin Stephens, and Agnes Moorehead as Samantha's meddling magical mother, Endora.

The bronze statue that honors the show and its star features Elizabeth Montgomery in a basic dress, her hand lifted high as she sidesaddles a broom across a smidge of cloud, a large crescent moon behind her back. It's not an interesting statue. It looks more like a weathervane than anything else and is not a great likeness of Montgomery. In the words of one of my tour guides, "Elizabeth Montgomery was a beautiful woman, and we ended up with Willem Dafoe in drag. Like in *Boondock Saints*." The story of the statue, however, is very interesting.

It was installed by TV Land, the cable channel dedicated to old sitcoms. They had a project for a while where they would make a permanent place for those sitcoms on the American landscape by sticking bronze statues of their stars in cities where the sitcoms took place. Like the Fonz in Milwaukee. Ralph Kramden in New York. Bob Newhart in Chicago.

The unveiling of Samantha in Salem took place on a rainy day in June 2005. A stage was set up for the event in Lappin Park and speeches were given by the president of the channel, the mayor of the city at the time, and William Asher, the producer and director of *Bewitched*, who was also the husband of Elizabeth Montgomery. The surviving cast members were there as well: Barnard Fox, who played Dr. Bombay; Kasey Rogers, who played Louise Tate, the wife of Darin's boss, Larry Tate; and Erin Murphy, who played Samantha and Darrin's daughter Tabitha. She was also the grand marshal of the Haunted Happenings parade that year.

A few hundred people showed up, despite the rain, along with lots of news cameras . . . and protestors. Although most seemed to dig the party, a few groups weren't happy with the statue. One sign dangling from an adjacent window read, simply, "Shame," while in the crowd floated a few signs reading, "Tragedy Does Not Equal Whimsy" and "Salem: We're Better Than This, Much Better" and "Is There No Limit to the Schlock and Hype?"

Some Witches thought it was another example of the city belittling

Bewitched Statue, Lappin Park

their religion. Some residents thought it trivialized the city for immortalizing an actor without connection to it in one of the most prominent parts of town. After all, *Bewitched* was set in Westport, Connecticut, and Elizabeth Montgomery was born in Los Angeles. Others didn't like what they saw as more capitalization on a tragedy in a city already full of it. Historians found it troubling. Richard Trask wrote an editorial for the *Boston Globe* where he compared the act to erecting a statue of Sergeant Schultz outside Auschwitz, a reference to *Hogan's Heroes*, a sitcom about POWs in Nazi Germany.

And, honestly, all these concerns are pretty much right on. I mean, the first-ever statue of a witch in Witch City isn't that of a Witch Trial victim or one of the founding mothers of modern Witchcraft. It's a 1960s sitcom character. And while part of me likes the idea of Salem bronzing fictional witches and setting them up all over town, I could see how that would upset the always teetering balance of what the "witch" in Witch City really stands for.

Except for one thing.

Bewitched might have had a not-insignificant role in the Witch City we know today.

The year was 1970. The show was to start filming its seventh and—although they didn't know it—penultimate season. The previous one was the first full season with Dick Sargent replacing Dick York as Darrin, due to the latter's health condition. Season six had also been the lowest-rated season to that point in the show's history, which has been attributed to everything from the audience not warming up to the new Darrin to the show's plotlines growing repetitive. And to top it off, a part of their set in Hollywood had been damaged by fire.

For all these reasons, the creators decided something new was needed. It didn't take much brainstorming to come up with the idea of some on-location shooting in Salem for this show about witches. And so was born the Salem Saga, a storyline that covered the first eight episodes of the seventh season.

Filming took only a week or two in the summer of 1970. But it was a big deal in Salem. People mobbed the stars during filming and gathered around the hotel where they stayed. Newspapers wrote articles about it and interviewed Salem's famous visitors. Looking at all the press coverage of the filming, it seemed like a fun time.

The Salem Saga is a story arc that involves Samantha attending a witch convention in Salem, and bringing Darrin along to multi-purpose it into a vacation. Throughout their stay, they get chased around by an enchanted bedwarmer from the House of the Seven Gables, Darrin gets turned into the Gloucester Fisherman's Memorial, Samantha gets a doppleganger, Paul Revere gets pulled into present-day Salem, and Darrin and Samantha get sent back to old Salem where Samantha ends the Salem Witch Trials herself. One of Samantha's last lines in the saga is, "Good news, I don't have to go back to Salem."

On our first night in Salem, we were invited by Tina Jordan and Stacy Tilney to attend a talk at the Salem Witch Museum by the local "*Bewitched* guy," an author named Peter Alachi. Unfortunately, we couldn't attend because the event coincided with the Haunted Happenings Grand Parade, but I later contacted Alachi for a private tour of *Bewitched* in Salem.

"Meet me at the bathrooms in the lobby of the Hawthorne Hotel," read his email. Such instructions should really be a red flag, but being color-blind, I agreed.

I arrived first. The bathrooms at the Hawthorne Hotel are near its Essex Street entrance, in an alcove past an honest-to-god public telephone bank. A sign near the entrance of the bathroom alcove states, "For hotel guests only."

I'm unsure if that sign also applied to the collection of framed objects on the wall across from the bathroom doors. It's a mini-exhibit of *Bewitched* in Salem. The Hawthorne Hotel, back then called the Hawthorne Motor Hotel, was where the cast and crew stayed during the shoot in real life and where Darrin and Samantha stay for the story.

The exhibit included a photo of Elizabeth Montgomery and Dick Sargent, as well as a facsimile of a script page from the "Samantha's Hot Bed Warmer" episode that mentions the Hawthorne Hotel ("CUT TO: EXT. HAWTHORNE HOTEL — STUDIO"). There was a Christmas card to the hotel manager from Montgomery and Asher. And a placard that explained why all this stuff was on the wall in the first place.

The most fantastic thing on the wall was a menu. The restaurant at the Hawthorne Hotel created a special menu in honor of its guests. The front of the menu had a witch on a broom below the title *When Witches Get Together.* Cocktails included Witches Brew (a "caldron" of punch), an Evil Eye (vodka martini with a purple onion), a Sabbat Stinger (a Tom Collins with green menthe), and Satan's Sip (a "very, very old fashioned" with black and green fruit). Some of the ghastlier hors d'oeuvres were jellyfish au gratin (baked stuffed clams), lizard gizzards (chicken gizzards), fried salamander (shrimp), and pickled elephant tail (Vienna sausages). Beneath its sneeze guards, the buffet had Green Goulish Stew (fish chowder), Python Eggs Sauté (fried rice), Jack O'Lantern Beams (candied carrots), and Sea Serpent à la Bourguignon (lobster in cherry sauce). And then for desert it was Passion Berry Surprise and Amazon Water Brulee, a tart and coffee, respectively. I guess they ran out of names there toward the end.

As I occupied myself with the exhibit, I realized that I didn't know what Peter Alachi looked like. There was no way I was going to make eye contact with every guy headed to the bathroom, so I moved around the corner to the payphones. When he arrived and each of us figured out who the other was, I was surprised to hear his accent. It wasn't a North Shore accent. Not even a Boston one. Salem's *Bewitched* guy is Syrian.

Alachi came to the United States in 1979 to further his college education and moved to Salem in 2003. Today, he's a microbiology professor at Salem State University.

"So how did a microbiology professor from Syria became the *Bewitched* guy?" I asked him.

"When the Samantha statue came to Salem about two years after I moved here, I was intrigued. Why is she in Salem? What is all this chaos?"

He was compelled to research the topic like his tenure depended on it and ended up writing a trilogy of booklets on the topic, one of which came packaged with cardboard 3D glasses: *Salem's Summer of Sam.* "It was really just academic curiosity. I'm a microbiology guy, which is mostly petri dishes, but I'm always interested in finding other things out."

"Did you know about *Bewitched* before that statue arrived?"

"Oh yeah, I watched it as a kid. It used to be on Lebanese television. Everybody knew about *Bewitched.* It was dubbed in French with Arabic subtitles, so I could read it. Samantha and Darrin were called Cassandra and Jean-Pierre in that version."

My own familiarity with the show was completely due to the pre-cable days of summer syndication, back when school was out and there was nothing to do during the week days except go outside or hang with friends. Instead, I caught *Bewitched* and *Gilligan's Island* and *I Love Lucy* and *All in the Family* and *I Dream of Jeannie*, often back-to-back episodes of each. Basically, I did summer electives in the American sitcom.

Alachi and I walked out the side entrance of the hotel onto Essex Street and looked up. The red-brick exterior of the Hawthorne Hotel was never used during the show. Instead, a dull, gray cement facade was faked back in Los Angeles. The only parts of the hotel that actually made it into the show were the lobby elevators, which have an old-fashioned brass mailbox between them that is still there today. They showed the elevators in one episode as part of that old gag where two people miss each other by seconds as one goes up one elevator and the other goes down another.

Alachi opened one of his booklets and showed me a tiny, blurry, black-and-white photo of Elizabeth Montgomery, Dick Sargent, and Agnes Moorehead leaning out a window of the hotel and waving to what must have been a crowd of fans below. He pointed to the corresponding window of the hotel above us. "Their view of Salem was from up there," he said.

From the hotel we walked a few paces down Hawthorne Boulevard to a towering bronze statue with a billowy greatcoat and a stern countenance, the namesake of the boulevard, Nathaniel Hawthorne. Again. The mustachioed gentleman sits regally atop a rock with a hat and a walking stick in his hand. He is elevated six feet in the air by a stone pedestal.

The statue made it into one of the episodes, albeit merely as an insert shot as Darrin and his boss Larry Tate, played by David White, see some of the sites of Salem while Tate tries to convince Darrin to slip in some work on his vacation. Today there's a massive tree shadowing the statue that turns bright orange and red in the fall and blocks the hotel behind him. During the filming, that tree was barely a sapling, and the hotel rose large behind the statue, forming its entire backdrop.

We decided to walk to the *Bewitched* statue first. As we did so, he told me about the local cable access show that he hosts called *Showcase Salem*. About a *Bewitched*-themed bed and breakfast that someone he knew unsuccessfully planned for Salem. About a computer program called Bio-

BASE that he wrote for identifying microbes. On the ground surrounding the statue were pumpkin shards. "This morning they were all over her," he told me. I had seen it myself. I had been killing time at Rockafellas that morning drinking one of their beef-straw Bloody Mary's and gazing out the window. Someone had arranged pieces of pumpkin rind all over the statue. It was almost more decoration than vandalism. As I drank my Bloody Mary through the miracle that is a beef straw, I watched a family knock them off the statue so that they could get a clean photo with her. Throughout October, a permanent crowd surrounds the statue, as if the year were 1970 and formulaic sitcoms produced superstars. For the millionth time, I wished the sculptor had depicted her dressed as a witch.

We continued down Essex Street to the Witch House. This historic property popped up in passing when Darrin, Samantha, and Endora arrived in Salem, Endora perched on the top of the backseat of the convertible as though she were in a parade.

"Isn't this one of the places where they held the Witch Trials?" asked Darrin, in the driver's seat.

"One of them," said Samantha, incorrectly. "Let's drive on."

"As long as we're here, wouldn't you like to go in?"

"Darrin, that's like asking Napoleon if he'd like to revisit Waterloo."

After a bout of canned laughter, Samantha and Endora explain to Darrin that there weren't any real witches in the Witch Trials, just "mortal prejudice and hysteria."

"They were going to film here," explained Alachi, "but it rained so they couldn't. Fortunately, they had already taken footage of the landmark and just projected it behind the car on a stage."

That happened a lot throughout the filming of the Salem Saga. Most of the landmarks of Salem were used as insert shots, shown either without actors at all or projected behind them on a screen. Some of that was because of the weather, which was rainy off and on throughout the shoot. Most of the interiors were sets, and even many exterior scenes were filmed in California. You can tell because in real life, Salem has no palm trees, nor are there any mountains nearby.

"You've probably seen every single episode of the series multiple times," I said as he used his camera to show me the angles used in filming one of the Salem scenes.

"No, I haven't seen every episode in the show. I've seen the Salem Saga a lot of times, obviously." That told me his fascination had less to do with the fact that *Bewitched* filmed in Salem than in the fact that Salem hosted *Bewitched*.

From the Witch House, we doubled back east, this time making our way to Derby Street toward the central site used in the Salem Saga.

En route, we passed In a Pig's Eye, a small barbecue joint that could have been straight out of the south . . . except for the black and white Tarot-card portraits lining its walls. "Wait. Look at that." Alachi pointed to a band flyer taped on the window. It was for an act called The Darlings, their name laid out in large white letters against a blue-tinted picture of Elizabeth Montgomery. It was the fourth time I had seen her face that day in the city, what with the Hawthorne Hotel bathroom exhibit and the statue and the episode guide I saw sitting prominently on a shelf of Wicked Good Books.

Finally, we made it to The House of the Seven Gables. Adjacent to this attraction is the patch of Salem most used in the Salem Saga, both as a filming site and as a plot point.

We turned down Turner Street, a side street that parallels the Gables property and offers the best view of it this side of a purchased admission. In fact, the house is technically on this street, and its doorway here used to be the front entrance of the house, which is now accessed via Derby. A dozen paces past the doorway, Turner Street dead-ends at the harbor.

This cul-de-sac was used more than any other site in Salem and across two different episodes. In one, Samantha and Darrin visit The House of the Seven Gables and run into the enchanted bed warmer. The interior shots were all sets, but once they left the house, with the bed warmer floating behind them through a window and into the back of their convertible on an invisible length of fishing wire, they were on Turner Street. The other episode had Darrin and Larry Tate hanging out in front of the entrance, for real this time as opposed to at the Hawthorne Statue, as Tate continued to attempt to get Darrin to work on his vacation. At one point, Tate walks across the back lawn of the property and stares off into the harbor.

Turns out, Alachi is also a big fan of *The Munsters*, another '60s supernatural sitcom, possibly liking it even more so than *Bewitched*. "I got to meet Butch Patrick two years ago in Salem," he said. That's Eddie Munster, the child werewolf in the family of monsters. "I also met Al Lewis, Grandpa Munster, at a convention. I told him that people say I look like him. He told me, 'I look a little better than that.'" "I grew up in Syria but, like most Syrians, was exposed to American culture. We watched *The Love Boat, Columbo, McMillan and Wife.* All these shows were on television in the 1970s."

"Coming from Syria, was Halloween a shock to you?"

"A little bit—not so much for my wife. She's from New Jersey."

"Do you like Halloween?"

"I do. It's gotten bigger since I moved here in 2003. But I like the trick-or-treating part more than the downtown scene, so I stay at my house and wait for the kids. I like to get dressed up. I've been Batman, I've been John Belushi from *The Blues Brothers.*"

"What do you like the most about your adopted city?"

"It's a beautiful community, the neighbors are friendly, it's clean, nicely maintained. It does have its kitschy side," said the man who prized kitsch, "but the kitschy side of Salem brings people in, and then they get to learn all about Salem. If you can put up with October, you're okay." That's the key, of course, and a not-too-inconsiderable one at that. While my family was at the children's costume parade, Lindsey got into a conversation with a local woman. The woman said she had lived on a street off the Common for years, but her family was now in the process of moving. "I love the city, but I can't take October. We can't even get into our street most of the time."

After Alachi published his first booklet on *Bewitched,* he was asked to give a talk to a group of *Bewitched* superfans who came to Salem for a convention. That got him on television and in newspapers and suddenly cemented his role as the resident expert on *Bewitched.* "I didn't really want to be known as that at the time, so I let it go." But the group kept in touch, and he gave another talk when they returned to the area. They then asked him to give a talk in California for the fiftieth anniversary of the show. "I couldn't take off work for that one." Microbiology beats magic in the end.

We headed to the Common and hit a few sites on the way. The first was Immaculate Conception Catholic Church just down from the Hawthorne statue on Hawthorne Boulevard. Its steeple was used in an establishing shot in the episode that mostly takes place in Gloucester.

The Gloucester episode was probably the best one in the whole Salem Saga. In addition, more Gloucester sites were used in that episode than actual Salem sites throughout the saga, not counting inserted shots. Gloucester sites included an empty pedestal adjacent to the Gloucester Fisherman's Memorial upon which they erected the Darrin-ized version of it, the Gloucester House Restaurant, and Hammond Castle.

We headed down Charter Street, passing the Old Burying Point. "You would have thought they would have filmed at Charter Street Cemetery, but they didn't," he observed. The cast and crew would be two decades too early to film at the Witch Trials Memorial.

Next was a large condo building. Located at the intersection of Charter Street and Central Street, this building once housed the Salem Police Department. Harry Houdini performed an escape here in 1906. A corner of the exterior, just enough to get the "Salem Police" sign above the door into frame, was used in two different episodes, one of which also featured verbal references to the Peabody Essex Museum and the Salem Pioneer Village.

At the Common, a Hollywood equivalent of which was shown regularly throughout the show, the Roger Conant Statue made two appearances, both times as inserted shots. But it was the topic of conversation for both scenes, at least, one of which included the actor Jonathan Harris, who also played the lovably evil Dr. Zachary Smith in *Lost in Space*.

As we got ready to part ways, I said to Alachi, "Of all the things in Salem that you could have been hooked on, *Bewitched* is the one that got you."

"Yes. And it could have been nothing," he replied. And it might have been, had he ended up in any other city in the United States.

The Salem Saga episodes aired from late September to the beginning of November in 1970, the same year that they were filmed. And while there wasn't a lot of actual Salem in the saga (in fact, half of the episodes didn't feature any shots of Salem), most people around the country—and I guess the world, judging by Alachi's childhood experience—who watched the show didn't know that.

Suddenly, a chunk of the TV-viewing audience saw Salem as a place to take a vacation, just like Darrin and Samantha, and Salem saw a bump in tourism as a result. More important than that, though, is that *Bewitched* did its part to further bind the idea of Salem and witches in the popular consciousness. And that is really what the Samantha statue in Lappin Park signifies.

Of course, going by that standard of tourism, the city should also place bronze statues of the Sanderson sisters in the garden behind the Ropes Mansion.

Over the years, most of the statue's critics have acknowledged its validity as a Salem landmark, although few, critic or supporter, find the statue artful. In fact, the only thing that seems to still gall its detractors is the prominent piece of real estate it holds. In January 2016, a local blogger named Donna Seger—a professor and chairwoman of the History Department at Salem State University—who has been known to regularly rail against the cheesier and history-insensitive aspects of her city, wrote a post on her blog, Streets of Salem, called "Samantha Should Go." In it, she writes, "My feelings towards Samantha have evolved: I don't really want to destroy her anymore, I'd just like to move her—to a less prominent and more appropriate place—where she can represent Witch City rather than *Salem*. Maybe in front of the Witch Museum?"

I think I know a better spot, one more tied to the show and still near tourist traffic: The cul-de-sac at the end of Turner Street. You're welcome/I'm sorry, House of the Seven Gables.

The Samantha statue and the Danvers meetinghouse are much alike. They are both physical traces of ephemeral moments in the unique history of Salem (and ex-Salem). They've also both transcended their original roles. They were each originally part of a specific story, but today, they help tell the larger story of Salem and the Witch Trials. And they stand as a lesson to all future film and television storytellers.

If you want to film a story about witches, do it in Salem. It means more there.

10

THE REAL WITCHES OF ESSEX COUNTY

Witches in the Haunted Happenings Grand Parade

I was in a narrow alley, one of the walls of which was covered in large green, red, and blue dragons. In front of me was a round black table with a yellow pentacle painted on it that was barely discernible beneath the chaos of candles and statuary and instruments on top. A tiny black cauldron sat in the middle. A young woman beside me was finishing an incantation. She threw a powder into the cauldron, and a fire flashed. She said, "Now let's open the circle and get to Walkin'. Like Christopher." I had just experienced my first spell.

There are three types of witches in Salem. The first is the soul-selling, demon-worshipping, anti-Christ type that never existed in the first place.

The 1692 witches. The "Thou shalt not suffer a witch to live" witches. The witches of superstition.

The second is the supernatural, broomstick-riding witch. The Halloween witch. The ones that are in our fictions and films. The Wicked Witch of the West. The Sanderson sisters. Witch Hazel on the Bugs Bunny cartoons.

And then there is the third type of witch, the religious Witch. This Witch is the only one of the three kinds that is real.

And I was on my way to interview my first real Witch.

I didn't know what to expect. I knew the basics of the religion. That it's a nature religion that worships two main deities, a goddess and a god. That it really caught on in the United States during the counterculture surge of the 1960s. That it reaches as far back as it can to pull traditions and ideas and symbols from pre-Christian religions. That it uses much of the same terminology usually assigned to fictional witches, like *spell* and *magic* and *coven*. That it is an extremely varied religion, about as hard to pin down in its particulars as Christianity is. That it is duly recognized by the US government. Witches buried in veteran cemeteries can get pentacles on their tombstones, and Witches have performed the opening invocations of government sessions. As recent as 2013, it was touted as the fastest growing religion in America.

My first interaction with her, over email, was promising in its strangeness. She asked me to make sure that I scheduled our meeting during the waxing phase of the moon and when Mercury was not in retrograde. My Outlook calendar didn't have those features.

Her name was Gypsy Ravish, and she runs a Witch shop on Pickering Wharf called Nu Aeon. Pickering Wharf is a horseshoe of bland-looking retail shops and restaurants on the water, the insides of which are anything but bland. It includes Witch shops and seafood restaurants, a haunted attraction, and some of the usual unusual Salem giftshops.

Gypsy Ravish's name is half stage name and half married name. She got the Gypsy during her career as a club singer, when she used to open for the likes of Dizzy Gillespie. A short-lived marriage (not the Ravish one) brought her to Salem in the mid-1970s, where she started taking classes and became what she called a "lineaged Witch." Today, besides running her shop, she is also the High Priestess of the Temple of Nine Wells.

Her shop was small, although about the same size as all the Witch shops I had seen in Salem. On her shelves were books and candles, jewelry and statuary. She pulled a chair out for me to sit on and then settled herself side-saddle on a full-sized statue of a white goat. Somebody had placed sunglasses on its face and wrapped a pentacle around its neck.

"I was ready for something mystical," she told me about how she got involved in the Witch culture of the city she found herself in. "Before I came to Salem I'd already read Allan Watts and Baba Ram Dass and was interested in things like reincarnation and higher levels of consciousness. So I almost feel like I was guided here."

"You said something earlier about being a lineaged Witch. What do you mean by that?"

"Lineaged just means the line of teachers before you. You know, who taught you and who taught them. In a lineaged family, there's some sort of egregore, a group soul. I've been taught by a number of different teachers and they've all made a beautiful impact on me."

"Ok, so that's what you meant by lineaged. What about Witch?"

"Isn't that an interesting word, Witch, in 2015. People will define it according to their own belief system or etymological research, but Witchcraft comes from the old ways of working with the spirits of nature. It's about a sensitivity to what is around us and how to communicate with it. The neo-pagan movement was a revival of these old ways and an envisioning of us as not alienated from nature, which I think is more like Christianity, but as a part of nature. That's the magic." She then went on to list a variety of techniques that practitioners use to access that magic, from eggs in water to bones and tortoise shells to Tarot cards and runes and crystal balls. She even told me that she did a reading on me prior to meeting up using a form of divination called I Ching, where she tossed coins with symbols on them.

"There seems to be a lot of flexibility in this religion or craft or what do you call it . . . "

"A spiritual path."

"With all that flexibility, people are going to be doing wildly different things as they follow their own spiritual paths. Does that make for a lot of friction?"

"I think that most or all of the friction today between groups is about the people themselves more than the actual beliefs. It's more like who did what to whom and who said what about whom. That can create drama."

"You came here four decades ago. That means you were part of the original influx of modern Witches into Salem. What was it like back then?"

"It was really fun. Big, big fun. It was inspiring to meet people who had beautiful gifts like psychic vision and who had been living the lifestyle of the mystical. There was so much going on, it was so brilliant and exciting, it was so inclusive, it was like family. I wrote a whole music album about those experiences. It was an amazing journey for me."

"How has it changed in your time here?"

"The big change was when people didn't need to come to Salem in the same way they had to before. In those days, people came to Salem to practice Witchcraft. You couldn't be an open Witch in many other places in the country because of misinformation and propaganda from other religious groups." I had read that going public with one's Witchcraft beliefs was often phrased as "coming out of the broom closet." I couldn't bring myself to ask her about the phrase, though. She continued: "You could come to Salem and wear a pentacle, a cape, you could dress the part. Not like a poser, although there are plenty of those, but to find that part of yourself that really wanted to connect with the magic in life. Visitors might say things like, 'I always knew I was a Witch' or 'I feel like I'm coming home.'"

She went on to explain that today, in the teenage years of the new millennium, people can do that anywhere, in New York or Vermont or Texas, wherever they are. Many neo-pagan organizations have been created, a library's worth of books have been written, and with the Internet, "everything has gone completely cosmic. The Internet was so huge for the craft."

She then thought for a little bit, as if traveling back to those days in her mind for an answer that was more personal, "You know, people around here weren't teaching Witchcraft as a religion in those days. It was put out more like techniques that worked—I used to call them survival skills—but techniques that worked for healing yourself and others, for prosperity for yourself and others. Very inspiring, very beautiful."

I asked her, "So you walk around Salem, and everywhere you look there is a witch caricature. Hooked nose, warts, the whole deal. Is that something that bothers you?" In my head I was thinking about the scene from *Bewitched* when the first thing Endora does on arriving in Salem is to change all the witch signs from grisly old hags to beautiful young witches.

"It's a misogynistic propaganda ploy. It wasn't just that the church was against practitioners of the arts, it was against women in particular. Taking the most grotesque images of the wise woman of the village and making her the monster was an attempt to disempower and demonize her. So when you see this ugly crone riding a broom, we have mixed feelings about it." On the one hand, she kind of resented it. "It's an image that is derogatory, to see powerful women portrayed as monsters." On the other, she kind of dug it. "Yet, it's extraordinary that in Salem, the image of the witch has become something so beloved."

"How do you interpret that, this act on the part of Salem to really claim the witch as a symbol?"

"People here love their history. Not the horrors of what I call the Witch Hunter Hysteria instead of witchcraft hysteria, but the fact that it ended, that people finally found their sanity again. I really think that Salem is proud of the fact that they stopped and evolved. At least that's my take on it. It might be a little more optimistic than what others think."

"But do you feel that way personally, when you see somebody walking down the mall with the silhouette of a witch on their shirt or you see the symbol on the sides of the cop cars?"

"Put it this way, I just came from Martha's Vineyard. I have a mug that says 'Martha's Vineyard,' and all down the street there were Martha's Vineyard T-shirts, dolls, everything. That kind of commercialism that people have in destination places, we have here. I don't begrudge it so much as I'm just aware of it."

"And now as a shop owner, you're kind of a part of that, right? Tourists walk in here every October."

"Well, the Witches never called it Witch City. It wasn't our idea to exploit or utilize the dark history of Salem to make money. It's just commercialism of the sort that is natural in cities like this."

I looked at the variety of mystical objects surrounding me. "I don't see any cartoony witches."

"We don't have any of that that here. You can get cartoony witches everywhere else. There's a gift shop next door that has plenty of them."

"Tell me about Samhain. I know it's one of your sabbats and that it coincides with Halloween. And that it has some similarities. But that's about it."

Ravish alighted from her goat and walked over to a rack of CDs. She grabbed one of her own, called *Enchantress*. On the cover was a black and white photo of a much younger Gypsy Ravish. She had dark curly hair, a dark dress, dark eyes. Ravish popped open the plastic case and showed me the artwork on the surface of the disc inside, spinning it with a beringed finger. It was a circle divided into eight slices: The Wiccan Wheel of the Year. Each slice was a sabbat, each one corresponding to an annual astronomical event, solstices and equinoxes and others. On each one is held a festival. Samhain is often considered the Witch's New Year.

"Samhain is when the veils are thin, when it is time to reach out, to become aware, to feel and to attune to your loved ones who have gone beyond the veil, in the spirit world, like my husband." That was Richard Ravish, who gave Gypsy the other half of her fantastic name. She met him in 1981, and they started the business together. He died in 2012. I had seen his picture in the shop window as a memorial when I walked inside. "We've had a circle out at Gallows Hill for Samhain for many years now. Non-Witches would attend and tell me how they felt the spirits of their loved ones during the ritual. It's really powerful."

"I've read that Wicca is the country's fastest growing religion. Why do you think that would be?"

"I think people are looking for alternatives, for something genuine, and maybe they find it in the magical and the mystical. Is it on the rise? Yes. Do I see as many people here for ceremonies as we used to? No. But again, that's because these days people are freer to practice Witchcraft anywhere."

"Then do you foresee a time in the future when Salem stops being the Wicca-mecca?"

"I don't see Salem changing out of its mystical persona. As a matter of fact, I think we're at the point now where a lot of us elders, people who have been on the scene a while, we're starting to archive things. We're establishing foundations and libraries." She described her unique personal collection of Witchcraft art and artifacts that she had been able to amass from individual artists and artisans because of her role as a retailer. "Now with my husband gone, it's all left in my care. Who's going to take care of it when I'm gone? So some of us are now really thinking about legacy, not individual legacy, but the legacy of the craft. We'll be the ancestors someday, and what are we leaving to our children to light the path for others? What are we leaving behind to tell our history?"

"What specifically do people come in here to buy?"

"They often don't know what they're looking for. It has to call to them. Something catches their eye, maybe it's a dragon or a pentacle—so many people lose their pentacles and need them replaced. But they're not looking for the macabre or curses here. They may be looking for protection, or love."

"And maybe just a souvenir?"

"Some are. But there are souvenir shops everywhere in Salem. They're looking for something different here. People want talismans. They want something that does something, that has some juice. Everything in here has a function besides just being pretty or Witchy. Come over here."

She took me on a quick tour of the shop. She showed me jewelry and explained the power of each stone. She showed me a shelf of books that was packed with works on Italian Witchcraft, Alexandrian Witchcraft, Green Witchcraft, Celtic Witchcraft, books on how to become a Witch, books on the Kabbalah, the Golden Dawn, the mystical orders, angelic languages, hermetic magic, Egyptian code, feng shui, fairy magic. She showed me candles wrapped with spells, some of her own devising. She took me to a rack of cloaks. "When you wear something like this, you feel different. You feel grand and fun and special."

"You said you did a reading of me before I came. What did it tell you?"

"It was a good reading. That your project is important and a good thing for the craft."

"So if the reading had come up bad, you wouldn't have invited me in here?"

She laughed. "No, I would have still met you."

My first actual psychic reading in Salem was done by a retired contractor from the North Shore with a bushy white moustache named, let's say, Murray. Don't get me wrong, I wasn't exactly expecting a stereotype. You know, a woman in a glittery turban and silk robe, jewelry dripping off her wrists and neck and fingers, long fingernails scratching the globe of a lighted crystal ball and telling me dire things in a husky voice. But I certainly wasn't expecting a Murray.

Murray almost wasn't my first Salem psychic. I'd originally chosen a shop that looked a little bit more in line with the classic psychic storefront you see in the movies. An old house, an exotically named woman, a neon sign depicting a crystal ball. But after Yelping her and seeing some controversy online, I decided she might not be my ideal first Salem psychic experience. The moral of that story is that I Yelped a psychic.

Murray was set up in a curtained alcove at the back of a New Age bookstore. We sat on opposite sides of a small table on which was stacked a well-used deck of Tarot cards. I briefly wondered if you had to break those things in, like sticking a new baseball glove under your mattress. He introduced himself, asked me if I was looking for anything in particular from my reading, and when I answered in the negative, he explained how his readings work.

"It's not the cards that do the work," he said, shuffling them in his hands. "They're pieces of paper. It's the spirits working through them. I won't tell you your life history. That's for gypsies at the county fair." That must be where the turbaned women were. "I want to talk about your life now and in the near future. I often don't know what I'm talking about, and that's okay. I'm just a messenger, I don't have to understand the messages."

He had me shuffle the deck, which he then spread face-down in front of me in a line while I picked out a certain number of cards. He flipped those cards over in a pattern on the table.

From that point on, it was mostly an exercise in vagueness. General questions about job and relationships and life, accompanied by vague suggestions. My favorite part was when he told me the spirits thought it a good time for me to do some contracting work on my house. That's when I learned what he used to do for a living. But I do dig the idea of practical spirits. One thing he nailed was that I had taken a major southwest trip, although he seemed perturbed that I had taken it eight months ago instead of more recently.

Eventually, our fifteen minutes was up, and I parted the curtain and left. It was to be my first of many Salem readings. After all, this is how Witches connect with muggles (or fleece them, according to one insistent bullhorn I heard on Essex Street) instead of evangelizing or proselytizing. But I wasn't participating in them to play the part of debunker, nor was I trying to learn anything about my life. I was just trying to learn about Witchcraft. And, as a fan of outré experiences, I wanted a variety of them.

It turns out, though, that the city of Salem is papered with Tarot cards. In most cases, I had to specifically ask for other forms of divination, a question that was often met with blank stares and appeals to other staff members. That's how I found myself in Artemisia Botanicals. The shop was one of the few, if not the only, place in town that I found actively advertising tasseography—tea leaf readings.

Artemisia Botanicals is on Hawthorne Boulevard, a few doors down from the Hawthorne Hotel. It's a cheery two-story yellow building. Inside, it looked nothing like any of the Witch shops I had seen so far. It was bright and open. No incense smell weighted the air, no skulls or strange statues eyed my entrance. It had some magical items, but they weren't the focus of the store. That's because Artemisia Botanicals isn't technically a Witch shop. It's a herb retailer . . . run by a Witch.

Along three walls ran shelves that nearly stretched to the ceiling filled with hundreds of large, glass jars full of flakes and powders. The contents were all labeled with both a common name and a scientific name and arranged in alphabetical order. Some were basically cooking ingredients, chili powder and cornstarch, vindaloo. You could find many of them on spice racks in any kitchen. Some were recognizable but of obscure purpose, like dandelion root and elderflower. Others sounded more exotic and completely incomprehensible to me without a search engine—lungwort, benzoin, grindelia. There was also a range of teas. The one that caught my eye right away because of the pair of full, bright red lips on the label was Rocky Horror Spice. It had bits of candy in it. A Halloween tea.

The reader took me to a small, closet-like area and pulled down a hinged plank between us for a table. She had me choose a tea and scooped an ample portion of loose grounds into a delicate cup. She poured a trickle of hot water over them, making more of sludgy soup than a tea. Since I only wanted a fifteen-minute reading, she explained to me, she wouldn't be brewing a full cup and having me take my time with it. Instead, she had me drink a few spoonfuls and then swish the cup around. She flipped the cup over, letting the tea soak into a paper towel and the excess grounds drop, and then righted the cup. She peered inside at what was still clinging to the interior surface.

The reading followed a similar template as Murray's. Questions and answers, vague suggestions about family and travel and work. She asked me if there was anything I was looking for in particular. There wasn't. She showed me the shapes she was focusing on, a snaking tendril of damp grounds that extended to the rim, a bulbous bit at on the bottom, individual specks on the side of the cup. It all felt . . . civilized. Not at all dangerous. Not like I was messing with Forces That Should Not Be Poked. But tea will do that. Tea can make a political rally seem like a librarian conference and a prison riot a chess tournament. Tea's like magic, man. I felt like I could slip a tea reading into a church potluck and everyone would be amused, as opposed to the horrified reaction I'd get slamming a deck of Tarot cards beside the green bean casserole.

I ended up talking to the owner of Artemisia Botanicals. Her name was Teri Kalgren, and she'd been running the store for almost two decades. Kalgren was born in the Bronx and spent a good portion of her life isolated out on Long Island with her three daughters. She had been a Witch for a long while at that point, but one of the solitary kind that I would hear about from other Witches. Sometimes those Witches stay private practitioners because that's the way they like it. Other times, when there is no Witch community near them to connect with, they're forced to. The latter was Kalgren's situation on Long Island. "I would wear my pentacle so people would see, but I never met any other Witches. The only people that noticed were the cops. 'You know what that means?' they'd ask me. I told them, 'It's a star. It means I've been a very good girl.'"

Kalgren had a cousin who lived in Salem, and somewhere in the late 1980s she moved here herself. She opened the business seven years later.

"I noticed that all the herbs in the Witch businesses were meant for spells, and that's fine. We use ours for spells, too, but the herbs they were selling were in plastic tins and couldn't be used for very much else. We needed more organic herbs, more fresh." Today the store stocks over four hundred herbs, one hundred teas, and seventy-five essential oils.

"So how did you fit in here in Salem? It must have been a real change for you from a Witchless Long Island."

"I took some classes when I got here and got along pretty well. I'm not the 'knock this pentacle off my shoulder'–type of person. But I also volunteered with the chamber of commerce, so I wasn't just in the pagan community. I had three children whom I wanted to fit in with their classmates. You can't be flying around on a broom if you want your children assimilated into a community. I wanted them to be who they are, but also have the freedom to have a life."

Today, her youngest daughter works in the shop with her. "She's part of a north pagan tradition through her father's side, which is Swedish and Danish. I'm more Celtic myself. But she's comfortable, and that's what I want. Witches don't raise children to become what we are. It's more about leaving them to be what is right and perfect for them."

Her oldest daughter was a First Degree Witch, but she let her Witchhood lapse. Her middle daughter is more hands-off when it comes to Witchcraft. "When she wants a spell, she calls me to do it."

"How has the Witch community changed in your time?"

"It's always been a varied group. It used to be more of a hub than it is now since you can find communities in every state. What usually changes is thc type of Witch. Back in the '60s, it was a lot more about the goddess and feminism. In past decades we'd have what I called Megadeth witches—goths playing at Witchcraft. We've also had ren faire witches." I imagined people in bodices and tights using turkey legs for wands and putting st's and th's on the end of the verbs of their spells. "But whoever it is, they either change into being a real Witch or drop Witchcraft entirely. It's like that with a lot of religions. We create god in our likeness, not the other way around."

"How about the city of Salem? What are the changes there?"

"Salem's economy has changed dramatically. October isn't what it used to be. We used to do a feast of Samhain for twenty years as a charity event, and we stopped that last year. We used to see people fly into town just because they wanted to be here on Halloween. Twenty years ago, the costumes that people wore here were amazing. It was fabulous. Now every town has a haunted hayride. The only people that stay here for a full week are Witches." She told me that sometimes tourists will come and ask to see a ritual. "But it's a like on a random Tuesday. There's no reason to have a ritual. We might meditate or pray, but we only have eight sabbats and the new and full moon."

"Do you still like it here?"

"Yes. I love the fact that if I have a beef, I can walk right over to town hall and talk to somebody. That there's history everywhere I look. On Long Island we were homogenized, all the same. And anything interesting was down the road in the city. But there's a real pride of place here."

"Who exactly is your clientele for Artemisia?"

"Health-conscious people, vegetarians. If you're buying a free-range chicken and then putting store-bought chicken rub on it, that doesn't make sense. Pagans, of course. Spells are also better with fresher, better produced ingredients."

"I came into your store because you were offering tea leaf readings, and I've been looking for readings outside of Tarot. I've found some variety, but the one thing I can't seem to find is a crystal ball reading. I see the crystal balls themselves for sale at the shops, but nobody seems to using them for readings, or at least not advertising it. Are crystal ball readings a myth?"

"No, they're real. Crystal balls are just boring. If I take out this ball that's clear crystal and we're spending 15 minutes looking into it, it's not exciting for you, and you start wondering if I'm actually seeing anything. People want drama with their reading. Tarot cards have it, and you can explain the symbology and how the cards work together. And you're involved by cutting and choosing the cards."

"What's your method of choice?"

"I'm not a reader. I believe everybody has the gift, but depending on how you embrace it or are afraid of it, it will manifest itself or not. When I was a kid, I used to know when people would die, and I didn't like that, so I squashed it and did probably too good of a job. I have it sometimes, but not enough to make a living off it."

"The big criticism I've heard of the Witch culture in Salem is that some Witches seem to appropriate the victims of 1692 as martyrs in their own cause of religious acceptance. Is that true?"

"No, they didn't die for Witchcraft. They died for being good Christians. But the thing is, those Christians were part of a religion that told them that there was nothing worse than being a witch, that witches by definition hang out with the Devil. That's sad to us. And religious people still feel that way today. You'll see them on Halloween."

The first night tour I took in Salem was a Witch walk. Our guide was a young redheaded woman who spoke with a practiced but seemingly sincere enthusiasm that reminded me of an elementary school teacher. Lindsey and I were part of a group of about a dozen, and she led us through a gate and into the alley beside Crow Haven Corner. It had mural of dragons on one wall, and the guide called it the "magic alley." She asked us to be mindful of the fact that it was a sacred space.

At the end of the alley was a round black table with a yellow pentacle painted on it. Atop the table was a pile of candles and gourds and goblets and statuary that included a black bird and an Egyptian deity. There was a bowl of polished white stones, and a tiny black cauldron sat in the middle near a crystal ball and a fake skull. A ring of sistra—musical instruments that look like small tennis rackets strung with metal discs that rattle against each other when they're shaken—lined the edge of the table. A stereo somewhere played music heavy with drums.

The group gathered around the table while the Witch introduced herself. Her name was Sammy, and she had been a practicing Witch her whole life. She explained that we were about to do a "non-denominational ritual" to raise the energy that we needed in our lives. And then she asked if anybody had ever been involved in a pagan ritual.

"One time when I was drunk in college, I think," said a middle-aged woman in the circle.

"Best answer ever," said Sammy, and then she explained that she was about to cast a circle, using the 1996 Paulie Shore movie *Bio-Dome* as a metaphor for it. "Too bad people don't know *Bio-Dome* anymore," she said.

I did, and I still love the *Safety Dance* montage. Basically, the circle she, or I guess we, were about to cast was meant to keep out negative energy. Besides *Bio-Dome*, she also likened it to a force field around a spaceship and Glenda the Good Witch's bubble.

To cast the circle, she lit the candles on the table and whipped out a small dagger called an athame before calling on both the male and female gods of Witchcraft, as well as any deities any of us worshipped. It was an EOE circle, and I imagined the gods sitting awkwardly next to each other to watch their respective acolytes like parents at a play date. Sammy then "called the quarters" and had the group face all four cardinal points with our non-dominant hands (because that, she said, is the side of the body that draws energy in) to invite their elemental properties of fire, water, air, and earth. She said that at the end of the rite the bowl of white stones on the table would be charged with positive energy.

She then had us practice the phrase, "So mote it be," which she explained was just like saying amen at church.

Once the circle was cast she handed out the sistra and told us to chant and clap and stomp and repeat the phrase, "Earth, air, water, fire, bring to us our desire." We were to visualize what we wanted, "Like when you blow out the candles on a birthday cake."

At the end, she threw a powder into the cauldron, which flashed dramatically. From there, she opened the circle, which was the same routine, but in reverse. We each grabbed a positively charged stone, which she instructed us to keep on the dominant side of our bodies or rooms to draw good energy.

When it was over, she gave us the moral of the exercise: "Did you like the part where the alleyway fogged up, clouds of bats flew through, and a giant demon appeared to try to get you to join us?"

And then we started walkin' out of the alley like Christopher.

The rest of the tour was similarly designed to explain the tenants of Witchcraft using sites around Salem and to show us that the religion wasn't scary or macabre and had nothing to do with the Devil. It was also a less-than-subtle commercial for three of the Witch shops in town. "That sticker you got for the tour also gets you 20 percent off at Crow Haven Corner, Hex, and Omen."

At the Roger Conant statue, she explained that Witches dressed the way they did for a lot of the same reasons Conant was dressed the way he was. In addition to their aesthetic benefits, cloaks kept them warm during outdoor ceremonies. "They're like wearable blankets and look cooler than parkas." The tall hat was a status symbol, just like like the pope's, and the staff was for balance, although in the case of Witches it's to balance energy. They wore black, she said, because it absorbed energy, just like the color absorbs light.

At the park by the visitor's center, she explained about the Wiccan Rede, "Do what thou wilt, harm none" and the Law of Three, according to which whatever one puts out into the universe in thought or word or deed is returned 27 times (3 x 3 x 3). She used *My Name is Earl* to illustrate her point. "Basically, we're a bunch of tree-hugging hippies."

At the *Bewitched* statue, she explained how annoying it was to be a Witch named Samantha, because of the constant stream of jokes, which I guess is why she went by Sammy. She took us to the storefronts of Omen and Hex, two of the Witch shops owned by her bosses, and used them to explain the difference between dark and light magic. Omen catered to light magic, and was bright and yellow inside. Hex—the shop's sign provided the subtitle "Old World Witchery"—catered to dark magic, and its decor used a lot more reds and blacks. She said that light and dark don't equate to good and evil. They are just different, "the way nature is both dark and light."

Later, I would return to Crow Haven Corner for what was possibly my most interesting reading. It was another Tarot reading, but my interest had to do with getting it done in one of the oldest continually operating Witch shops in the country. I went in, paid for it, and was directed to the back of the store to one of about ten mediums sitting almost shoulder-to-shoulder at their tiny tables.

The woman did the usual Tarot thing, having me pick my cards, any cards, but kept coming up with the idea that I'd just been through something extremely heavy with my family. I hadn't, so I asked her if it was a possible future event. She insisted it was in the near-past or present. She

Crow Haven Corner

realized soon that the reading wasn't working, so she said, visibly frustrated, "I probably need to hand you off to another medium, but let me keep trying." After the cards came up wrong again, she handed me off to a second medium.

The new medium asked more questions and played off more of my answers, and it turned into one of the typical readings I'd been having—positive, vague, generally applicable advice. Later, I would get to ask the owner of Crow Haven Corner herself about the whole experience.

Lorelei Stathopoulos is a third-generation witch from Revere, Massachusetts, and has the accent to prove it. "As a little girl, my mother would teach me clairvoyance, Tarot cards, automatic writing, and other magical techniques." When Stathopoulos was a teenager in the late 1970s, she would hang out with the daughters of Laurie Cabot, Salem's original Witch. As was my habit, I started the conversation by explaining the book project to her.

"Oh, great. It's good for people to know that Salem is still Witch City," was her response. "It has so much to offer, and I love cross-promotion. However, there's a stigma within Salem about it being Witch City. And we want to make sure that we never lose the magic of this city."

When Stathopoulos moved to Witch City, she eventually took over one of the shops that Cabot started. And by "one of the shops," I mean the most conspicuous example of the species in all of Salem. Three stories tall, cauldron-black, and in a prime location across from the Hawthorne Hotel, Crow Haven Corner is often the place tourists get their first experience with Witchery.

"If we expect to turn tourists into clients, we need to let them have a little fun with us. When somebody from Kentucky asks, 'Are you going to fly on your broom?' they might get thrown out of another shop, but we joke with them. How else can we connect with them to educate them?"

And Stathopoulos has seen her share of tourists. She's been operating Crow Haven Corner for almost 20 years. "What's it like running the most famous Witch shop in a city famous for them?"

"This house is full of spirits, and I have been blessed by them with wonderful clients. I take a lot of pride in this building. If you come into my store, you come into my home." She meant that literally. She lives in the top two floors of the shop. "The man who owned the building before me wasn't planning on giving it up as he owned a lot of property in Salem, but I told him for ten years that someday I would own it." Eventually the property owners decided to sell it, so Stathopoulos "did a spell" on her home to make it sell fast. It went within a month. Getting a commercial loan was much more difficult, so, again, she turned to magic. "On the new moon, my fellow Witch and friend Christy Faris and I snuck upstairs and magically claimed it. We did a full magical circle and used sage to neutralize the incorrect energies that were holding us back from buying the place, and promised the spirits of the home that we would take care of it forever." She eventually got the loan.

One of Stathopoulos's passions is animals. The topic came up sixty seconds into the conversation. Stathopoulos co-founded Salem Saves Animals with fellow Witch Leanne Marrama. The organization helps animals in need, educates people about animal neglect, and pushes for tougher laws against animal abusers. "I want Salem to be Animal City, too. When the victims of 1692 were persecuted, so were the animals." The records show at least two dogs were shot on account of the hysteria, and villagers were certainly wary of animals during the trials. Witches were supposed to have familiars and be able to turn themselves into animals. "As a Witch who believes in reincarnation, these animals need to be honored in Salem as well."

Inside Crow Haven Corner, you might run into one of her Chihuahuas, Chico and Dolly, and she keeps a trio of cats upstairs. She also allows her employees to bring pets to work. "They're all my familiars, the cats and the dogs. All pets are familiars, actually. They're sent to us from above to protect us, but owners don't always know it." She then told me that Laurie Cabot adopted Chico into the Cabot tradition and gave him third degree paperwork as a high priest.

I explained to her what happened to me in her shop. "Is that normal?" I know, I realize I was asking if it was normal that a stranger couldn't tell me intimate details about my life with a stack of laminated paper.

"Somebody who's been reading for thirty years would never hand anybody off like that. But you were at our psychic fair, so it was a little different." She then explained that they bring in extra readers for the busy October season and sometimes it takes time for new readers to get used to working with the full-timers in such a small space that is "full of energy" while a line of people wraps around the building. “Most of the time, our readers are experienced enough that it’s not an issue, but if a reader is tired or not connecting, we always want the client to leave satisfied with their reading experience, so we move them to someone who is fresher.”

Speaking of psychic fairs, my first was inside the Museum Place Mall at the Annual Festival of the Dead Psychic Fair and Witchcraft Expo. It wasn’t affiliated with Crown Haven Corner’s psychic fair. In fact, there were psychic fairs all over town. Almost every Witch shop hosted one. So I wasn’t surprised to find one in the mall. I also wasn’t surprised because I had been handed a flyer for it by the same girl probably once a day while walking the Essex Street Pedestrian Mall.

It was time for me to go to it.

The fair and expo took up a single room in the mall. Rows of chairs and tables were set up in the middle, each station numbered, and around the edge of the room were vendor tables selling magical items. I paid for a reading and was directed to a table. It was a weekday night, so the attendance was sparse. The young psychic to whom I was assigned may have been legally blind, judging from the way she held the Tarot cards millimeters from her face. Her reading involved a combination of Tarot and rune stones, rocks with symbols carved into them that she spilled from a bag to read how they fell.

I grabbed one of her business cards as I sat down and noted she was from Ohio. A lot of psychics and mediums are imported from out-of-town during October. High demand and all that. The reading itself was of the usual sort, but by this point in my reading experiences, I found myself really rooting for the psychics and feeling bad when they stumbled into a dead end or tried an interpretation that didn’t resonate. Happy with a clean bill of psychic health and finally checking rune stones off of my list, I got up and started perusing the merchandise tables.

Eventually, I made it to a back corner where a strange-looking camera was set up on a tripod pointing at a black backdrop. A barefoot girl walked up to me and asked, “Do you want your aura photographed?”

I did in fact suddenly want that.

According to Witchipedia, an aura is a “subtle luminescence that surrounds all objects, hinting at the energy contained within.” So it’s like what happens to Bruce Leroy and Sho’Nuff when they fight at the end of *The Last Dragon,* or anytime Olivia-Newton John gets to dancing in *Xanadu.* Many Witches and spiritualists believe that auras can be read like palm lines and head bumps, but since the energy leak is invisible to most of us, it takes special devices to reveal it. Like a camera.

The girl sat me down, wrapped a black cloth around my neck, and walked over to the camera. I didn't recognize the make or model, and unfortunately Lindsey—who is a photographer—wasn't there to help me. After a few seconds of adjusting the camera the girl hit a button. Nothing happened.

"Did that flash?" she asked.

"No."

She tried again. Nothing. Finally, she got the flash to work. The Polaroid came out almost immediately and, after flapping it around a bit, she showed it to me. My head looked disembodied, thanks to the black background and black neck-wrap. It was also completely enveloped in a cloud of yellow tinged with red. I was apparently not very energy-efficient. The splotch of glowing color looked like an overexposure or a special effect from the original *Star Trek* series.

"What does it mean?" I asked her.

"Hm. I'm . . . not . . . sure."

That was worrisome.

Fortunately, a gentleman from a nearby vendor table saw her struggling with the interpretation and came over and looked at. "Oh man, you're way into sex," he told me.

"That's cool, right?" the girl asked me.

The man then handed me a little pamphlet about aura interpretation called *What Colors Mean* that had been printed in Indiana. Yellow, apparently a creative color, was described with a word cloud of about twenty words that ranged from joy and imagination and hope to dishonesty, cowardice, and jealousy. Red had a much longer description, but it seemed in general to be characterized as an aggressive and self-centered but also tender and warm color. "Vitality, nervousness, and glandular activity" was the phrase that stuck out to me.

It was probably my least interesting experience of all the psychic readings, but I did get a souvenir out of it.

The Festival of the Dead referenced in the name of the psychic fair is almost a mini–Haunted Happenings within Haunted Happenings. This slate of rituals and Witchcraft events is open to the public and runs throughout October. It was created by a self-described "power couple" of Witchdom, Christian Day and his husband, Brian Cain.

Day is from Beverly, while Cain is from Spokane, Washington—almost as close and as far as you can get from Salem on the continental United States. Day is the more talkative of the two, although Cain isn't at all demure. It's just hard to compete in a conversation with a man who can converse almost completely in taglines. Day is also quick with the metaphor and has a lot to say about the craft, as if he has had to defend it in general, and his own style of it in particular, for a long time.

As to how he styles himself, Day told me, "I'm more of a cauldron-stirring, hocus pocus Witch. I deal with it mostly as magic with a side of religion."

Meanwhile, Cain takes a different tack: "I'm an initiate of Alexandrian Witchcraft. I belong to a priesthood that is a fertility cult. Christian and I work together, but I approach it more as a religion than he does."

"Witchcraft is a nascent religion in a modern world," Day explained. "It's reconstructive—I don't think there's an unbroken line of practice—but I think we are a collection of ideas and rituals that are ancient. We haven't hashed out our definitions yet. It's all branding and identity, at the end of the day."

Day knows a little bit about branding. He has a past in agency work in Boston. Cain's career history is in retail management. These days, the two channel those skill sets into making their money solely from their craft. And they do pretty well. "We have oodles of money," said Day, providing me that rare opportunity to type "oodles" in a book. "Less than ten Witches in the world make what we make on Witchcraft, but," he made sure to add, "This was my faith for seventeen years before it was my career, and it was Brian's faith for twenty-five years before it was his career. We're Witches and we want to be Witches all the time, and this is the way we can do that."

They make that money through their two stores in Salem, Hex and Omen, as well as through a tour company, a psychic hotline, and the Festival of the Dead events. They've also opened a store in New Orleans—that one's called Hex, as well—and a sister festival to the one in Salem, called HexFest, which takes place in the summer. The pair have probably the closest thing to a commercial Witch empire on the planet. When the two met, Day had already been working for years on building it. "But when Brian came in, he tripled profit in three years," Day said.

That success probably sets them apart from most of the Witches on the Salem scene. However, the bigger thing that does so is . . . Day isn't a Salem Witch anymore, and Cain never was.

The husbands live in New Orleans where they both met and where Cain had been living. After getting married in 2014, the two decided to settle in the Big Easy. At one point, Day was splitting time between the two cities, but now that they've officially started a life together, the pair only make it to Salem for the last two weeks of October, plus a visit here or there throughout the year.

"I hate the weather, the cold," Cain explained.

"I like the weather, but I hate the drama," said Day. And drama seems to follow these two around, mostly, again, because of the pagan Christian ("I don't consider myself a pagan," Day explained to me. "I can't resist wordplay," I'm going to have to explain to him after he reads this). It's hard to research Day, not because he's a man of mystery, but because there is a ton on him out there, and it's full of feuds and stunts

Witch Altar at Hex

and opinions and issues, all of which seem to be welcomed by him in an almost Aleister Crowley kind of way. It doesn't take too long searching his name to see some Witch or other describing him as a media-monger or a poor public face for the craft. "I have been called terrible things in the pagan court of opinion. None of it is true. But at least they're talking about us."

During my stay in October, Day was making headlines before he even arrived because of a lawsuit brought against him by a former business associate, who claimed Day was harassing her. The court hearing received lots of press. After all, what headline writer is going to resist, "Witch Sues Warlock."

But neither he nor Cain shy away from the controversy. Without my even asking about it, Day brought it up. "She got a restraining order based solely on her testimony. It was 1692 all over again."

"Witches are still convicted on spectral evidence," said Cain.

"New Orleans is like being on a remote island," said Day. "We don't get the publicity here because people don't care. Brad Pitt could come down and the locals wouldn't care."

"It's too hot and everyone's drunk," agreed Cain.

"It's one of the reasons we moved to this city," said Day. "And I don't need to be in Salem because we are in Salem. You can't go around that city without feeling our presence, negatively or positively. Some hate us, some love us."

Then Day brought up Salem's "Psychic Wars" from about a decade ago, when the city found itself with an overwhelming number of psychics within its borders and a feud between those who practiced year-round and those who carpetbagged in October. The city had to get involved to figure out a licensing compromise. Things got really weird when one of the practitioners left mutilated raccoon corpses on the stoops of two of Salem's Witch shops as either a form of intimidation or as part of some bad magic.

Day and Cain might not like the drama (or at least profess not to), but they do love the dramatic. In late October, you won't catch them without their billowy capes and tall pointed hats on. Day has even been known to jump on a Segway in full regalia and float around Salem like he's reinvented the broom.

At some point in his life, Day started calling himself a Warlock, a controversial term in Witchdom. In popular culture, the word means a male witch (although within the religion, the word *witch* isn't a gendered word). However, some in the Witch community believe it to mean *traitor*. Day vociferously maintains that the popular culture definition is closer to the actual origin of the word, and that any etymology around the other definition is just Christian (as in the religion) baggage. Still, Day embracing the term tells you pretty much everything you need to know about his skills at marketing and ability at creating a sensation. But that put Cain in an awkward position.

"I never called myself a Warlock, and I don't do it usually today, but I've come to adopt it somewhat. I mean, if I'm a Witch and my husband is a Warlock, that kind of insinuates that I'm the bitch, doesn't it?"

"All right, so all this behind-the-beaded-curtain stuff aside, tell me what you think about the city of Salem in general," I said.

"I think of Salem as a tapestry," said Day. "And for years all its threads—1692, haunted attractions, maritime, architecture, literature, chop suey sandwiches at Salem Lowe, the donuts at Ziggy's—have been very focused on themselves and on promoting the city in each one's image and missing out on a bigger opportunity. Over the past ten years, there's been a melding of all of those things in Salem, and its true uniqueness is getting out there now."

But Day, of course, couldn't leave it at a nice, inoffensive quote. "In 2003, I tried to join the board of Destination Salem, but my business partner at the time and I were rejected and told that we did not fit the model of Salem's art and culture direction. So I thought, if they don't like Witches, we'll give them something worse." Day said they scoured the area looking for a "trashy vampire model" to use on their advertisements for the Vampire Ball, one of their past Festival of the Dead events. They found what they were looking for and created posters of her, bloody and in a bikini. "We put the posters up everywhere and then took an Acela train to New York for an alibi. We used shock tactics quite a bit back then." He explained that the purpose of the tactics was to help them get a foot in the door of Salem's commercial scene, in addition to just being ornery because the city didn't like Witches. "We don't do that anymore, though. Now, the city is very accepting of Witches."

"What about you?" I asked Cain. "You came to Salem with a fresher perspective than Christian."

"My experience with Salem has always been in October, and it's like stepping onto the red carpet. When I'm there, I have to put on the full persona of who I am in the Witch world. The first year I went there, I had people coming up who knew me, but whom I didn't know. It's not an experience I've had before. It was like instantly being a celebrity, without any experience at being a celebrity."

Day chimed in: "The number one question the media asks me is, 'Why are you in Salem when 1692 wasn't really about Witches?' There is an implied tone under it that we don't have a right to be there or that we're capitalizing on it." He went on to say that he didn't believe that there were Witches in the full sense of the term in Salem in 1692, but that there were probably people practicing folk magic. He's right about that. Mary Sibley's witch cake is a good example. She got the idea for that from somewhere, although oddly enough she was only accused of bad judgement for that, and not for being a witch.

"The relevant thing about 1692 for modern Witches is that the word *witch* has been polluted," he continued. "The idea of witches as bad in the community has percolated through millennia, thanks to Christianity. Besides, I don't recall anywhere reading that Muhammad made a pilgrimage to the McDonald's in Dearborn, Michigan. Jesus didn't roll his stone at the Cracker Barrel in Virginia Beach. There's no Wailing Wall in Brooklyn." That quote sounded too practiced, so I Googled it later and found it was a go-to comparison for him. "So to say why are we in Salem is bigoted and prejudiced and hateful. But people tell us that all the time. 'Why do you have to be there?' We don't need a reason."

But he did have one, just in case.

"The city of Salem is more associated with the word *witch* than anywhere else in the world. If it is branded with that word, albeit a false definition, then doesn't that make it the most powerful place for Witches to be to educate people about the truth of modern Witches? We could decide tomorrow that we want to set up shop in Las Vegas. But the reason for us to be in Salem is to fight the false definition of *witch*."

I asked them where they thought the major driver of their success lay, especially in a town with a Witch shop on every corner.

Day said, “The reason why Witchcraft shops fail every time is that they don’t understand their market segments. Of the three segments, the smallest one is the practitioner, the second largest one is the souvenir seeker, and the number one market segment, the one that’s like 89 percent of Salem visitors and the one that is ignored by most shops in Salem, is muggles seeking magic.” That word again. Day was referring to those people who aren’t Witches and don’t want to be Witches, but still have hope that maybe magic works in some way. Day used the example of someone who takes a charm to Foxwood Casinos in Connecticut hoping for good luck, or to a trial in hopes of receiving justice.

The way to reach muggles seeking magic, Day explained, was to make the shop and the items in the shop extremely accessible to them. That meant good customer service and simple educational elements like clear labels for what things are and what they do. “Visitors shouldn’t be scared to enter a Witch shop.”

“One phrase I’ve heard describing Salem’s October 31 celebration is that it’s a Halloween Mardi Gras. You two seem like the most perfect people on the planet to address that comparison.”

“Yeah, that’s not an accurate statement,” said Cain.

“I used to say that until I actually saw Mardi Gras,” said Day. “If I won the Powerball, I would fly the whole Krewe du Vieux parade to Salem. If people in Salem saw what went on during Mardi Gras, they would all have heart attacks. Salem’s much more conservative than they realize.” I looked up images from the Krewe du Vieux parade later. Let’s just say it’s not safe for this work.

Before his and Cain’s “blessed be”-s, Day had one more thing to say. “Listen, that ‘who Salem is’ thing, even though it’s gotten much better, is still going on today. And that same crisis is inside the Witch community as well. In fact, the identity of the Witch might be in an even bigger identity crisis than Salem’s is.”

I visited both Hex and Omen while I was living in Salem. Even got a reading at Omen. I walked into that shop devoted to light magic and asked for anything except a Tarot reading. The staff froze for a few moments, looking at each other. “Are you looking for something in particular?” one of them finally asked me.

“I don’t know. You got any palm readers?”

He plucked what looked like a baseball card from a pile. It had the photo of a Witch on the front, and their gifts on the back. "Oh," he said, "Audrey does it. She's here tonight." Like Murray, that's not her real name.

In Omen and Hex, you get your readings done in the shop window. It's a great idea and illustrates the marketing savvy of Day and Cain. You become both a paying customer and a free advertisement at the same time.

The first thing Audrey did was to leave the window alcove, which was separated from the interior of the shop by a curtain. She returned a few seconds later with a bottle of hand sanitizer. "It's the law," she explained apologetically. After we were both de-germed, she took my hands in hers and scrutinized them wrist to fingertip, back to palm. She had silver rings on every finger, black and red fingernails. I don't remember what her face looked like. The reading was vague and general like every other reading, but here the vagueness and generalness were at least connected to the marks and contours of my own body parts instead of pieces of paper and bits of stone or herb. At one point, I thought I heard thunder and got excited that I was getting my palm read in a thunderstorm, like the crystal ball scene in *Pee-wee's Big Adventure*. "It's the haunted house next door," Audrey explained. I ended up giving her a nice tip, even if she did say I had short fingers and shallow lines.

I had one more reading in my future. I really wanted to do a crystal ball, despite Teri Kalgren's warning. I went into another Witch shop on Essex Street and asked for it. The young girl behind the counter looked at me strangely and then brought over an older colleague and passed on the question to him. "Yes, we have somebody that does crystal readings, but he's not here until tomorrow."

"I'll come back."

The next day I came back, and it was pouring rain. This time, I thought, I'd get my *Pee-wee's Big Adventure* scene. I asked again. It was the same girl and the same guy, but they didn't seem to recognize me. The crystal reader was in. "Is he prepared to do a crystal reading?" the girl asked her colleague. The guy went back to check. When he returned, he said, "He is, but he's starting with somebody else right now and it'll be a while before he's free. If you want, I can call our sister shop. I know the medium on duty there only does crystal readings."

A phone call later, and I was making my way through Salem in the pouring rain without an umbrella and really sad that my bicycle had been stolen. I was headed to Pickering Wharf, to a Witch shop called Enchanted, not too far away from Gypsy Ravish's Nu Aeon.

I apologized to the man behind the counter for getting the floor all wet and told him my name and business. "Okay," he replied. "You know that she doesn't use a crystal ball, right? She throws crystals." He shook his right hand like it had dice in it.

I pretended that I knew exactly what the medium did and that it was exactly what I was looking for. It was mostly my own fault. I had, in fact asked for a "crystal" reading instead of a "crystal ball" reading. I guess I felt silly saying the full phrase, somehow. Inside I was a little crestfallen, but I took consolation that it was a style of reading I hadn't yet experienced. He directed me around the end of the counter to a small alcove behind it.

The medium explained why she used crystals. "I grew up in Hawaii—so, on a rock—and that's why I throw rocks." She laughed. Also unique in my experience, she pointed at a tiny pad and pencil on the small table, "That's for you. I encourage you to take notes."

She then tossed the crystals. I can't remember if she threw them from her hand or from a bag, but either way, she spilled tiny stones all over the table. They were of all different shapes and sizes, textures and colors, some faceted and some rough. She pointed out the names of a bunch of them, but I only remember pyrite.

But this medium, alone of all the mediums, nailed right away that I was a writer. This reading was also unique for me in that it turned into a medical reading. That's because I mentioned that I once had cancer years ago. I thought the confession would take the reading in a fun, new direction. She held her hand with her palm toward me and moved it up and down, while asking me to keep saying my name. By the end of it she was giving me prescriptions for various crystals and herbs, pointing me to some Indian rhythmic breathing exercise, and offering the web address of a homeopath in Marblehead.

I didn't know it at the time, but Enchanted would be the site of the interview that I was the most looking forward to/trepidatious of in this entire book.

When I visited that second time, the guy behind the counter directed me to the same area I had been directed to before. Except this time, the area had been transformed by a makeshift hallway made of floor-to-ceiling black sheets.

I entered the hallway, and there she was at the end of it, sitting at a small table with a lit candle atop it. She didn't rise, just sat in a high-backed chair waiting for me to approach. She wore billowy black robes, had long, two-toned hair—white in the front and black in the back—a pair of thick-framed black glasses with large lenses, and a faded spiral tattoo on her left check. This felt the most like being with a Witch of all the Witches I had approached.

I mean, of course, it was. The woman sitting in front of me was Laurie Cabot, the most important Witch in the history of modern Salem.

Cabot started publicly practicing Witchcraft in Salem back in the early 1970s and, perhaps, was a catalyst for its national uptake. She opened the first Witch shop in Salem. She started groups and events and businesses that carry on to this day, albeit under different management. She was everywhere on TV during her prime. Looking around online, I saw mentions of appearances on Oprah Winfrey and Phil Donahue and Johnny Carson. In 1977, state governor Michael Dukakis somehow awarded her the title "Official Witch of Massachusetts." I'd even heard her called the "Elvis Presley of Modern Witchcraft."

She's in her eighties these days and has pulled back from the spotlight, as well as from her earlier business endeavors. She ran multiple shops at one point but closed the last one in 2012, although she does have a few lines of her own products that are carried by some of the Witch shops in town. She still does readings, too, on a limited basis. I was told by Day during our conversation, "People have been writing her epitaph, speaking her eulogy, writing her off for twenty-seven years. But she's still going."

I had no idea what to expect of Laurie Cabot. She could have been anything from unapproachable to arrogant to guarded to, well, plain weird beyond any attempt at conversation.

But then we started talking, and I immediately found her both gentle and sweet. She talked to me almost as if I were doing her a favor instead of the other way around.

"Are you an already published author or is this your first book?" she asked me.

I explained to her my publishing history. Cabot is an author too, with various books about her craft, and we commiserated a bit about that struggle. Her latest book had just come out, *Book of Shadows*. It was her first book in twenty years. "That's everything I've ever taught in my entire life. Our whole tradition is in those pages and there's so much stress wondering if I left something out or said something wrong in it." Surprisingly, she hasn't put out a personal memoir yet, although, she told me, she's working on it.

"So why did you pick Salem four and a half decades ago?"

"I didn't pick Salem. I didn't want to come here because of the Witch Trials." Cabot had become a Witch on the younger side of her teenage years. She picked up the craft, she told me, from a British Witch. Cabot was born in Oklahoma, spent her formative years in California, and came to Massachusetts as a teenager. Her mother wasn't a Witch, but she was open to her daughter pursuing whatever caught her fancy. Once Cabot hit the later teenage years, she sloughed Witchcraft for later-teenage-years interests. Fast-forward a few decades through two divorces and two children, and Cabot found herself in the midst of some good old-fashioned soul-searching.

"I said to myself, 'Who am I?' 'What am I?' And the first thing that came across the screen in my mind was *Witch*. And I went, oh my god, I am a Witch, you know? And I started thinking about what it would be like if I went public with that."

While she was figuring that out, she was living in an apartment in the North End of Boston, but she wanted to move because of her two daughters, Jody and Penny. She met another woman going through a divorce who also had children. They became friends and decided to move to the suburbs together and share a place. "She knew I was a Witch because I'd already sort of started coming out, and I told her that I'd move anywhere but Salem. But then she comes in with a rolled-up newspaper with a notice on it circled. It was in Salem, on Chestnut Street. We couldn't pass it up." Turns out, that house was 18 Chestnut Street, a home Nathaniel Hawthorne himself once inhabited. So I have to run into this guy even in the Witch chapter. "We were there for a year, and I wasn't outed yet in Salem. I hadn't yet opened my Witch shop. But I had a couple of kitties."

She then told me this wild little origin story that involved one of those cats, a black one, natch, named Molly Boo. The cat climbed up the tree next to the house, about three stories up, and then couldn't come down. According to Cabot, Molly Boo was up there for three days, so she called the Salem fire department, the police department, and the animal rescue league, not because she thought she needed an army to get the cat out of the tree, but because each one turned her down in turn. One of them told her, "You'll never see a cat skeleton in a tree." She then called up the *Salem Evening News*. "I told the guy who answered the phone my story, and then I just said it. I told him I was a Witch and Molly Boo was my familiar and then before I knew it, outside was a fire engine, a police car, and the animal truck. A picture of me and Molly Boo was in the paper the next day." She told me that the photo got picked up by the Associated Press and drew a lot of attention. And it was right after that when Cabot decided to open a Witch shop.

"I didn't have any money, I just did it. I rented the place and lived upstairs. It was 100 Derby Street. Downstairs was the store. I made everything in there except for the pentacles, which I got from a local woman who made them for me. I don't know how I did it financially. What was I thinking? I had no money, a very fixed income . . . "

"And no population of practicing Witches, right, to be your clientele?"

"There were none. And not even in hiding. I'd seen Witches interviewed in California, but it wasn't really a thing out here and there were certainly no Witch shops."

"But it gradually caught on?"

"Well, at first I had zealots telling me I was going to burn in hell. I'd be walking down the street with my two little girls, and people would lean out the car and yell, 'They ought to hang you again.' I was in the supermarket around Thanksgiving once, and a man put his hands on my cart and said, 'You shouldn't be in here with these good people.'"

"Did you dress as dramatically as you do now?"

"Oh yes. That was another thing that happened when I asked myself, 'Who am I?' I made a vow to our god and goddess that I would wear the black robes of a Witch and never take them off. So I was wearing that when I came to Salem. See, I wanted to teach the craft, and I thought how are other Witches or people who want to explore the craft going to find me if I'm in sweatshirts and jeans?"

"When did you realize that it was turning into something bigger?"

"Not until it was too late. Not until all the newspapers and TV shows started calling me. I did a few shows like Oprah and Donahue, but turned down a lot. I realized I'm not an entertainer and I've got to keep my eye on what's important to me. At first I didn't know what to do about it, and then I thought it was a platform, I can explain who we are."

She got her break as a teacher when she ran into a drunken man at a club in Rhode Island. He approached her and said, "You're a Witch, aren't you?" She talked to him just enough to not be rude, and that turned out to be a good thing, because he was head of continuing education at Wellesley High School. He signed her up to teach a 10-week course on Witchcraft. "I also ended up teaching at Salem State University. The dean was going to put me in with credit on the next year, but the board of directors didn't like the publicity. I still have my library card that says 'Faculty' on it."

After that, she started teaching her own classes, which she still does to this day. "It's different today, because they attend on Skype and can come from anywhere in the world. I'm a rock star in Brazil." She laughed.

"What has changed in the Salem Witch community from when you started to now?"

"Well, it's changed a lot. There are lots of people who come here legitimately who want to learn, but there are even more wannabes. It's like politics. Everybody wants to be the grand poohbah or know more than the other one when they don't know anything about our ancestors and the history. They just see Salem, they see television, and they think it's going to rub off. They want to be famous." She didn't say it outright, but I'd heard it from other Witches and seen it myself: Lots of Witches wanted to be Laurie Cabot.

She told me that her temple was the first to be established as a federally recognized temple in Salem, although temple is a bit of a misnomer. "We don't have an actual temple. We don't have the money for it. But we meet at the Moose Lodge because it's a nice big place."

"Let me ask you this. Today Salem is in a different world in that Witchcraft is more accepted everywhere, and there are plenty of places that you can be a Witch without problem. So is Salem still a point of pilgrimage for Witches?"

"Yes, it is. I mean, Witches are everywhere, but there are still places where it's not as prominent. Witch shops don't last long in the Bible Belt."

"From what I've seen so far, the Witch journey emphasizes individual paths, is that right?" I meant it as an innocuous question, but was surprised by her answer.

"Well, it shouldn't be, but it is because few people are properly educated. They don't know Celtic mythology. They don't know that Witches are only European. The word *witch* doesn't represent magic in any other culture. They're using the word with a Christian definition. That's not who we are. Every day I feel like I hear about a new tradition. They don't know what tradition means."

She then explained that she draws her lineage from the Witches of Kent, who claimed their blades were touched by Excalibur and therefore carry the light of Excalibur from blade to blade across the centuries. "When my letter opener was touched by my teacher's blade when I was a teenager, I had the light of Excalibur, supposedly. If it's true, fine. If it isn't, fine. It's still kind of an amazing idea. So when you're initiated into this tradition, my blade that has been struck strikes yours and it carries on the light of Excalibur."

"How do you feel about Halloween? Is it just a parallel thing for you here in Salem?"

"I enjoy that people are out there being idiots and running around having fun. It's not our holiday, though. It's a Christian idea to run around as a monster with blood dripping all over you. We dress up like what we want to become, so it's not going to be that. It brings in tourism and helps people learn who we are by coming to the real Witch shops. We still observe our changing of the season, Samhain. It's a nice ritual."

"When you walk around the city and you see the caricatures of witches, the cartoon Halloween witches, are you okay with that as a draw for tourists?"

"Well, we don't allow them in our stores if they're green-faced. It's too derogatory. Devil costumes, out, that's a Christian idea. Vampires are ridiculous, but we're okay with them. We don't agree with the gore and the evil. That's not what it's about. It's about opening the veil to the other world, which is not zombies. That's just old programming from other religions."

"What do you think looking back on your work? It's been almost half a century now, so how do you see it continuing?"

She thought for a little while. "Salem is very accepting, but it still feels like we're the low group on the totem pole. And it might be us. I've never seen a religion where everybody wants to be the pope. They want to be famous because of what happened to me. I still don't know how it happened to me, but it happened, and that and $2.50 gets me a cup of coffee. That's all it did, really. Hopefully, it allowed me to educate a few people, but the ones who become a Witch for publicity and it doesn't happen, they become bitter and fight. I don't know how it's going to change."

"Even if it doesn't change, is there a strong enough core of authentic Witches to continue the Salem Witch community?"

"Yes, certainly. I do believe that."

"All the materials I've read that map out how Salem came to be what it is today include 1692 and the explosion of Halloween nationally, your own advent here, and the sitcom *Bewitched*. The Salem episodes aired right around the time you moved to Salem. Did you happen to see them before you moved here?"

"No, I'm the only one that hasn't seen those episodes, I think. I did watch the show before, though. I liked it. I thought it was cute. But I didn't watch it all the time. I found out that it brought tourists in after I came here. Some people are opposed to Samantha in the park, but I think it's fine. *Bewitched* put a positive light on magic out there in the world. I see nothing wrong with that."

I told her about the scene in the Salem episodes where Endora changes all the ugly witch signs into beautiful witch signs.

"Oh really? I've been trying to do that all my life. I used to go into card shops and if they had cards like that or those signs that hang on the wall, I'd just turn them around. I'd probably still do that if I got around."

"So what's next for you in your work?"

"I'm pretty much trying to wind it up. I'm at an age where I'm soon going into the other world. Which is fine with me. You worry about how, you don't worry about going. People from the other side say, 'There is nothing wrong over here, you guys are the ones in trouble.' So I'm just trying to leave something behind of value. Witchcraft still hasn't really made its mark yet, but the Aquarian Age is two hundred years away. If the world makes it that far, it'll be fine."

Thus ended my time among the modern-day Witches of Salem. I

don't have much by way of conclusion. But it surprised me, even though it probably shouldn't have, how parallel this strange religion is to the more conventionally accepted ones in this country. How similar are the basic practices and beliefs of the people on either side of the megaphone. Sure, the Witches' costumes are showy, but no more so than those of the Catholic priesthood. Sure, the economics of it in Salem are highly visible, what with a Witch shop on every corner and tip jars at the elbow of every psychic, but there's little real difference between that and Christian bookstores and the offering plate touching every person in the pews. And I've paid plenty of admission fees to tour historic churches in my time. Casting spells and saying a prayer are pretty much the exact same act. And fortune-telling and speaking with the dead? I haven't heard a Christian prayer that wasn't asking for supernatural guidance. And Heaven and Hell are full of the living dead.

I'm not saying that Witchcraft doesn't have its con artists, but the fact that it does probably legitimizes it as a religion more than anything else.

But forming a conclusion was never the point of my sojourn into sorcery. What I really came away with is just how important the Witches of Salem are to Witch City. They make that nickname resonate a bit more than it would by itself. They make Salem more Salem, somehow.

Also, the fact that you can go to Salem and trick-or-treat at a Witch shop? That's god- and goddess-damned perfect.

11

MORE THAN WITCHES TO FEAR IN SALEM

Zombie Walk

I was standing in line with a bunch of monsters, waiting to see more monsters, when a parade of monsters went by. Salem.

It took a good five minutes for me to realize that a horde of zombies was streaming past me on the street. Call me obtuse if you will, but at this point in my Salem October, I was used to crossing crowds of nightmares. To knowing that around any corner, something ghoulish might step out. To seeing monsters dotting the crowds like I was wearing the sunglasses from *They Live*.

I'd never witnessed a zombie walk firsthand before, and, of course, my first time happened in Salem.

I was standing in line with some friends to get into a haunted house. The establishment had its own zombie stumbling around and entertaining the line, when suddenly he got competition. Or backup. I'm not sure which. Flowing down Derby Street behind him was a dingy crew of walking corpses with gray faces and ripped clothes, spangled in red from rotting head to rotting toe.

As they shambled and jerked, they mugged at the audience. Made guttural noises at each other. Lunged at the living when they strayed too close. Every once in a while, a zombie would check its phone. There were zombie brides and zombie delivery people, Victorian zombies, zombie hunters, and even zombie kids, their strollers and onesies sprayed with blood instead of the usual pureed vegetables. Also regular-looking people, who I assume were there for either solidarity or as a food source.

So what did I learn from this plague of zombies in a city of witches? Well, first, that I want to be in a zombie walk. But really, that the best part about a zombie walk is that brief instant where you can convince your brain that the zombie apocalypse has finally happened. Here they are, coming down the street. This is it. No escape. Brad Pitt or not, the world as you know it is over. As is probably your life. Wait. Never mind. Just a zombie walk.

Also, I learned that with a zombie walk, there are no levels of good or bad costume, just levels of good or bad enthusiasm.

But this slow, shambling introduction is just to say that it makes sense that Salem would be Monster City in October. We've already talked about how the mythology that built up around the Salem Witch Trials itself was a terrifying catalog of monsters, that in addition to witches there were ghosts and demons and hairy imps and other creatures. That the Witch Trials is both human history and a genre horror story. Now that it's Halloween City, Salem's claim as a horror hub is that much more entrenched. After all, you can't have Halloween without monsters. And of course films like *Hocus Pocus* and *The Lords of Salem* and *Horror Hotel* and the dozens of horror movies that take place in Salem or a Salem-like city continue to add to its monster mystique.

So it should come as no surprise that there's a monster museum in Salem. But that monster museum itself holds a few surprises.

Count Orlok's Nightmare Gallery is on Derby Street, right across from the Haunted Neighborhood. Inside the atmospherically lit and creepy corridors of Count Orlok's are more than fifty full-size reproductions of film fiends from every decade of cinema. These reproductions are made from resin, latex, and silicone, sometimes full-body, as with the devil-like Darkness from the movie *Legend* or the Gill-man from *Creature from the Black Lagoon,* and sometimes just a face, with the rest being movie-accurate costumery.

Looming inside are monsters from the era of silent firm (including the vampire for whom the museum is named), Universal Studios monsters, Hammer horrors, '80s slashers. Vincent Price is in there a couple of times. As is Christopher Lee. Every fiend from Pennywise to Pinhead, Freddy to the Fly. There's a whole room-gone-mad full of zombies. Carrie's in there, as is Regan from *The Exorcist.* If you've never seen a horror movie, you'd still probably recognize Anthony Hopkins as Hannibal Lecter or Jack Torrance from Stanley Kubrick's *The Shining* or the mother from *Psycho,* Alfred Hitchcock himself standing dutifully by her side.

The owner of the museum is James Lurgio. I go back a ways with him, having written about his place a few times in my life. What I like the most about his museum—aside from it catering directly to one of my major interests—is that it's a private collection placed on public display. In other words, the attraction wasn't put together for the purpose of capitalizing on either Salem or Halloween. It was put together out of passion. If Lurgio had no museum, he would still have these creatures—gathered around his dining room table, I assume.

I sat down with James in the foyer of his museum to talk about his unique perspective on Salem. Behind him loomed the Tall Man from *Phantasm* and on a chair beside him was Billy the Dummy from *Dead Silence.* Over my shoulder was the Universal Studios Frankenstein monster and his bride. I could see one of my favorite pieces in his collection, Pumpkinhead, just around the way. Towering over both of us was the Phantom of the Opera at his organ. And that's what you see, give or take a monster, just by walking in to buy a ticket.

Lurgio was born in Jamestown, Rhode Island, and has lived in that state almost his entire life, a streak he broke only recently, as he and his husband had just moved to Massachusetts before the 2015 season. Previous to the move, he commuted to Salem for eight years from Cranston, Rhode Island, eighty miles one-way. "Salem has never been my city," he told me. "It's just been the place I work."

And, when that work involves the care and display of monsters, it might be one of the few places you can work full-time.

Lurgio says he teaches history—the history of monster movies. That also means that, since monsters have been such a part of Salem's history, he also inadvertently runs a Salem history museum. Elvira is in his museum because she's the Mistress of the Dark, but she was also in Salem in 1986 shooting an MTV Halloween special. Vincent Price might be in there because, well, he's Vincent Price, but Price also narrated a video tour of The House of the Seven Gables back in 1989. Bette Midler? Her Winifred Sanderson is in there. And I guarantee just about every creature in Lurgio's museum has walked the Essex Street Pedestrian Mall during one Halloween or another.

"I always liked monsters," Lurgio said. When he was 11, he was introduced to his first home haunt, an amateur haunted house created in someone's home for trick-or-treaters to go through and get a little more than just a fun-sized Milky Way. "Some home haunts can look spectacular," said Lurgio, "Others can look like a Spirit Halloween store barfed everywhere." This home haunt was of the former type and run by a guy named David Albaugh. The young Lurgio visited a few years in a row and then contacted Albaugh, who invited him over to see his collection. "I brought my older brother just in case the guy was a weirdo. And David was definitely a weirdo, but in the best possible way. He taught me what to collect and how to be discerning and who to call and write to. He's still in my life." I can vouch for that. I actually ran into Albaugh myself when dropping by Count Orlok's later in October to see how the museum was faring. Lurgio introduced me, and Albaugh had to shift the severed head he was carrying to his other hand so that we could shake.

Lurgio started calling people in Los Angeles and elsewhere who were making odd things. "That's how it started. Spending my allowance on monsters. Before you knew it one of my bedroom walls was filled with shelves holding nineteen or twenty heads."

Once he had all that spooky stuff, he started putting it to use in his own humble haunted houses all over Rhode Island. His first was at a bird sanctuary during his high school years. He continued making small haunted houses while majoring in theater at Dean College in Franklin, Massachusetts. He even started a haunt at Belcourt Castle in Newport, where he worked as a tour guide.

"You're calling it a collection, but you're using it for haunted houses. I assume the collection was much different than this one we're sitting in, right? You weren't using movie-related items?"

"Right. At that point there were a lot fewer movie-related items. I had several artists who did and do phenomenal original monsters. Everything is centered around that collection, though, because without it, none of this"—he waved a hand to encompass more than a century of horror movie characters—"would have been possible."

His foray into movie monster displays started in a dumpster behind a Gap store. His husband, Mark Waldron, called him up one day and let him know that the store he managed was about to throw away all of its mannequins. "He knew what a weirdo I was. And mannequins are expensive." It took two trips for him to rescue about fifty-three of the dumpster mannequins.

He needed those mannequins because he was about to create a new attraction, one that wasn't a haunted house. He called it the International Monster Museum, and it was part of a seasonal haunted-house theme park. The small display featured about a dozen or so full-size movie monsters from his collection. "It got a great reaction. People started asking where the collection was displayed the rest of the year. I thought, 'I'd love to do this for a living.'"

He soon got that chance. The man who ran the theme park, John Denley, who these days runs the Witch Mansion on the Essex Street Pedestrian Mall, invited him to Salem to see about opening a museum there.

At the time, Denley had an attraction on Pickering Wharf called the Museum of Myths and Monsters. He thought having a second monster museum in Salem could make for an irresistible combo ticket. So Lurgio drove to Salem for the first of what would be many, many commutes. "Denley showed me this building and introduced me to my landlord." And then almost as soon as Lurgio moved in, Denley's museum closed down, going the way of so many Salem attractions.

"That's interesting," I said. "Because one of my questions to you was going to be, 'Why'd you pick Salem?', fully expecting you to say, 'Where else would you open a monster museum?'"

"It would never have dawned on me to come here if Denley hadn't suggested it."

"But you grew up in New England. You were a monster fan. Salem wasn't on your radar?"

"No. I hadn't been up here since I was ten, for a school trip. And I only went to a couple of things, the Witch Museum and Seven Gables. The only thing I wanted to see was a haunted house called Dracula's Castle, which was in a building smaller than the Lobster Shanty. But it was closed for the season, like every haunted house in every other city, so it didn't seem that different to me." Dracula's Castle has since closed for good.

Undaunted by these failing attractions, Lurgio opened Count Orlok's Nightmare Gallery in 2007—in a space previously occupied by another short-lived attraction, the Museum of Hawthorne and Poe.

"So you moved your collection to Witch City and named it after a vampire."

"Well, he's public domain. And it's a neat name. I also thought I could assume the persona since the name's a bit esoteric. Initially, it was just going to be Nightmare Gallery, but another attraction was called Nightmare Factory. But that worked out because that business is gone." Of course.

"And you opened with zero witches in your museum."

"That's right. Although I have three now." That included Meg Mucklebones, the slimy green swamp witch from *Legend*, the Grand High Witch played by Angelica Huston in *The Witches*, and, as I mentioned, Winifred Sanderson—which, by the way, means that no jaunt to the filming sites of *Hocus Pocus* is complete without checking out Count Orlok's.

"So if you hadn't been shown this space in Salem, would you have opened up a museum at all?"

"I'd always wanted to. I thought about it every time I passed an empty store in a strip mall. I've also toured mills and old nursing homes looking for spaces. I would have opened it closer to home—and I would have lost my shirt. It has to be part of a destination city."

"What happened when you opened?"

"We immediately attracted a lot of people because we opened in September, so close enough to October that we were getting traffic. Still, we barely survived that first year. We just didn't have enough of a street presence and people would come in looking for a haunted house. I was also trying to stay open every month, as well, but in the middle of winter I'd be sitting here twiddling my thumbs."

The museum has really hit its stride now, with nine seasons under its cape in a place where spooky attractions are, somehow, a fragile business. The museum also gets a lot of repeat business from people who are into being surrounded by movie monsters in a spooky setting. It's not something a horror movie fan would ever get tired of. Count Orlok's was the number one site in the city on TripAdvisor for three years, Lurgio told me, and has stayed in the top eight out of fifty-six things to do in Salem. It might sound weird touting an Internet site score, but I didn't go to a single attraction or join a single tour where I wasn't asked to rate it on TripAdvisor after my experience.

"Tell me about Haunted Happenings. What do you like or not like about this month in Salem?"

"It's the month that my husband and I look forward to and dread at the same time every year. October represents a lot of seventeen-hour work days. And that's not just for me. Mark is as dedicated to it as I am." They generally divide the labor between them, with Waldron managing anybody that breathes (the staff) and Lurgio managing anybody that doesn't (the characters). "But I like that I can exist for the rest of the year because of that. I like that because of the haunted house, the museum can exist. Without the haunted house, I don't think the museum could, although we're experimenting year after year. We are actually cutting some Fridays out of our haunt schedule. And after years of doing a monster museum, people are finally getting the concept—mostly because it took us getting the concept first."

We also got onto the topic of his neighbors across the street, the Haunted Neighborhood. He's not a big fan. "Often people go to that first, because why wouldn't you? It's always packed and looks like a party, but then they have a bad experience and don't bother to try my place. You can look it up. They're not very well rated on TripAdvisor. I don't love having a reputation we don't deserve because of something they've done. That's something I don't love about Salem."

"I can see why you wouldn't want visitors lumping your attraction with others."

"But there is a positive side to it, I guess. The more stuff Salem has, the more people it attracts. And that unified front is unique, which is pretty cool, but the downside is that everybody's not playing their part in that front. But it's a beautiful city. Salem in October is gorgeous, the crisp air, the fall leaves, the scents. It has its own mystique."

Lurgio doesn't just raise silicone effigies of monsters at his museum, he also brings them to life. Over the years, he has hosted a range of horror movie actors at Count Orlok's, many of whose monstrous alter-egos reside in his museum. He's brought in Doug Bradley, who played the spiky-domed Pinhead in *Hellraiser.* Dee Wallace, whose horror credentials include everything from *Cujo* to *Critters, The Hills Have Eyes* to *The Howling* and, of course, Rob Zombie's *The Lords of Salem*. Kane Hodder, the hulking stuntman who brought Jason Voorhees to life in many of the *Friday the 13th* movies. Count Orlok's is where Peter Alachi saw Butch Patrick. Even Victoria Price, the daughter of Vincent Price, has visited Salem thanks to Lurgio and his museum.

At one point, I took some friends through Lurgio's haunted house, and we exited to find a young man named Nicholas King sitting at a table. I didn't recognize his face, at least not the one above his shoulders, but I recognized the one on the table in front of him. It was death white, with long, stringy black hair and sunken, black triangular eyes and no discernible mouth. It was the face of Bughuul, from the recent *Sinister* and *Sinister 2* horror movies.

King is a stuntman, and the 2012 *Sinister* was his first acting foray as a horror villain. That means he gets to ride the autograph circuit, because us horror fans are like that. You put a thin piece of rubber on your face in front of a camera and make stabby motions with your arm, and we'll want to take a photo with you. I examined his Bughuul mask and we talked a little bit, just enough to learn that he was from California, and it was his first trip to Salem, which he found "wild" or "crazy," I can't remember which. I didn't think to interview him at the time. I'm not sure why. Maybe because I was hyper-focused on interviewing

Lurgio's next horror guest, who happened to be the first horror actor Lurgio ever brought to Salem and the only one he brings back every year . . . Tony Moran, the nicest guy to ever wear William Shatner's face inside out.

Now, if you're not a horror fan, you won't recognize that name. And if you are and saw his real face, you might not recognize it either. But you would know his other face, horror fan or not. Moran's bone structure fills out the mask of Michael Myers in the final scenes of John Carpenter's 1978 *Halloween*. It's Moran's face we see when Jamie Lee Curtis rips off Michael Myer's mask, one of his eyes jacked up because she just shoved a wire coat hanger into it. The mask was only off for a few seconds, and was quickly yanked back on before Donald Pleasance blows a bullet in his back. Yet, of almost a dozen *Halloween* movies to date, it was the only one to show his face. Tony Moran's face.

I sat down with Moran at his autograph table outside the museum to hang out and talk. He was a big presence, with a boisterous voice and an extremely friendly demeanor. He talked with almost a New York accent despite being born and raised in southern California.

It might have been the most Halloween moment of my October stay. Here I was, in Salem, outside of a monster museum, sitting beside the guy who tried to strangle Jamie Lee Curtis in the original *Halloween*, while a speaker above us blared a soundtrack that included *Thriller*, the theme from *The Rocky Horror Picture Show*, the violent violins of *Psycho*, and Elvira doing some rapping. I set my phone on the table to record our conversation, where it was almost lost among his photos and merchandise, which included masks and hats and T-shirts. A pair of *Halloween* panties. He picked up my phone and held it to his mouth like a microphone.

"You've been coming here for how many years now?" I asked him.

He looked at Lurgio, who was taking a short break from the million tasks he had to do in running the museum to hang out with us. "Six years, right?"

"Yes, 2009 was the first time you were here," said Lurgio.

"Was that your first time in Salem?" I asked.

"It sure was."

"Am I interrupting an interview here?" This was from a young guy who had just exited the museum. He was with his girlfriend. They were from Bucks County, Pennsylvania, outside of Philadelphia. "No, no," I told them. "Come talk to Tony. I'm the one interrupting."

"We're going to see the original *Halloween* in a theater later this month," enthused the fan to Moran. "I've never seen it on the big screen."

"It's really a trip," said Moran.

"I was only four in 1978, so I don't think my parents took me," said the fan.

"Everybody's younger than me," said Moran. "Every single person."

And that's kind of how the interview progressed. People exiting the museum and getting excited or intrigued when they saw Moran and the signage that explained his long-ago alter ego. At some point I just started acting like his handler, asking them if they wanted an autograph, sometimes taking the photos myself, but mostly trying to smooth over that first awkward hump of conversation between them realizing who he was and trying to figure out how to start a conversation with a famous killer. Every one of them shared a story from their life about the mask or the movie.

"What were your first impressions of Salem?" I asked Moran during a momentary lull.

"I immediately fell in love with it. And James is a great host, and I'm not just saying this because he's standing over there. I can't wait to come back every year."

"And I guess it's a place full of familiar faces for you. There's a guy right now on Essex Street dressed up as Michael Myers for tips. I mean, I'm assuming that's not you, anyway."

"You know what they do," he said, and by "they" he meant his fans, "They actually Facebook me and say, 'I saw you in Salem,' even if I wasn't there that week. And they'll argue with me over it."

Lurgio jumped in, "Yeah, you should check out his page. They say, 'I saw Tony Moran on Essex Street dressed up as Michael Myers and doing the Macarena for tips.'"

"How many appearances do you do every year?" I asked.

"I average probably ten at haunts and conventions."

"And October has got to be a busy time for that, I assume?" I was leading the witness.

"Yeah, I'm usually booked every weekend."

"But you still make time for Salem and James?"

"Yeah, of course, I mean this is a tradition, the only one I have as far as October appearances go. I brought my daughter and girlfriend here this year. My girlfriend's been here a couple of times, but my daughter, she's fourteen, she's never been here before. She's out there right now, walking the streets." Probably tipping the other Michael Myers for keeping the ancient art of the Macarena alive.

A few more fans came out of the museum, and I halted the questions. As they spoke to Moran, I saw another girl come out, she must have been nineteen or twenty, something like that, which would have put her at like minus-seventeen when *Halloween* debuted. She stared at Moran but continued past. A few minutes later she returned, but kept me between her and Moran and didn't say anything. "You want to talk to Tony, right?"

"Yes."

"Go for it. He's a nice guy. Just don't let him catch you in a closet."

She didn't buy anything from his table, but Tony still posed enthusiastically in a photo with her.

"You've made my day," she told him as she left, obviously overwhelmed.

"Since there's been like a dozen Halloween movies and remakes, how do people see you fitting in now? I mean, you were the face of the Shape, but you were only in the first movie."

"It's amazing. It doesn't matter how many sequels or remakes there are, nobody really gives a damn about any of them except for John Carpenter's original. His was done so brilliantly."

"And it was the only movie that they gave Michael Myers a face. Your face. Was that your only scene as him?"

"No, I started from the strangling scene all the way to the end." Another actor (and later writer and director), Nick Castle had played Michael Myers for much of the movie, but apparently he didn't have the face of a psychotic murderer.

"So you got some solid Michael Myers time in, then."

"Well, the whole movie only took twenty-one days to film. Donald Pleasance was on set for like a week, something like that. I was on set for one day."

"And you came in to play exactly the scenes that you played?"

"Yes. They auditioned me, John Carpenter and the producer. They hired me for my face. They liked it."

Lurgio picked up one of the photos showing a younger, shaggy-headed Moran from a stack on the table, "I mean, look at that face."

"Why would they cover it up with a white mask?" I agreed. "What happens to you when you're done here for the night?"

"I'm going to take my daughter over to the Village Tavern, and she's going to have oysters and Boston clam chowder for the first time. And then Sunday we're going to go to Swansea, and my girlfriend's going to get a tattoo."

That launched us into a conversation about Moran's tattoos. He apparently has seven or eight of them. I asked the obvious question. "Is the mask of Michael Myers on your skin?"

"It is." He reached down to the bottom edge of the left leg of his jeans and pulled it up to reveal the iconic horror movie mask on his calf, half in shadow, the name of the movie in its distinctive typeface below it. It was only a piece of latex away from him having his own face on his leg. "I got that done four or five years ago."

"So, decades after the movie came out?"

"I was late to tattoos. Shit, my first tattoo I got was by a nine-year-old girl at a convention in Florida in 2009. She was the daughter of a famous tattoo guy there. She did a four-leaf clover on my ankle. She reminded me of my daughter, and the tattoo guy showed me a couple of things he let her do on him, 'cause she's aspiring, so I asked for one and she did it right there at the convention."

"You're like one of those people who lets student doctors work on them."

"Here's the problem though. I had never had a tattoo before, and I didn't know how painful it was to get one on your ankle. And they announced it over the PA system before it happened, so I had a crowd. I had to look brave, couldn't whimper or cry or nothing."

Moran wasn't happy just staying on the pointy end of the needle, though, and one day got his chance to start defacing other people. "What happens these days is tattoo and horror is crossing over. So they do these tattoo horror conventions where they have tattooists doing live tattoos. So people will come and go, 'Hey, man, will you autograph my arm? I'm going to have it tattooed right now.' And five or six years ago, I started saying, 'Cool, but if you want I'll ink it for you myself.' And they let me."

"I mean, I've seen your work with a kitchen knife. That's pretty scary."

He told me about getting one of his first tattoos. It was in Boston, and after the tattooist finished with him, the tattooist asked Moran to return the favor. "At that point, I'd never done a signature or anything before. Maybe it was the first year I came to Salem. I said, 'Shit, dude, I've never done that before.' And he says, 'I don't care.'" The tattooist was similarly laid back about what the tattoo should be. Moran thought about it for a bit, and then asked for some orange ink. "I did the most ghetto angry pumpkin face that you can ever imagine, but it says Tony Moran under it, and that's where the gold is."

"I don't have a tattoo," I admitted. "And there's no reason for me to not have one. You want to do a jack-o'-lantern on me?"

"I'd do it in a heartbeat. Put it right on your ankle."

The other part of the answer about why he waited decades to get a Halloween mask on his calf was that it took decades for him to realize what he had been a part of. "I never knew that *Halloween* and Michael Myers were such a huge deal. I mean, I didn't tell my family or my friends or the people in my acting workshop when I did the movie. I was ashamed of it. I got out of acting in my early thirties and went underground. I had a regular job for years and started having kids and stuff."

"But you must have noticed all the *Halloween* movies coming out every few years."

"I did, but I was like, whatever. But they kept coming out and eventually I started doing conventions. The first one where I really understood what was going on was at Chiller in New Jersey. I was like, 'Wow, are you kidding me? You're going to pay for this shit? You only saw my face for like two or three seconds.' But they'd go, 'We don't care, you're Michael Myers.' My little sister, she didn't even know I did the film until we were at the same convention in 2006." Moran's "little sister" is Erin Moran, as in Joanie Cunningham from *Happy Days*. As in Joanie Cunningham from *Joanie Loves Chachi*.

Here we were joined by a four middle-aged British tourists squinting in the light of day as they exited Count Orlok's. The two couples each got Moran's autographs from him. "For our kids," they said. And then one of them added, "We bought the mask today, too."

Lurgio told me that Count Orlok's month-long haunted house exhibit came about for purely business reasons rather than any particular passion on his part. To me, it was a revelation, the idea that a monster museum owner pulls up his QuickBooks account and then correlates the dollar signs and decimals there to trending attendance stats, hits a few buttons on a calculator, and then concludes that he needs to be a haunted house. Even better, I'm hoping that it's his accountant who is advising him in this matter. And that it's a guy in the same wrinkled suit that he's been wearing since the mid-eighties, his knit tie loose down the front and stained with sad dinners past, eyeballs a permanent pink color from trying to make complex equations cooperate and wishing daily he had been a poet instead of a numbers man. "James, I've crunched the numbers. I've done the math. I've also performed a few other clichés with calculations. You need to pay people to dress up as monsters and ghouls and freaks on these set days in October to increase revenue 80 percent." Salem, you know?

I love haunted houses, but not for the adrenaline. I almost treat them like art museums. I try to linger, squinting into the darkness to get a closer look at the animatronic reptile-man jumping out of glowing barrel of toxic waste. Or the trembling, eviscerated corpse spewing blood all over the cardboard tiles of the morgue. But that's only about 40 percent of why I like haunts. The other 60 percent is simply that I like watching people get scared. I have that much in common with very bad people. At least I don't scare them myself, right? But I wanted to talk to somebody who does—a Salem haunter, someone who volunteers his or her free time for very little money to spend nights dressing up and scaring people until he or she is hoarse and exhausted.

It wasn't too hard to find a haunter. There are probably half a dozen haunts downtown during October. I got in contact with Steven McCaw because he dropped a message on my OTIS Facebook page after I sent out a call for any locals with interesting connections to the city. Turns out, McCaw wasn't just a haunter. He was a firsthand expert in Salem's haunt scene.

I met him at the Witch's Brew Café on Derby Street. I was living at the Essex Street house at the time, and he also lived at that end of Essex, so it was a good meeting point. Plus, the place served this apple cinnamon sugar martini that became my dessert of choice throughout my stay, and sometimes my entrée and hors d'oeuvre as well. I sat at the end of the bar closest to the front door and waited for him. Behind me, the windows were painted with horror characters for the season: Chucky, Michael Myers, Jason Voorhees, the Ghostface killer from *Scream*, and Twisty the Clown from the fourth season of *American Horror Story*, all hoisting drinks at their own bar. Had I been sitting on the restaurant side of Witch's Brew, I would have been surrounded by windows with characters from *It's the Great Pumpkin, Charlie Brown*. Because they're all underage, I guess.

I didn't know what to expect from McCaw, but the guy who walked in was freshly pressed—clean-shaven, a tie—and a family man, with a

wife and a trick-or-treat–aged daughter. By day, he was a geologist who specialized in ground-penetrating radar applications. By night, he was an evil clown who jumped out of hidden doors in the darkness and tried to make adults scream and run.

"Do your colleagues know about your haunting double-life?"

"It is impossible to know me without knowing that I am a clown," he said. "Honestly, there are days I come into the office that I still have little traces of white on my face, and they'll be like, that's right, October."

McCaw has haunted at almost all of the haunted attractions in Salem, past and present. He's also haunted outside of Salem in seasonal theme parks like Spooky World in Litchfield, New Hampshire, and Fright Kingdom in Nashua, New Hampshire, right by my own home. His full haunt history needs to be recorded at some point for posterity.

Born in Seattle, McCaw moved across the country both as a child and as an adult. His parents eventually settled in Wellesley, Massachusetts, about an hour and a half southwest of Salem. McCaw wanted to be closer to them, so in 2005, he picked Salem. "Why?" I asked.

"Because it's Salem. How can you not love Salem?"

He was moving from Carbondale, Illinois, which, he said, had "a *Footloose*-esque policy where Halloween was more or less illegal due to riots on the main drag in the past. But I've always been a spooky person. Always into horror. I came out to Salem as a reversal of polarity, so to speak."

"And you just love haunting?"

"I love being in haunts. I do."

"What was your first haunt in Salem?"

"The Museum of Hawthorne and Poe. That would've be a couple of months after I moved here. It's not around anymore."

"I've heard of it. That place was a haunt as well as a museum?"

"As far as I know, that's all it ever was. I mean, honestly, it was horrible. And to call it a haunt is going too far. They just had to do something to pull people in."

"Where are you haunting now?"

"Count Orlok's, over on Derby Street. It's the best haunt in town. Been haunting there for years."

I wondered briefly if Lurgio had planted McCaw on my Facebook page. "I know the place. I've been there a ton of times for the museum, but I did it for the first time as a haunt the other day. I guess you were that clown."

"Did I call you Beardie, tell you I was going to shave you, and that you'd look like a big baby?"

A repressed memory burst in my head. "That . . . did . . . happen." I changed the subject. "What do you think about the haunt scene in Salem?"

"There is a lot of haunt-related politics in town." A story I dug up in the *Boston Globe* from 2011 seems to back that statement up. The story was about a feud between two haunted houses, Witch Mansion on Essex Street and the now defunct Nightmare Factory, which was inside of the Museum Place Mall. In fact, the exit for Witch Mansion was across the hall from the entrance to the Nightmare Factory. The feud included screaming matches and smear campaigns and attempts to pull visitors away from each haunt. It even went so far as physical assaults.

"I can actually go through the major Salem haunts one at a time for you," said McCaw. He then gave me capsule reviews of each. I'm redacting some of the names here for obvious reasons. The first one he described in the following way: "Imagine you go into somebody's basement and there are no lights, and then there are a bunch of kids running around yelling at you, wearing masks they got at Walgreens. Except you can't see them because it's pitch black."

Another went like this: "The guy who runs that one has a very specific philosophy, which is one of the reasons I stopped working for him. He thinks human haunters are horrible and animatronics are better. He just wants to put a *Scream* mask on a pneumatic mannequin. And it shows."

"What about Chambers of Terror?" I had just recently visited that one. It was on Pickering Wharf and advertised itself with the phrase "Bringing scary back." My wife and I jumped into it one night after a few dirty martinis and a raw bar tower at nearby Finn's seafood restaurant. "That used to be where the Museum of Myths and Monsters was, and there have been three or four haunts in that same space over the past decade. Chambers of Terror is cool, but small. A big chunk of that site was sold to another store before they moved in." I had also brought that one up specifically because throughout the month I would sit on a bench near the haunt's rear entrance to jot down notes. I'd watch people run out flushed, with the tail ends of screams dying on their lips or turning into relieved laughter in the sunlight. They would quickly look around as they realized they weren't in the haunt anymore, and then attempt to walk away as casually as they could, as if they'd just walked out of a quaint giftshop instead of a scare attraction.

"The strange thing to me about the haunt scene in Salem," I said, "is that it's not where you go in New England when you want to do a haunt. There are much better, bigger haunts elsewhere. I feel that shouldn't be the case. Salem, which is already used to that October-only business model and has a spooky reputation and multiple haunted houses on top of that, should be the place you go when you want a haunted house experience. Why isn't it?"

"Haunts like Fright Kingdom and Spooky World are multiple haunts in one big attraction. All our haunts here are small. You go to Spooky World, you're spending the whole night there. In Salem, you do a haunt for a few minutes and then go do something else. That's because the rents are high and you have very little space to work with downtown. Don't get me wrong, I'd be happy if somebody opened a big haunt here."

"You've been in Salem for ten years, and you live right on Essex Street. What do you like the most about Salem?"

"That is a tall question. Where do I even begin? I am a spooky person. I have always been a spooky person. And here's finally a place I can live and be spooky and it's a normal thing."

"But spooky's not normal in March, though, right?"

"October drives up the spooky factor, but it's still here year-round. I'm not saying every day is Halloween. It's not. But that spookiness really is there. I mean, here we are at the Witch's Brew Cafe, which is open year-round. It's like that sign you see in the tourist shops, 'As far as anybody knows, we're a nice normal family.'"

"So if Salem wasn't spooky, would you like it as much? Like if it was just a nice place with cool restaurants and history?"

"I don't think I would have moved here in the first place, to be honest, but I'd still like it."

Despite the direction this chapter has taken, not everything spooky in Salem spiderwebs back to Lurgio and Count Orlok's. For instance, at one point I discovered that Dacre Stoker, the great-grandnephew of *Dracula* author Bram Stoker, was giving a talk in Salem. Despite his interesting first name, Dacre isn't straight outta Ireland like his forebear. He's from Canada and lives in South Carolina. At some point he realized his connection to the gothic author and it became a passion for him. He's now a Stoker expert. I mean, a Bram Stoker expert. He's probably also a Dacre Stoker expert, I guess. Either way, he has co-authored a sequel to *Dracula* and gives talks all over the world about his famous grunkle.

Dacre was brought to Salem by a Connecticut-based film production company called Historical Haunts that makes films based on local folklore and history. *The Vampires of New England* documentary that was playing at the Salem theater all month was produced by them. Hence the tie-in with Stoker.

The talk was being held at the old YMCA building, which dates back to 1898. And it's, natch, on Essex Street. Inside the auditorium, the foot of the stage was lined with lighted vampire-themed jack-o'-lanterns. As Dacre began his presentation, it became apparent that this was a travel-themed tour of the places that inspired and influenced Stoker in writing *Dracula*. Basically, Dacre was a spooky travel guy, meaning he was my kind of guy. Lindsey and I stuck around afterward to talk to him.

Dacre has been to all of the sites related to the author and his most famous work, more than once, and was currently at work on a *Dracula*-themed travelogue. "You go to a country like Romania, it's scary as heck to an outsider. It's easy to get ripped off there. A lot of folks want to take full advantage of anybody from the West who wants to see a castle, and they'll say Dracula lived here. So I want to clear up that myth, show the real places that Bram visited or was inspired by or show the places that are only possibly connected but are still great experiences."

"What about St. Michan's?" I asked him. It hadn't been featured in his presentation. The seventeenth-century church in Stoker's birth city of Dublin has an amazing crypt. Lindsey and I toured it years ago. Inside, they show you desiccated corpses that were uncovered when their coffins rotted away around them. They even let you touch the finger bone from a hand held out in macabre greeting by one of the mummies. It's been worn to shininess by so many years of tourists making contact. At the time, I'd heard that the crypt was supposed to have been visited by Stoker and may have inspired him in writing *Dracula*.

"Scholars say there's no written record that he ever went into St. Michan's and looked at those bodies. But just because you can't read about it, doesn't mean it didn't happen. But they were there when he was there, and even though there's no written record of him walking in there, there's no written record of you walking in there, either."

I don't think I'd told him at that point that I was a travel writer.

"But regardless, it's still cool," Dacre continued. "People should go see it. Go into the crypts under St. Patrick's, too."

When I was in Dublin I didn't see any real Stoker memorials. A couple of plaques on houses, but nothing in proportion to his influence on culture. I asked Dacre about it.

"It's just politics. They look at Bram as this second-tier writer and turn their noses up at him, 'It's only horror.'"

I found out it was Dacre's second time in Salem. "So what's it like being a vampire guy in a witch city?"

"I put a little spiel around it. I say that if you've had enough of witches for the weekend, come and see something about vampires." The next day I saw him at a table on Essex Street, not too far from Steve the Vampire, meeting people and signing books and advertising his talk for that night. "I sold out of all my books," he told me. Salem in October.

Every city has a ghost tour these days. But Salem, especially in October, has droves of them. They're almost the fauna of Salem, moving slowly and in concert like passing herds of grazing beasts across grasslands or like starling murmurations, expanding and contracting themselves around and through the Salem crowds or past other tour groups. We would walk around at night to take in the spooky ambiance of the city, and we would see them rambling toward us up darkened streets or huddled around their guide at the base of this or that historic building. The groups could be as small as five or swell past thirty. Sometimes each member of the group held a candle in a plastic cup in front of them like they were performing some kind of rite.

There were other tours besides ghost tours, like history tours and crime tours and Witch tours, but the subject matter often overlapped to the point of being indistinguishable. When we were taking Rob Velella's Hawthorne tour over the summer, a local woman on the Common stopped us to find out what the tour was about. When she learned it was a literary tour, she said, "It's so good to see people taking a civilized tour of Salem instead of a kooky one."

My favorite kooky tour was the Voodoo, Vampires, and Ghosts tour put on by Spellbound Tours. It was a mix of history and folklore, the macabre and the paranormal. The tour guide called himself Dr. Vitka. He wore a top hat, glasses, and lamb-chop sideburns. I'd see him just about every night in October in the small park across from PEM. Eventually, I became a part of one.

Vitka was entertaining, his spiel both dramatic and funny and delivered in a cadence that I recognized but couldn't put my finger on. The

tour started after dark, and he set the mood right away. "On this tour, people have been scared. We've had people faint. The stories get scary, and people can internalize them, but they also have experiences. I don't know what you believe in, but you might want to take a moment and protect yourself. In the past, people have claimed to have been followed home by the energy they encountered at the sites that I am about to show you." Here there were unsure titters from the crowd. "If you don't believe anything I tell you tonight, I encourage you look it up when you get home." And then he gave the usual TripAdvisor appeal.

Vitka walked us over to the Old Witch Gaol site, where he explained how the experiences he had gone through while working in one of these offices turned him into a believer in the paranormal. "As you can see," he said, pointing to a sign on one of the windows of the front door advertising vacancies in the building. "There's always space available. You can have an office in here tonight if you like, but I don't recommend it."

And then he said something really interesting.

"There are some people in this city, politicians and old-time townies, who wish we would stop talking about the Witch Trials, that it's still a stain on Salem's reputation. They try to brush it under the rug and forget it. And that's why the original witch jail is no longer here. The city tore it down and sold the land. They ordered that the wood from the jail be sold as firewood. They burned that history away."

Throughout the rest of the tour, he showed us more sites related to the Witch Trials, took us to purportedly haunted sites, found ways to fit vampire stories into Salem's own, talked about the Boston Strangler's relevance to Salem, and brought up Houdini while we were standing in front of the old police headquarters.

At one point we stopped behind PEM, Yin Yu Tang rising above us white and ghostlike in the gloom. Vitka explain what a great museum PEM was, but that it wasn't what it used to be. He listed some of the items that had been on display in the past—cannibal forks from Fiji, pins that poked accusers during the Witch Trials, shrunken heads, Blackbeard's skull. "They are a lovely museum worth checking out, but all the cool macabre stuff is in the basement."

Later I met Dr. Vitka for drinks at the Hawthorne Hotel after one of his tours. His fiancée, Jenny Suomela, came along.

I ordered off the specialty cocktail menu, like I always do, especially in Salem during October. This time I went for a Strandbeest. Suomela ordered a Scarlet Letter. Vitka, parched from his hour and a half of declaiming for tourists, ordered a large glass of water. Three beats later, he said, "And a large gin and tonic, too."

His full name is Mike Vitka. "The doctorate is in divinity and was bestowed by the venerable Universal Life Church. It's the same doctorate that Hunter S. Thompson had," he told me, laughing. It turns out he was both the owner of Spellbound Tours and its only employee.

I'd heard there that the competition in the tour business was even more intense than the competition in the haunted house business. And I'd seen it myself. During my conversation with Richard St. Amour at the Charter Street Cemetery, a man in a black hat and long black coat that immediately pegged him as a tour guide came racing across the cemetery toward us waving a lit cigarette and yelling, "He can't do that here. You have to stop him." I thought he was talking about me at first, that there was some law about interviewing people in a graveyard, but he was talking about a guy leaning against a nearby tomb. The man was talking to a young couple who seemed to be only politely listening to what he had to say. By his elbow on the tomb was an empty plastic cup.

"He's not doing anything wrong right now," St. Amour said.

"He's unlicensed and he's giving a tour. You have to kick him out."

"He's just talking to those people."

"That cup is a tip jar. I know him. The city will give anyone a tour license, but they still turned him down. He just listens to the other tour guides and then gives their spiel. And he's dressed like a hangman. In a cemetery. In Salem. That's just disrespectful."

I looked closely at the man in question, and he was in fact wearing a noose around his neck. Later I'd see him walking down Essex Street with that noose in his hand and a black hood on his head. It's probably the only costume that's offensive in this city. Bravo to him for finding it.

Back in the Hawthorne Hotel, I was getting more insight into the tour guide landscape.

"A lot of the personalities that get involved with the tours are people who wouldn't necessarily fit in well other places. A lot of the tour people, in a normal walk of life, would be weirdos. And in Salem, they've managed to carve out a pretty good niche for themselves," said Vitka.

"Is it competitive out there?"

"It's intense. But at this point we all, at least on the surface, get along."

"Seems like there's plenty to go around in October."

"In October, it seems that way. But during the year, we're fighting for crumbs. When I started people would call each other out on tour and it was really rude and stupid, but most of us are friends now. The days of physically fighting in the streets are long over."

Vitka grew up in Groton, Massachusetts, and moved to Salem in 2002 to attend Salem State. "I liked the idea of Salem. I remembered coming here as a visitor and I enjoyed the fact that it had the crumbling graveyard and the haunted houses and the kind of reputation it has."

"So you moved here for the spooky."

"Oh yeah. If there wasn't spooky stuff in Salem, I wouldn't be here. Take away the spooky from Salem, there's no point living here." Growing up in the area, his father would take him to the Peabody Essex Museum, back before it had merged into one museum and was still proud of its shrunken heads. Those visits, Vitka told me, gave him the idea that Salem was a spooky place with exactly the type of culture that he was looking for. When he finally moved here, he found otherwise, at least outside of October.

"I like living in Salem a lot because I love what I do and I love the history, I love the ghost stories, I love the old cemeteries and the architecture, the monster museum, the store that sells human bones, the fun stuff like that. But when I moved to Salem, I was like, what did I do? I moved into this angry, little blue-collar town. Like I thought coming here was going to be vampires gliding down the street but it was Sully from Lynn, dude." He spoke the last few words in a Boston accent that sounded exaggerated, but which wasn't.

Up to this point, Suomela hadn't really said anything, just politely sipped her Scarlet Letter. Still, ordering that drink had been enough to tell me something interesting about her. She had a Swedish accent. "How did you guys meet?" I asked her.

"I went to school in California with a friend of Mike's from Salem, and I really wanted to see Salem in October."

"You knew about Salem in Sweden?"

"Yes, we knew about the Witch Trials."

Turns out, that school was a clown school, and when she finally made it to Salem in 2009, Vitka was nowhere to be seen. "That was my first time here," she told me. "But it was December. I didn't meet Mike because he was in Florida doing sideshow stuff."

"Wait. Sideshow stuff?"

"I work for the World of Wonders sideshow during the winter as the outside talker for the freak show." That was it. That was the cadence I had picked up on during the tour. The guy talked like carnival barker. "I actually brought a freak show to Salem for a while and did very well."

Suomela continued her story, "I came back and we met on Halloween through our mutual friend."

"So you met him and sacrificed all your dreams of being a clown?"

"I do physical theater still. No clowns, anymore."

"And now we're getting married over the dead bodies at St. Peter's," said Vitka. He then told me how he got involved with Spellbound Tours. It started at the now-defunct Spellbound Museum, which he described as a supernatural dime museum. He met the owner, Molly Stewart, who was active in the paranormal field, and struck up a relationship. Soon enough he found himself both a tour guide for Spellbound and an apprentice paranormal investigator. In 2011, he bought the tour company. "For me, the fun part is always the historic research, but the investigations are really great, too. Most don't yield anything, but creeping around trying to find something is almost better than finding anything. Just the experience of it."

"I dig that," I answered. "I'm not a paranormal guy, but I've given talks to ghost hunter groups before. I tell them that I love ghost stories and research and tromping through old buildings and cemeteries in the middle of the night, so basically, I have everything in common with ghost hunters except for the ghost hunting part."

"When I started, I went in as the biggest believer you'd ever meet, and now, after 15 years, I'm so skeptical," said Vitka. He told me that the tour's best years as far as the paranormal went were between 2004 and 2007, when everybody seemed to be paranormal-obsessed. "During those years, when I'd say I'm a paranormal investigator, people were like,

'Wow.' Now, when I say it, people are like," he adopted the Boston accent again, "'Yeah, so am I. I'm one of them paranormals, too.' It went from something that was sort of a strange field of science to something you could pick up at the flea market."

"You mentioned on the tour the destruction of the Old Witch Gaol. You almost had a conspiracy theory around it."

"No conspiracy. The city just said, 'This building's falling apart, we should get rid of it.' But they never really liked the Witch Trials' association with it. Most of the timbers were sold for firewood. Isn't that awful? We're trying to preserve everything that exists, and they outright burned that place."

"It's like Salem can't allow itself to become too odd."

"Salem has a really bad habit of doing things halfway. Salem's attitude is mostly like, 'We're making money, but we're not going the extra mile to do better. Let's not rock the boat, let's not risk it. We see it's good now, so we don't have to try.' And it's really kind of weird."

"And now you have to take tour groups to a plaque on an office building."

"Yeah, a lot of people in Salem don't get it. People come to hear that story. With my tour script, I ended up adding a lot more history than my initial one because people wanted the Witch Trials. I remember there was one tour company that had a slogan, "No more weights," like they thought people didn't want that story anymore, and they bombed."

"How many tour companies are there?"

"Year-round—and that's April to November—I'd say about fifteen. People that open up just for the month of October, I have quite some resentment for." He named a few names and had some choice words to say about those tour guides, calling them "interlopers who take business from others in October."

"What has changed in Salem since you took over the tour company?"

"I guess Salem's economy as a whole has gone way up. Which is good and bad." He told me that Salem's growing economy meant that people are doing better, but also that property values are increasing. "Some people in the tourist industry are starting to feel the pinch because the people who are buying up the condos are the fancy Peabody Essex Museum folks who don't like the kind of stuff we do. I mean, I like the museum, because I like art. I don't like the museum because they're snobby. When I'm out on the street selling ghost tour tickets and I see somebody with a Peabody Essex button, I either ignore them or try to mess with them, 'Did you see Blackbeard's skull?'"

"They don't always like talking about that side of the museum."

"I like both sides of it. I like the culture and I like the corny stuff. But if the Peabody Essex Museum were to turn one of those sheds they own into a Witch Room, can you imagine how many people would go there?"

"I've had that discussion with a guy from PEM. But they don't want witches anywhere near their brand."

"They don't have a brand. Here, so close to Boston, you can go to the MFA to see beautiful art. You can go to the Museum of Contemporary Art, you can go to the Isabella Stewart Gardner Museum. You can go a little afield to the deCordova. We live in an area filled with art. And if the Peabody Essex Museum wanted to differentiate itself, it could do that by sticking with some of the unique history, which they are neglecting."

Vitka stopped for a moment and seemed to pull back. "Listen, I'm trying to be a Salem cheerleader, but I feel like I'm sounding bleak. Or at least inconsistent. I feel like I'm telling you that I love Salem, and then on the other side, that it could be so much better." He thought for a bit more. "You know what the word for Salem is? Potential. Salem has so much potential. I saw a sign in a local business one year, 'Is it November yet?' October is the time of year we should all be grateful to be living here. October is the month people come here and enjoy themselves. This is when most of us make most of our money for the year. If you don't want a month-long Halloween party, if you don't want to see people in costume, if you don't want to hear about ghosts and the witches, move out. If you're going to own a business in Salem and put up a sign like that, you have no place doing business in town."

We talked for a while after that, on less heavy matters. Hell, we shut down the hotel bar. We got on the topic of our mutual admiration for *The Abominable Dr. Phibes*, the art of Tom Kuebler, Vitka told me a few more sideshow stories. I mean, two Scarlet Letters and a Strandbeest later, and I'm pretty sure I monologued about the philosophical changes in Scooby Doo over the past fifty years.

I talked to Vitka again later, after October, and it seemed as if some of that potential he talked about was already starting to be realized. Or he was just in a good mood due to his recent nuptials with Suomela. "Recent developments in Salem give me great hope," he told me. "The fact that the Gallows Hill site has at long last been officially recognized and will be getting a memorial is good news. Any time the city overtly acknowledges the Witch Trials legacy is great. Also, since the new Harry Potter material will be dealing with a fictionalized version of Salem, I predict an influx of visitors looking for fun. I see a good future for Salem."

Man, do I love the spooky side of Salem. I keep returning to that same idea that was repeated a couple of times in those discussions. Michael Vitka phrased it as, "Take away the spooky from Salem, there's no point living here." It was carnival-barker hyperbole, but it has truth in its tent. Even with the Witch Trials history. Even with Halloween. If that's not all bound together with, I don't know, a milieu, an atmosphere, a mise-en-scène, a reputation, if Salem doesn't have that united front that James Lurgio talked about, then it's just so many unrelated oddities, easily skipped or quickly experienced and forgotten.

But I can certainly tell you without any hyperbole that, take the spooky out of Salem, and this book you hold in your hands doesn't exist.

12

THAT'S HAWTHORNE, WITH A "W," AS IN "WITCH"

Nathaniel Hawthorne Statue

One day during this Salem October, I decided to skip Witch City. To avoid any attraction with an ugly hag on its sign. To not follow any crazy costumes around with my camera. To lay aside my ripped and creased copy of the Haunted Happenings brochure. Instead, I stuck a volume of classic American short stories under my arm and went out to explore Hawthorne City.

They're the same streets, give or take, but in Hawthorne City, the welcome sign is spelled out in scarlet letters. All the houses have a legally mandated seven gables. A marble faun is erected on the Common. Every minister at every church wears a black veil. Its favorite Halloween decoration is the scarecrow instead of the witch. The bars have names like The Great Stone Face and The Elixir of Life, and the hotels names like The Ambitious Guest and, well, the Hawthorne Hotel. And the high school mascot has a high forehead and a moustache.

This could have been Salem had the Witch Trials never happened. I mean, not literally, but Salem would most likely only have been famous for being the city that gave us Nathaniel Hawthorne, the author who gave us *The Scarlet Letter* and *The House of the Seven Gables,* "Young Goodman Brown" and "The Birth-Mark," "Ethan Brand" and "Wakefield." The author who Herman Melville called the American Shakespeare. Whom Edgar Allan Poe called "one of the few men of indisputable genius to whom our country has as yet given birth."

On the other hand, had the Salem Witch Trials never happened, we might not have had the Nathaniel Hawthorne we all are supposed to read in high school.

Hawthorne's work is black with sin, guilt, remorse, and all the icky parts of the human soul, what Hawthorne biographer Brenda Wineapple calls the "secret horrors of everyday life" in *Hawthorne: A Life*. "Shall we never, never get rid of this Past?" exclaims one of Hawthorne's characters in *The House of the Seven Gables,* "It lies upon the Present like a giant's dead body." Life is a corpse, and we all suffocate underneath it. That's Hawthorne.

And that makes him the perfect native scribe for a city under the constant shadow of a nine-month event in the late seventeenth century.

His stories are dark enough, in fact, that people sometimes try to categorize him in the horror genre, which would make him even more perfect for Salem (he himself called his stories "romances"). It's a stretch, of course. The supernatural in his work, when used, appears more often as exercises in symbolism than anything else—a living scarecrow, a ghostly patriot, a wilderness meeting with the Devil. Still, when Roger Corman was scraping the bottom of the Amontillado barrel by filming the works of Edgar Allan Poe back in the 1960s, he stuck Vincent Price into an anthology movie made up of Nathaniel Hawthorne stories called *Twice-Told Tales,* named after a two-volume collection of Hawthorne's short stories that had been previously published in magazines. The movie dramatized "Dr. Heidegger's Experiment,"—about an elixir of life that restored youth—"Rappaccini's Daughter,"—about a poisonous woman—and even *The House of the Seven Gables* and its generational curse.

Back in Hawthorne City, I wanted to see some of the sites associated with the author. I had to be choosy, as just about everything in Salem has a Hawthorne connection. The author lived more than half of his sixty years in the city, and even when he moved away—not counting his work as the US Consul in London—it wasn't to go far, with stints in Boston and Concord, western Massachusetts and coastal Maine. And he and his wife always had family in the city.

Pretty much any surviving building that dates to before, say, 1850, he probably visited, walked by, knew somebody who had lived there, toilet-papered at Halloween. He was familiar with all its streets, every one of its institutional buildings—the Essex Historical Society building, the Salem Athenaeum, City Hall. Even the Salem Witch Museum was built while Hawthorne was living there, although it was a church back then. That means anybody who visits Salem is on a Hawthorne tour, even if they don't know it. And that's why the guy has kept popping up uninvited in every chapter of this book.

Hawthorne was born on Independence Day in 1804, a sixth-generation Salemite. His parents were Elizabeth and Nathaniel Sr., the latter being one of Salem's many ship captains. Hawthorne was born in a two-story house at 27 Union Street, a site a couple of blocks off the Common and near the Hawthorne Hotel. That's the first place I went. Except that the house is not there. The original site is a backyard beside a parking lot in a residential neighborhood. So I didn't stay long. But that wasn't a surprise, nor is it a "cutting up the Old Witch Gaol for firewood" kind of story. His birth home was moved and preserved. We'll find it later.

He didn't stay at his birth home long anyway. His father died in Surinam of yellow fever in 1808, so his mother grabbed four-year-old Nathaniel and his two sisters and moved to the next street over, Herbert Street, to live with her family, the Mannings.

I walked back up Union Street to turn left at Essex and head down Herbert. However, at the intersection of Union and Essex, I noticed a black awning above an empty storefront in a large brick building to which I had not previously paid any attention. But on this day I had Hawthorne on the brain. The awning simply read, "Sophia's." That's the name of Hawthorne's wife. At first I just figured it was because it stood across the street from the Hawthorne Hotel, but then I saw a plaque on the building announcing that Sophia lived in the building in her early childhood. She was born five years after Hawthorne, and they probably crossed paths at some point in childhood, even though they wouldn't officially meet for another three decades.

The Manning house is at 10 1/2 Herbert Street, although in Hawthorne's day it was probably numbered 12. This was the house where he spent most of his life in Salem, in a room in the attic, composing the lion's share of his short stories and his first novel, *Fanshawe*. He grew to hate the place. He called it "Castle Dismal" and once sarcastically wrote of it, "In this dismal and squalid chamber, fame was won." It was the same attitude he often had toward Salem. In one of his later letters to Sophia, he wrote: "I am intolerably weary of this old town . . . Dost thou not think it really the most hateful place in the world?" Sometimes you just get tired of your home town. Especially if it keeps pulling you back in and seeping into your stories.

These days Castle Dismal is an unimpressive gray-green house shoved sideways into the neighborhood. Like its neighbor houses, it towers three stories into the air, plus Hawthorne's attic, the window of which overlooks Herbert Street. It's tangled in phone lines and divided into apartments. An oval plaque on its flank touts its Hawthorne connection. It doesn't use the phrase, "Castle Dismal," but the building hardly even seems worth any evocative title these days.

Hawthorne got a few breaks from Castle Dismal over the years, living for a little while with an uncle in Raymond, Maine, and then returning to that state for a four-year stint at Bowdoin College in Brunswick, where his classmates included such future notables as Henry Wadsworth Longfellow and Franklin Pierce. He moved to what is now 26 Dearborn Street in North Salem, but was, as always seemed to happen, still pulled back to Herbert Street.

Most of what he wrote during this time he published anonymously, even *Fanshawe*, and he's often portrayed by biographers as an introverted man, the kind who wouldn't answer a knock on the door, or who would head down a side street when he saw somebody coming at him. He lived off a family stipend and the small amount of scratch he got for his stories. It seems he spent his decades in Salem wafting—writing, walking, checking local history books out of the Salem Athenaeum. His life wouldn't take a really exciting turn until 1837, when he was thirty-three years old, one year past the age at which his adventurous, seafaring father died.

That was the year the first volume of his *Twice-Told Tales,* a collection of his previously published stories gathered together under his actual byline, was published. The anthology jump-started his reputation as an author, even if it didn't line his pockets with enough to leave Salem behind permanently. It was also the year that he met Sophia Peabody.

Peabody was an artist and somewhat of a shut-in at the time due to her chronic headaches. She met Hawthorne through her sister Elizabeth, who dug the writer's work and possibly had romantic designs on him herself. And that courtship happened in what today is not at all called the Peabody House in Salem. It's called the Grimshawe House.

You remember that place, right? The spookiest-looking building in all of spooky old Salem? The decrepit edifice at 53 Charter Street shares a wall with the Charter Street Cemetery and is overgrown with evil-looking weeds right out of Rappaccini's garden. Its white, peeling facade makes it seem like the ghost of a house. And it gets its name from a Hawthorne story. A creepy Hawthorne story. Natch.

Actually, the house is featured in two Hawthorne works, both novels and both unfinished at the time of his death. The first, *The Dolliver Romance,* would have been a story along the lines of "Dr. Heidegger's Experiment" in that it would have involved an elixir of life. The unfinished manuscript for it was placed atop his coffin during his funeral service. The other story, the one from which the house gets its name, is *Doctor Grimshawe's Secret,* which also pulls from other of his works and is about a spider-obsessed doctor, a secret chamber, and a bloody footstep. Maybe Hawthorne *is* a horror author.

At one point in time the front doorway of the house was removed and installed a rear entrance of the Phillips Library. A blue plaque above the white doorway touts its literary heritage as part of the Grimshawe House. I assume, due to the appearance of the house that it came from, that the doorway was a portal to a hellish dimension and that PEM yanked it from the building and hid it behind the library to safeguard it. I also assume that it hired the most powerful Witches in the city to cast protective charms on it. I can write ridiculous sentences like these because Salem.

I once overheard a tour guide tell his audience that the house was left to decay out of spite. That the man who had owned it had tried to turn the place into a bed and breakfast, but had been stopped by the city after pressure from PEM across the street, which wanted the house and its contents in its collection. The man died, his dream of a B&B unfulfilled, and left his will structured in such a way that the house was never to be renovated. It was to sit and rot unused, right in PEM's backyard. I have no idea if any of that is true, but I do hope that it's one of a hundred legends and tales that the spooky old house inspires in Salem.

Still, the best thing about the house is that its side yard is a graveyard. It is said to have inspired the setting of horror author H.P. Lovecraft's story "The Unnamable." In fact, the whole fictional Massachusetts town of Arkham that Lovecraft used throughout his stories is rumored to be Salem itself. "The Thing on the Doorstep" features the Crowninshield-Bentley House on Essex Street, and one of his more famous stories is "The Dreams in the Witch House." I should have dedicated an entire section of the previous chapter to mapping Lovecraft's Salem.

Grimshawe House

The more I learn about the Grimshawe House, the more I like it. I mean, it's an abandoned, seventeenth-century house by a cemetery, in Salem, that inspired authors to fill it with giant spiders and monsters that could not be named. I hope that whole will thing is both true and ironclad and that the edifice never gets refurbished into blandness.

For Hawthorne, though, the Charter Street Cemetery was more than just spooky atmosphere for his story. As he sat in the Peabody home, hanging out with the Peabody daughters, looking out the window, his eyes would have been drawn to one gravestone in the cemetery, the same one that draws everyone who visits the cemetery today.

It's the gravestone of his great-great-grandfather, Jonathan Hathorne. Judge Jonathan Hathorne. Witch Trials judge Jonathan Hathorne. Nathaniel Hawthorne had witch hunter blood in his veins. Some say that's why Hawthorne added the *W* to his surname during his twenties, to distance himself from the shame of his ancestor. Others guess that Hawthorne just wanted to throw the spelling back to an even older form of the surname because it appealed to his romantic nature. Some claim it was a way to make the pronunciation match the spelling. There are a lot of theories behind that one letter, which is apt. It's Hawthorne. He wrote a whole book about one letter.

Eventually, he got engaged to Sophia. In accordance with Hawthorne's usual withdrawn manner, it was a secret engagement. An almost three-year-long secret engagement. During that time, he moved to Boston to work at its custom house, moved to West Roxbury to try his hands tilling soil at a commune. And, of course, he got pulled back to Castle Dismal.

In 1842, at the age of thirty-eight, he married Sophia in Boston and then got the hell away from Salem. For three years, he and his wife lived in a house in Concord, Massachusetts, at what would come to be called the Old Manse, rented from the family of Ralph Waldo Emerson. He soaked up the history of the town where the first shot of the Revolutionary War was fired. It inspired his *Mosses from the Old Manse*. His first child, Una, was born there.

Eventually, the Hawthornes needed money, so back to Salem (and Castle Dismal) they went. You can see that for most of my tour of Hawthorne City I just sat cross-legged on the sidewalk on Herbert Street. "Here am I again established in the old chamber where I wasted so many years of my life," wrote Hawthorne.

In 1846 he landed a job at the Salem Custom House. I didn't need to put that on my itinerary. I'd already thoroughly explored the site during the Maritime Festival and had walked by it countless times in October itself. In addition to the giant gold eagle inside and the tale of the origins of *The Scarlet Letter* and the scandalous reception of the introduction, the one thing I left out is that the National Park Service has an exhibit of Hawthorne artifacts in one of the rooms, including his walking stick, his pens and inkwell, his desk, and the seal with which he marked cargo. It was a metal stencil with his name, the name of the city, and the year 1847 on it.

While he worked at the Custom House, he lived in a few different places. Like 18 Chestnut Street—Laurie Cabot's future house. And 14 Mall Street, where he wrote *The Scarlet Letter.*

In 1849, Zachary Taylor was elected President and fired everyone from their cushy government positions who wasn't a member of his party, including Hawthorne. *The Scarlet Letter* was published the very next year.

In 1850 Hawthorne left Salem, never to return as a resident. He had finally escaped Castle Dismal.

He lived fourteen more years, had a total of three children. He lived in Western Massachusetts, where he befriended Herman Melville. Melville would dedicate *Moby Dick* to him. Salem stuck with him for a little while, however, as he published *The House of the Seven Gables* in 1851. He moved back to Concord, where he bought his first house, called the Wayside. His lifelong friend Franklin Pierce became President and appointed Hawthorne US Consul in Liverpool, England, a position he held for four years. When Pierce wasn't reelected, Hawthorne resigned before he could get fired and traveled Europe with his family, hitting Paris and Rome and Florence and much of England. He returned to Concord and the Wayside in 1860. He died in 1864 in his sleep while traveling to New Hampshire. Franklin Pierce discovered his body.

I didn't learn about Hawthorne solely through house plaques, though. I talked to a Hawthorne expert as well to learn more about the American Shakespeare. But not in Salem. In New Haven, Connecticut. When I talked to Jason Courtmanche, he was halfway through his two-year term as the president of the Nathaniel Hawthorne Society, a forty-year-old group of more than four hundred academics dedicated to Hawthorne scholarship.

It was over Skype, so imagine the following conversation happening with lots of audio lag and screen interference.

"Have you ever been to Salem? You only live a few hours away," I asked Courtmanche.

"In 2006, when I was finishing up my doctoral dissertation on Hawthorne, my family and I spent a week there, saw the Custom House, The House of the Seven Gables, his birth home. It was August, but they were already gearing up for October."

Courtmanche grew up in New Haven and got a degree in English from the University of Connecticut in the late 1980s. "I loved books and I loved having a major where I could just grab a paperback and sit under a tree someplace." Eventually, he went back to UConn for his PhD, and that's where he ran headlong into Hawthorne.

"So how did your fascination with Hawthorne start?"

"Ghosts."

"Hawthorne's not really a ghost story kind of guy, is he?"

"That's the thing. I was really fascinated with supernatural phenomena in American literature. I wrote a term paper on it. It was going to be the foundation for my book." But that's a wide topic, full of sin and guilt and blood, and his book started growing to George R. R. Martin proportions. His refocused the project by comparing an early American author who deals with those themes to a later author: Hawthorne and Faulkner. Ten months later, the manuscript was still too big, so he had to bench one of the authors. "I really thought I was going to be more of a Faulkner scholar, but I ended up cutting him and sticking to Hawthorne. And that meant I was getting less into ghosts, because there's not necessarily a lot of ghosts in Hawthorne. Instead, I really started getting into sin and the way he's looking into sin in a way that was a progression from how authors had looked at in the past, in a secular way."

Courtmanche eventually got a paper accepted at the Hawthorne, Poe, and Emerson Conference in Oxford, and he was recruited into the Nathaniel Hawthorne Society. He then made his way to the board, and then to the presidency after he planned the society's international conference in Florence.

"What's your perspective on Hawthorne's life in Salem?"

"Everybody's going to have a different take on that story. How much of that stuff about the melancholy, reclusive youth is true and how much exaggeration? Who knows? Some people think he was creating a persona. We do know he said a lot of critical things about it, particularly in 'The Custom-House," but how much of that is him exaggerating his sentiments to create a character out of himself? I'd say nobody really knows for sure."

"Let me ask you this. We teach Hawthorne in school, and we put him on the shelf with the other original authors of American literature, right there with Washington Irving and Edgar Allan Poe and others. Yet in popular culture today, it seems he's the guy that always gets forgotten about. Washington Irving has a show on Fox right now. Poe's most famous poem is the mascot for an NFL football team. But Hawthorne doesn't seem to be a part of popular culture these days."

"I'd say his *Scarlet Letter* is," said Courtmanche. "You see scarlet letter references and parodies all the time." That immediately rang true to me. Months later, I did a quick Google News search for the phrase "Scarlet Letter," and found it everywhere. Pop star Taylor Swift had a song climbing the charts with the line, "We show off our different scarlet letters—Trust me, mine is better." At the 2016 Academy Awards, the writer who won the Oscar for best adapted screenplay said in his acceptance speech, "Big money is taking over our government, and until right and left goes, 'No more big money,' it has to be like a scarlet letter on these candidates." The Metropolitan Museum of Art in New York had just rebranded with a new modern logo with red letters, prompting backlash and headlines like, "Will the Red Letters in the New Met Logo Become Scarlet Letters?" Congress had just voted to place marks on the passports of sex offenders, which the media immediately started calling scarlet letters. It went on.

I still pressed the point. "But I guess I'm talking more about a coolness factor. Say you went to a thirteen-year-old kid and you said, 'Have you heard of the Headless Horseman?' They'd say yes. 'Have you heard of Poe's "The Raven"?' They'd say, 'Yes, I saw that *South Park* episode.' But you ask him or her about Hawthorne, and that kid's not really going to have a response yet, right?"

"Probably, and I think a lot of that is because of sex."

"Okay."

"I think about all my years teaching high school. The only book challenges I ever knew were people getting upset over sex. It's okay to tell a kid about somebody getting their head chopped off or somebody getting hatcheted to death. But sex? Oh no, we can't talk about that. Think about what we let kids dress up as for Halloween. You would never let a six-year-old girl walk out on Halloween night dressed like a tramp or anything suggestive, but if she wants to dress up as a vampire and wear blood and carry a weapon, that's okay, everybody's going to think it's cute. That says some really strange things about our culture."

His example sparked a bizarre image in my head. "Now I'm imagining sending out that six-year-old in a modest colonial dress with a scarlet *A* on it. You can't do that." I then realized somehow the conversation had progressed from ghosts to sex. In a conversation about Nathaniel Hawthorne. "So obviously I see the major sexual component in *The Scarlet Letter,* but is that really a theme for Hawthorne in general?"

"Absolutely. It's very pervasive. In *The House of the Seven Gables,* Alice is so-called 'ruined' by Holgrave's ancestor because she's seduced. It's all throughout that book, actually. In *The Blithedale Romance,* Priscilla was most likely a prostitute, and that's what she's been saved from. In *The Marble Faun,* Miriam is based on a character from one of Giovanni Boccaccio's stories who is the victim of incestuous rape. It's everywhere in Hawthorne's work."

Once Courtmanche called it out for me, I started seeing it everywhere, from "Ethan Brand" to "The Birth-Mark."

"So how often is Hawthorne in your head?"

"I think it's an inevitable occupational hazard that I see the world through literature, and I often see the world through Hawthorne's eyes. Take for example everything that's been going on with the Confederate flag controversy. I find myself thinking about Hawthorne because during the Civil War, he thought the country should let the South secede because it was just a culturally different place than the North. And we're still fighting that battle. I can't not think of the things Hawthorne said about that every time it comes up."

"You told me you've only been to Salem that one time, even though you don't live too far away. You don't feel that pull to go up all the time and see the actual sites related to this dead guy who's been such a part of your life?"

"Sure, and I'll make it back. But, honestly, if I feel a pull, it's more of a pull to Concord."

That made sense. Hawthorne spent more years of his life in Concord than he spent anywhere other than his home city, and the Concord years were probably the happiest. Today, you can still see the Old Manse window pane into which he and Sophia etched phrases. Most important to tying Hawthorne to Concord, though, is that Concord has his body—like how Salem's resonance is amplified for being the execution site for the Witch Trials victims. Hawthorne is buried in Sleepy Hollow Cemetery in a section called Authors Ridge, a short stretch of path that also includes the final resting places of Louisa May Alcott, Henry David Thoreau, and Ralph Waldo Emerson.

Back in Salem, I wasn't done visiting Hawthorne sites. I had two houses and a fountain left.

Hawthorne regularly used the landmarks of Salem in his works. Gallows Hill is the setting for "Alice Doane's Appeal." The steps of City Hall are the stage for "The Sister Years." And Hawthorne once wrote a story where the landmark itself was the narrator.

Collected in his *Twice-Told Tales*, "A Rill from the Town Pump" is a monologue by the town pump, located at the intersection of Essex and Washington Streets above Salem Spring. In it, the pump expounds upon how important it is to the town, as if it's running for office. In fact, it is so won over by its own case, that it eventually concludes, "when I shall have decayed, like my predecessors, then, if you revere my memory, let a marble fountain, richly sculptured, take my place upon this spot."

And goddamn if the people of Salem didn't do just that. Hawthorne City, guys.

In 1976, the people of Salem erected a fountain on the site of Salem Spring at the end of Essex Street, although these days it loses camera clicks to the *Bewitched* statue across the street. It isn't a marble fountain, and "richly sculptured" is somewhat of a subjective idea, but it's there. The tall concrete fountain is about the size of a large door. Its face is textured with a bronze relief sculpture of all the people and animals who had slaked their thirst at the spring, from Native Americans to cows to early Salemites. Four streams of water pour from it into a basin at its feet. A second bronze relief on the side of the fountain above a couple of drinking fountains depicts Hawthorne

The House of the Seven Gables

himself hanging out at the town pump. Above him, some explanatory text ends with, "This fountain is here at the suggestion of the town pump itself."

Most tourists might not know why that pump's there, and they probably won't see, except inadvertently, any of the sites I've mentioned privously. However, there is one Hawthorne site in Salem that nearly every tourist visits.

At 115 Derby Street is the Turner-Ingersoll Mansion, although nobody calls it that. Everyone knows it as The House of the Seven Gables. It's across the way from the Ye Old Pepper Companie, which calls itself America's oldest candy company. Tracing its history back to 1806, it's now a family business four generations in. The shop is about the size of a living room, but it is crammed with tooth-rotters from old-fashioned candies like Gibraltars—which Hawthorne himself referenced in his writing—and Black Jacks to New England tourist shop fare like gummy lobsters and salt water taffy to spooky stuff like chocolate witches and skull pops.

The House of the Seven Gables was built by Captain John Turner in 1668, a quarter of a century before the Salem Witch Trials. Later, it was sold to Captain Samuel Ingersoll, who removed four of its seven gables because the house was too big for his needs. He was also related to Nathaniel Hawthorne. Ingersoll's daughter, Susanna, who was twenty years older than Hawthorne, would tell the author stories of the house from back when it was crowned with seven gables. Hawthorne dug the phrase "seven gables" and wanted to do something with it. And he did. In 1851, he published *The House of the Seven Gables,* a novel about the last dregs of the Pyncheon family and the curse under which they live because their ancestor got a man hanged for witchcraft to take his land, upon which the hosue was built. Hawthorne adapted the curse from the final words of a real Witch Trials victim, Sarah Good. In Hawthorne's book, it was: "God will give him blood to drink."

In 1908, the house was bought by a philanthropist named Caroline Emmerton for its connection to the popular Hawthorne story. She turned it into a museum to fund her charity work in the Settlement Movement, which was an initiatve to help immigrants acclimatize to the country, to learn English, and to acquire relevant job skills.

Today, that work still goes on. In fact, the name of the organization behind the tourist attraction is The House of the Seven Gables Settlement Association. Ticket proceeds go both to historic preservation and to its work with immigrant families and at-risk youth.

The House of the Seven Gables is a massive, black, pointy house that seems imminently suited for trick-or-treating. It being October, the tour I was on was fast-paced and full-packed. We saw a fireplace in one room made out of original First Period bricks. A penny shop that opens out onto Turner Street that Emmerton installed in 1910 to better line up with the events in Hawthorne's book. We climbed a "secret" staircase that ascends to a small room interpreted by the site as servant quarters so that they can tell the story of the servants of the house. In the attic, we saw the original oak beams, over three hundred years old. We were shown a small model to illustrate how the house had changed over the years, losing and gaining gables, which were defined as any points on the roof that are tied into the main ridge line of the roof. We even saw the tables where Susanna Ingersoll probably changed little Nathaniel's diapers.

Eventually, we exited into the garden of the house, a magnificent spot which overlooks the harbor. And then we walked into Nathaniel Hawthorne's birth home.

Emmerton wasn't just a philanthropist and preservationist. She collected buildings. Ringing the garden of the Seven Gables property are about a dozen buildings that she bought and moved to the property. She turned the buildings into inns and tea rooms and antique shops, all for the purpose of raising money for her settlement work. After her death in 1942, the association kept up the tradition. In 1958, Hawthorne's birth home was in danger of being torn down, so the association bought it for a dollar, cut it into thirds, and reassembled it on the Seven Gables property.

Entrance into the house is included as part of the admission, and you get to take it at your own pace. Inside the maroon, two-floor home are various exhibits such as pieces of furniture that Hawthorne owned and art by his wife and first editions of his books. It's the only one of the many Hawthorne homes in Salem that the public can tour, as well as the only one in the shadow of the source of one of his greatest inspirations.

It wasn't my first trip to The House of the Seven Gables for the book, though. That happened earlier, when I found myself in the Retire Beckett house on the property. Built in 1655, it's the oldest building on the site and was built by a shipbuilding family. These days, the bottom floor is a giftshop, but I was headed upstairs for a staff meeting.

I was there to meet Kara McLaughlin, the site's executive director, and two members of her staff, Ryan Conary and Alyssa AlKhowaiter. I sat down with them in McLaughlin's office.

"I brought in Ryan and Alyssa because they know more about the history," McLaughlin told me. "They started out as tour guides here, and then we brought them into the operations."

"What exactly is the relationship between The House of the Seven Gables and Witch City?"

"We collaborate with other Salem institutions and Destination Salem to help promote Salem as a whole," said McLaughlin. "The more it's a destination city, the better positioned the Seven Gables is. But, because we're a multifaceted organization, we're often doing our own thing. For the most part, the only real connection to the Witch Trials that we have is through Hawthorne and his lamentation of the fact that he's descended from one of the judges and how that works into the novel *The House of the Seven Gables*."

"So this house was standing during the Witch Trials, but it had no connection to everything that was going on?"

"There were tenuous, small connections," said Conary. "There's a John Turner whom we think is John Turner II, the son of the original owner of the house. He's referenced as being thrown out of an apple tree by Ann Pudeator, one of the people who was executed for witchcraft. But like Kara said, although we have common goals and interests with other Salem sites, we have our own identity within the city."

"And that identity, like your activities, is also multifaceted, right? Even though it's famous for being a literary site, it's also an architectural site and a historical site and a maritime site."

"The tour focuses on all those themes," said McLaughlin. "And I would actually say there's another theme that we begin the tour with and that's more about our social work and our social service background with Caroline Emmerton."

"On my first trip to Salem, like a decade ago, from a town almost five hundred miles away and with an Internet still in its infancy, I knew two things about Salem. The Witch Museum and the Seven Gables. Why is this literary site so popular?"

"I think initially," said AlKhowaiter. "The book was very popular. So when Emmerton opened it in 1910, that really propelled the house into culture."

"Right," said McLaughlin. "It was in the late 1800s that people started to become tourists in the country. Before Emmerton, the Upton family was the last family to live in this house. They knew it was the setting for Nathaniel Hawthorne's novel, and they charged people a nickel to come through the house." McLaughlin said that the Uptons painted images on tea cups to sell as souveniers. The image they chose? A witch on a broom. "So the Uptons tried to connect the house to the Witch Trials, really."

"How does the witch reputation sit with you? Would you rather Salem be Hawthorne City?"

"Oh yes, definitely," said McLaughlin. "Even the witch sites want the city to be perceived as more than just the Witch Trials. The Witch Trials are a big piece, but the city is so much more."

"Also, a majority of our attendance happens in October," said Conary. "So I feel like it's not necessarily the Witch Trials. It's Halloween. If we did become Hawthorne City, I don't know if we would be able to have the scale of tourism that we get. It's like Lexington or Concord. Their tourism is mostly based on the Battle of Concord and the start of the Revolutionary War, but they have an incredible literary history, including the Hawthorne connection, which visitors can experience even if they are going for that one historical event. For us, it's the Witch Trials."

"I'll ask all three of you this. What are you trying to get people to walk away from these grounds with?"

"Well, a big one would be that we want them to know how Salem is so much more than witches," said McLaughlin.

AlKhowaiter was next. "I look at this place as a 300-year microcosm of not just Salem history, but American history. When you're walking through on the tour you start in the 1600s and the foundation of the city, and then you get to the Great Chamber and the Turners' connection to the Revolutionary War, and over time you're hitting these major events and this house is just always there and it's seeing all of this happen."

"You're so right," said McLaughlin. "It's far more than Salem. It's American history, and that's why we're a National Historic Landmark. That's a designation that's not given out lightly. It's reserved for the top 2 percent of historic sites. Those landmarks can be a building or a document like the Constitution. We're a whole district."

"What's the extent of the district?"

McLaughlin pointed at a map on her desk. "It's everything you see here. About 2.5 acres."

"That is big chunk of downtown Salem. Full of historic homes. And on the waterfront. That seems very expensive."

"Our organization has its challenges," said McLaughlin. "Maintaining three First Period homes and a couple of eighteenth-century homes is extremely expensive. Right now, there is half a million to a million dollars' worth of preservation work to be done." She got up from her desk and walked over to a window, where she pointed to various buildings. "That roof we put on there was $80,000. This roof that's going on Hawthorne's birthplace right now is $60,000." The building was under a spider web of scaffolding when I walked through it.

"All right, Ryan, what's your takeaway?"

"So Kara talked about Salem, Alyssa talked about the country. I would take it even further and talk about its importance extending to world history because of its connection to the China trade and the West

Indies and European trade. Money from that is what built this house in the first place."

"But Hawthorne—he's still, in 2015, the biggest part of the draw to the Gables?"

"People come specifically for him," said AlKhowaiter.

"Even though, aside from *The Scarlet Letter*, he hasn't really achieved the pop culture infiltration of some of his contemporaries?"

"*The Scarlet Letter* is a top-ten most read book in high school curriculum still," said Conary. "Although whether they actually read it, is another question. We get a lot of high school groups take the tour and we'll ask them, "How many of you have read anything by Hawthorne?" And the teacher will mention *The Scarlet Letter.* And then you'll learn over the course of the tour that none of the students actually read it." Turns out most people on the tours haven't read any Hawthorne, although they sell more of *The House of the Seven Gables* than anything else in the gift shop. "I don't know why he's not more popular. If you read any of his short stories, they're fascinating and would work well in today's culture."

"I mean, quality- and influence-wise," I said, "he's obviously right up there in American literature, but he just doesn't seem to have crept over the coolness threshold. He's not cool to culture today. Like Poe or Irving."

"It could be because he's known for his wordiness, and his prose is not exciting," said Conary. "And Irving and Poe are known more for their short stories and poems, more than novels. I don't know if anybody knows about, what is it, that *William Pym of Nantucket* novel, from Poe?"

"*The Narrative of Arthur Gordon Pym of Nantucket*," I said. The story is the closest Edgar Allan Poe ever got to a novel. It has its problems.

"See? I didn't even know the title. If more people read Hawthorne's short fiction, I think he'd be more popular today."

"Can you imagine if the guy had written full-on horror stories?" I said. "You guys would be set. It would be perfect for Salem."

"'Young Goodman Brown' is pretty terrifying," said AlKhowaiter. "I was reading that the other day sitting in his birth home all alone, and it got me."

The benefits of working at an historical literary site.

I had my chance to get a little spooked at the place after dark, myself. Every October, The House of the Seven Gables runs two dramatic programs on weekend nights. The first is called "Spirits of the Gables" and takes place inside The House of the Seven Gables. The second is "Legacy of the Hanging Judge," which takes place in Hawthorne's birth home and dramatizes some of the Witch Trials.

I was only able to attend one because of my schedule (there's always something to do on a weekend night in Salem in October), so, knowing I could get my fill of witches elsewhere in the city, I gave "Spirits of the Gables" a try. It was pretty fantastic. In almost every room of the Gables was an actor playing a character from the book. When our group entered the room, the character would address us as surprise visitors to the house and tell us a little bit about themselves and hint at their role in the larger plot. The ghost of Matthew Maule was dressed all in white with a powdered face and a noose around his neck. Hepzibah Pyncheon shoed us out of her penny-shop when she realized we weren't buying anything (and to get ready for subsequent groups, which came in every ten minutes or so). Clifford Pyncheon was in the attic, "fresh" from his thirty years of wrongful imprisonment. We met Colonel Pyncheon outside the house, trying futilely to get in. It's a great way to get a first feel for or to re-experience the novel.

Hawthorne City is a pretty big place with lots to see. Hawthorne's face might not be T-shirt-worthy like Poe's. Disney might not find his stories worth animating, like Irving's. And his reputation might not be able to beat all the cauldron-stirrers that surround some of the most important places in his life. But in many ways, that makes Hawthorne and his work a country ready to be re-discovered by the general populace. After all, just as the staff of the Seven Gables observed about the city itself, Hawthorne isn't only a Salem author. He is a New England one. And an American one. And, quite possibly, an international one. The Japanese Hawthorne Society, a sister society to the one Courtmanche is president of, currently boasts somewhere around two hundred members.

When Hawthorne published *The House of the Seven Gables*, the poet James Russell Lowell wrote him a letter that said, "Salem . . . will build you a monument yet for having shown that she did not hang her witches for nothing."

Lowell was prescient. Of all the Hawthorne sites in Salem, there's really only one place to look him in the eye. Even if you need a ladder to do so. The Hawthorne statue on Hawthorne Boulevard, where Alachi and I hung out during my *Bewitched* tour. The dramatic sculpture of the seated and bundled author was created by Bela Pratt and moved here for the opening of the Hawthorne Hotel in 1925 after twelve years at the Museum of Fine Arts in Boston.

Hawthorne might have had mixed feelings about his home city, but sure enough, that home has straightforward feelings about him.

I visited this statue many times in October. It was somewhat of a reset point for me in the midst of all the glorious Halloween chaos. And it always reminded me of a description of Hawthorne that I came across before moving to Salem. Evert Duyckinck, a nineteenth-century publisher, called Hawthorne "a fine ghost in a case of iron." Standing in front of that metal statue, it seemed the perfect description for an author who seemed to be both abashed by and obsessed with the hidden depravity of humankind. I could certainly see a ghost in that metal statue.

In many ways, he's the ultimate Salemite: a descendant of both salty mariners and sinful Witch Trial judges who can't quite come to terms with his home city, even as he is inspired by it. And in Salem in 2016, he's far from alone in that.

13

THE "CITY" IN WITCH CITY

Plummer Home

I was standing in the small kitchen of a community center for youth in one of Salem's poorer neighborhoods, holding up somebody else's phone to take a picture of the group in front of me. That group included the district attorney, a juvenile court judge, the chief of police, various officers, directors of the facility, and the mayor of the city.

I didn't really belong there.

The moment was during our stay on Chestnut Street. The night before the photo, Lindsey and I had been hanging out with Marshall in his house, talking about what we'd seen so far in Salem and what we were still aiming to see. At one point, I mentioned that I wouldn't mind talking to a police officer for the book. After all, they have witches on their shoulders every day and a front-line view of October and Halloween.

"What are you doing tomorrow?" Marshall asked me.

"Um, Salem?"

"You're coming with me. I'm on the board of something called the Plummer Home here in Salem, and I've have been invited to a small ceremony related to it in the morning. There will be officers there, and I can introduce you around."

The next morning, he drove me to the Point, one of Salem's lower-income neighborhoods, just south of the downtown area. There, he took me to a small building on the edge of Palmer Cove Park: the On Point Teen Resource Center.

On Point is a joint program run by the Salem Police, the Essex Juvenile Court, and the Plummer Home, the latter being a group home for troubled, orphaned, or otherwise needful kids. The main purpose of On Point is to provide impoverished youths who have broken the law with community service projects to pay off penalty fines and court fees and to avoid detention. But the center is also open to any of the neighborhood youth to use as a recreational facility.

Only a dozen people were present for the ceremony, at which the local district attorney, Jonathan Blodgett, awarded the On Point program a $16,000 check from funds that the city had accrued as a result of drug seizures.

Since I was the only one in the room who didn't belong in the photo, I took it for them.

It seemed a nice moment, and there was no press to document it. All press about Salem that month was, of course, of the black and orange variety. But for probably the first time that month, I was suddenly thinking more about the City part of Witch City than the Witch part. I mean, here we were, in an area of the city neither tourists nor locals make it to, yet still just a few blocks away from all the October madness. And while we all party on the Essex Street Pedestrian Mall, the city, the real city, has to keep ticking along. Crime has to be dealt with, reforms have to be implemented, budgets needed balancing, infrastructure needs maintenance, at-risk youth need to be cared for. And while there was a plastic orange pumpkin and some pumpkin-shaped cookies on the table in the On Point kitchen and all the officers had witches on their shirts, Halloween suddenly seemed far away.

I decided I wanted to talk to a few of those people in the photo to broaden—even slightly—this picture of Salem that I'm puzzling together. The first person was easy to get a hold of, since, you know, I knew a guy on the board.

We actually saw the Plummer Home before we'd ever heard of the Plummer Home. My family and I were spending the morning on Winter Island, a protrusion of parkland off the end of the broom, if you're still buying the idea that Salem is shaped like a witch. To get there, we drove up the broom handle that is Salem Neck, past the coal plant that was in the process of becoming a natural gas plant, and then rounded the end of Cat Cove.

Winter Island is surrounded by two coves and the Atlantic Ocean, with a tiny strip of land that all but prevents it from being an island. Still, in the fall, the small park feels like it might as well be an island, as secluded as it is. The park is only a mile and a half from the downtown, but people don't make it there much during the fall because they get stuck in the spiderwebs festooning the streets downtown. The beach on Winter Island is called Waikiki Beach, and dotting its interior are the remnants of an eighteenth-century fort called Fort Pickering. Off the coast, almost close enough to clamber over the rocks to touch, is the Pickering Lighthouse.

Winter Island is also the former site of a Coast Guard base. Its dormitory still stands, looming over the surrounding land, abandoned and overgrown, its white paint flecking off to show the red brick beneath. Around its base dashed tiny rabbits, and through the windows that weren't boarded up we could see graffiti from trespassers past.

On a bluff overlooking the ocean was a massive square green house. When we saw it from the beach, we assumed it was a private mansion because of its size and age and where it was placed, but the number of cars surrounding it made it seem more likely to be a bed and breakfast or boutique hotel. Turns out, that historic piece of architecture and ideal piece of real estate is the Plummer Home.

The Plummer Home was established in 1855 as the Plummer Farm School of Reform for Boys by a local philanthropist named Caroline Plummer—not to be confused with Caroline Emmerton, who preserved

The House of the Seven Gables. Originally, it cared for forty boys. However, in the last decade, it has experienced tremendous growth. It's now involved in the lives of two hundred youths a year, both boys and girls, with fifty staff and a $3.2 million budget. The Plummer Home encompasses five programs: the group home itself, a foster program, an apartment program within the home, a community apartment program, and On Point.

I eventually headed up to the Plummer Home to talk to its executive director, James Lister, whom I met at the On Point ceremony. Lister took me on a walk around the outside grounds to the community garden. He grew up in Haverhill and went to school for criminal justice so that he could become a probation officer for at-risk youth, but ended up in social services. He started as executive director of the home in 2005.

"So this was the original building that it all started in back in the mid-1800s?"

"Yes. And there is so much opportunity to learn about the history here that we haven't yet embraced. We're thinking about engaging Salem State to really dive deep. Plummer was probably one of the country's first female philanthropists."

"Why all the growth in the past ten years?"

"Well, that started with a lot of basic organization 101 tightening up, and then we got more focused about what we wanted to do at Plummer and planned a growth strategy around it."

"I was talking to Marshall about this place," I said. "And he told me there's a problem most charitable organizations and programs face called NIMBY, but that the Plummer Home doesn't really have to worry about that. Is that right?" NIMBY stands for "Not In My Back Yard." It applies to most development, but in this specific case, it means that even though people want the less fortunate to be helped, they don't actually want to see them or the mechanisms that help them. They want it to happen away from where they live.

"Yes, we're in a unique situation. We've been here for over 150 years, so we were here before most of those backyards were. And, of course, we're isolated out here on Winter Island, so in a good spot. But even so, the community support part of it is huge. We have people that bake cakes for kids on their birthdays and volunteers who do all types of things for the home and the kids." He told me the story of a kid named Joey who wanted to go to a truck driving school in Andover. However, due to the logistics and timing of the program, the Plummer staff couldn't figure out a reasonable plan that would accommodate it. But then one of the volunteers offered to take him back and forth to school. "It's the only reason that Joey graduated. No question. The community is so woven into this building in so many different ways."

"I guess I don't know how the foster system works. Is Plummer the only program for that in Salem?"

"The majority of foster care is done by state foster homes. For kids with higher needs, they mostly outsource that to nonprofit organizations like us, and there's no one else in Salem that does that."

We made our way inside the big, three-story building. The third floor held administrative offices, and the second was made up of personal living spaces. We stuck to the first floor. As we walked through, he greeted some of the residents and had quick conversations here and there. The first floor mostly contained rooms with communal functions: dining room, kitchen, living area. There was also a music room full of instruments.

"We offer a music program a couple of days a week, but kids will come in here to mess around for fun. Some have really embraced it. They learn instruments, play in bands, write their own music. We create a CD every year at the holidays and perform at open mic nights. It's pretty cool. We've performed at the State House three times."

"How are the kids' schedules managed? I assume that they're not on the same one, right?"

"Right. For the most part, when kids come home from school, depending on which school—they don't all go to the same school—they'll have dinner at 5:00. But the academic ability ranges here widely. For some kids we're paying for tutors because they're in advanced math classes, and with others we're hoping they'll get their GED. They all have their own individual treatment stuff, as well—therapy, substance abuse groups—depending on their needs."

"It seems pretty insulated from Salem, especially right now with all the October craziness downtown."

"Yeah, it doesn't impact us."

"Do the kids do anything for Halloween?"

"Yeah. I mean, it frightens us. It doesn't generally bring out the best.

So we try to gear up, but inevitably we have three or four kids that go AWOL and we worry about them, but then they show up at 1:00 a.m. or so."

A couple of teenagers walked by us and said hello to Lister in passing. "How do the kids see you? The guy who runs stuff?"

"That's pretty much it. I've been more removed from them over time. I used to be real hands-on with all the kids, and now I just get updates when we get new kids. I mean, each of our five programs has its own director, and in addition to that we have an overarching director of operations, a director of strategy and advancement, and a business manager, so I have a few layers between me and the kids. I do miss it, though. They're amazing kids and people when you get to know them. You can't help but be impressed by their resilience."

It was an idyllic site, doing great work, for some amazing young people, and it made me feel slightly guilty for focusing so much on haunted houses and witch logos. So I turned myself into the police.

I finally got to talk to a Salem police officer, just as Marshall had promised me. What I didn't expect was that I'd eventually find my way into the office of the chief of police.

I'm not a guy who has seen the inside of very many police departments, so all my preconceptions derived from 1980s New York City police movies. But what I found when I walked into the Salem Police HQ was a lot calmer than that. The waiting room was small and drab, and I was delighted to see on one side of the room a small display cabinet with a selection of Salem Police Department merchandise for sale, the witch patch featured prominently on all of it. They also sell it online and even had a table set up to peddle it on Essex Street one weekend.

I walked up the officer at his station behind a glass and metal partition. He asked for my name and made a quick phone call. He then buzzed me in and gave me directions to the chief's office.

The chief's office was roomy. A shiny shovel—of the type used at groundbreaking ceremonies—leaned in the corner. Near the end of its hilt on the window ledge was a bottle of wine with a Salem Police Department witch logo on it that I was later told was a gift on the occasion of the chief's swearing-in ceremony. Butler welcomed me warmly.

Mary Butler was born in nearby Lynn, but she grew up in Salem

and went to Salem State University. She was a long-time Salem police officer but was brand new to being chief, having only been appointed in April 2015.

"You and I met briefly at the On Point ceremony in early October," I told her. When she nodded remembrance—of the event, not me—I continued. "From what I understand the police department is part of the joint management of that center?"

"Yes, the property is owned by the city of Salem, and it ended up getting turned over to us. We considered making it a substation for the police department to make it easier for the neighborhood to reach us, but we didn't have the resources to staff it 24/7, and god forbid that a person ever comes knocking at the door for assistance when we're not there."

Instead, she told me, they decided to use it as part of the mandate of their Community Impact Unit, which they started in 2007 as a way to, according to the police website, "identify and address incidents that affect the quality of life of its citizenry." The On Point program fit the unit's goals. "What I love to see every time I go there," the chief told me, "is when younger siblings of these kids who have to be there are there, because it's sort of getting them engaged in the community early on."

"I've heard Salem described as a small city with big city challenges."

"That's true. We have an eight-square-mile city with forty-two thousand residents. We also have the largest hospital north of Boston, a power plant, a sewage treatment plant. We are the county seat for the Essex County court system, we have a number of state agencies here, we have a college that has around twelve thousand students, we have, like, fourteen parks. You have to wonder how we fit it all into those eight square miles."

But because of that, she explained, the city deals with all the issues of a big city—crime, infrastructure, poverty. "We have somewhere around 7 or 8 percent of people who make less than $10,000 a year in this city, so that's a challenge. And I can't imagine there's a crime that everybody else has that we don't have. Do we have them at a lower scale? Certainly." She used the national heroin problem as an example. Salem had fifteen people die in 2015 due to heroin overdose. "Fatals," she called them. "That's a huge number and really talks about what societally is going on. It doesn't matter where it is, whether it's Salem or Boston or San Diego or whatever. It's what's going on in our country at this particular point."

"Did you get a criminal justice degree at Salem State?"

"My degree was in social work initially, because Salem State at the time did not have a criminal justice degree. I eventually went back for a criminal justice degree, as well. But I truly believe my social work training was beneficial. Because if you think about law enforcement, what do we do? We're dealing with people. All the time. At some point I really hope somebody looks at melding human services and law enforcement together."

"Tell me about your path to the force."

"It was a long process, and a bumpy one." She explained to me that she originally took the civil service exam in 1981 when she was 21, and was met with resistance of both the political and prejudicial sort to joining the force. She met with one lieutenant who asked her what her parents' political claim to fame was. She was also told by a sergeant that the wives of the officers wouldn't like her working there. "I walked away going, 'Oh my God. I don't need this shit.' And decided I was going down a different path because this was insane." It wasn't until a new chief, Robert St. Pierre, was appointed in the mid-1980s that it seemed like things were changing in the police department. She took the exam again, and became a Salem police officer in 1987.

"So, witches. You've worn the witch patch most of your career . . . "

"I still do sometimes."

" . . . and the police uniform at its best is a symbol of authority and dignity and, for a lot of people, something to aspire to. Yet you guys here in this building have a cartoon monster on your uniform. Is there a general feeling about that on the force?"

"People who live in Salem and grew up in Salem, it has always been one of those things where we've always had it. It's a part of our upbringing. If you're on the football team or the basketball team or the gymnastics team, you're wearing a witch. You are a Salem Witch. But I have to say it is one of the most sought after patches in the country because it is extremely unique. I think people wear it proudly."

"Let's talk about Haunted Happenings and Halloween."

Throughout October, I had seen a lot of police. On the Essex Street Pedestrian Mall. On Derby Street. Each officer wearing a reflective yellow jacket over their uniform (unfortunately, it covered up their witch patches), driving around in cruisers with the witch on their doors. It felt like I was never less than a block from a police officer at any given time. But I have to say, it never felt like a police state. They clumped in loose, seemingly casual groups talking to each other. They were extremely approachable. I saw them giving directions whenever asked. I even saw them posing for pictures with tourists, despite the hidden witch patch. I told Butler about my observations.

"That's a purposeful strategy," Butler told me. "When you think about what's going on in policing today and how the police are viewed, you have to be careful. But it's also been a number of years of experimenting until we found what works in this unique situation. You have to be cautious as a police officer, but you don't have to be in people's faces. We're trying to make sure that people are safe and that they're enjoying their time here."

"But Halloween night, that's a whole different situation, right?"

"On Halloween night the strategy is still sort of hands-off. Unless people are hurting themselves or others, let them be, because crowds are volatile."

Another part of the Halloween strategy involves the large number of officers out on the streets. For the holiday itself, Salem brings in police from surrounding communities to bolster its resources. "If you saw the sheer numbers of people there, the size of the police presence shows that we are prepared for anything but hope for the best. Given the times that we're in, you really don't know, but I don't think we want to necessarily be so obvious that we're on edge. Because if we're on edge, then everybody else is going to be on edge. So the approach is, people need to be able to have a good time, and we're there if we're needed."

"Where are you Halloween, here in the office?"

"No, I'm on the streets."

She told me that the station has two command centers on that night, the usual dispatch they always have, which monitors the rest of the city, and then a special Halloween dispatch temporarily set up in a conference room and focused on the downtown area. They also have a team that does the booking for anybody brought in that night. They don't have the space to hold too many people, so they also have a bus out back so that after they're processed in Salem, they can be taken to facilities with more cells.

Later, she gave me a tour around the station. She took me down to dispatch, which was a bank of screens with real-life feeds from CCTV cameras around the city. She then took me back and showed me the processing room, the interrogation room, and the holding cells, which number only thirteen—nine cells for men, two for women, two for juveniles, and a large holding cell. They were all empty. The officer on duty told me that during the day, everybody is in the courts.

Back in Chief Butler's office, I had one last question for her. "Since you're so new as chief, do you have your own goals for the force?"

"I actually just unveiled to my officers my new mission statement. I didn't even show it to my husband before I gave it to the department."

"What does your husband do?"

"He's a police officer."

"A Salem police officer?"

"He is." She handed me a piece of paper from a stack on her desk. "This is our mission statement." It was a long document, more than a page in length in a small typeface, but as I perused it, I could quickly see both her criminal justice background and her human services background merging into a philosophy. She gave me a summary. "It talks about enforcing laws, protecting people and property, and helping people, but it also talks about reaching out to the community to be involved in it outside of high-stress calls. We deal with people, and I want officers to engage with them in a normal situation. And I want the people to see and engage with officers in a normal situation. We're guardians of the community, but only warriors when you need that. It can't be that we're pounding the pavement like we're pounding our chests. We're part of the community."

One consistent refrain I heard from almost everybody I interviewed was how much over the past decade the city had started to really embrace Halloween, and how good the city had become at managing Halloween night itself. Everyone also seemed to attribute it in no small part to the current mayor of Salem. Who just happens to have been mayor for a little over a decade.

The mayor was already high on my list of people with whom I wanted to secure an interview. But when I first started the project, the questions I wanted to ask were all about what it's like being the mayor of a spooky town and whether all the other mayors poked fun. I still wanted to know that. But everyone I talked to seeming to have such a high opinion of the mayor's attitude and vision around October altered the character of my line of questioning somewhat.

I found myself at City Hall on a snowy February afternoon. City Hall is on Washington Street, just steps from the Essex Street Pedestrian Mall and steps from the paved-over site of the Witch Trials courthouse. The edifice could only be more in the middle of things if it took over one of the pedestrian mall storefronts. City Hall is a two-story, red-brick building, with a gray-block facade featuring faux-pillars and topped by a small golden eagle, wings outspread. It could be an august-looking building it if weren't swallowed by the close-pressed shops of Washington Street.

But the building is extremely accessible, as is the mayor's office. I ascended the steps—the same steps where the personified Old Year meets her sister the New Year in Hawthorne's story *The Sister Years*—and then took a short flight of stairs just inside the entrance. That dropped me off right at the front door of the mayor's office. I was ushered inside and waited at a long table set up in front of the mayor's desk.

I looked around, saw a ceremonial shovel like I had seen in Chief Butler's office, another portrait of George Washington, a collection of law books, some family photos, and all kinds of other interesting odds and ends. This was an office with some history, and it was lived-in. The only witch I saw was on a small paper decoration stuck casually on a shelf. On one wall were portraits of the previous mayors of Salem, all graying white dudes. When the current mayor's portrait joins these, it's going to really stand out.

Kim Driscoll was born in Hawaii and grew up in Florida, thanks to a Navy father. She had grandparents in Lynn, and came to the area to attend Salem State University. "I wanted a change, to explore something different. And I wanted to know what changing seasons were like," she told me.

She got that change and then some. "I ended up falling in love with both the city and a husband." And then, of course, she became mayor of Salem. She was elected in 2005 and took office in January of 2006. As of my interview with her, she was less than two years from the end of her third term.

"I think not being from here impacts my perspective on the city. If you're not from here, you almost have a better view of the incredible assets this city has than if you grew up here. That's true of anywhere. Where you grow up you see more of the warts sometimes than the opportunities." I think the witch pun was inadvertent.

"You seem pretty accessible. Your office is just a stairway from the sidewalk. I realize it's a small city, but still, it's a city."

"I think that's good. One of the things that keeps people grounded who work in local government is that people have access. I mean, we're all on social media these days. That's one of the benefits of being in local government, I think, you're just closer to the people who are impacted by what's going on."

"Do you get angry villagers every once in a while knocking on your door with farm implements brandished in their hands?"

"Oh yeah, absolutely, and de-escalation is a good skill to have. It's one of the things that separates what I do from what a congressman does or what a state representative does. They're coming down if they're upset about something. And we have to address it, because there's a greater accountability. But that fosters this togetherness. We're collectively trying to figure out how to make our city work really well. People are super-engaged here. You're not going to feel isolated and alone if you come to Salem. It's welcoming."

"With the caveat being, if you can make it through October, right?"

"October happens here, yeah." It was a good answer, and possibly a good tourism campaign tagline, as well. "October in Salem has grown as Halloween has become the second highest consumer spending holiday in America. And we've ridden that shift up while trying to be mindful of the impact it has on residents, but also recognizing that there's a tremendous benefit for the local economy here. I think generally people understand that. There are residents who are purists, who love Halloween and wouldn't change a thing and think it's fantastic. There are others who I would say put up with it, and then there is certainly a group that despises it and thinks it hijacks our history. There's something to be said for that as well."

"I've seen that clash somewhat, but to me, the reason that it's happening is interesting, because it shows how vested in the community everyone is. They all see something worth fighting for."

"We're not going to change the fact that the first thing people think about when they hear Salem is witches. Our goal is to make sure there are other things, too, whether it's the maritime history or the awesome architecture or the dining scene. We know you know about witches, but here are some other really cool things that you may not know about our city."

"When you were first elected, I'm assuming you came in with a list of things you wanted to get done. Where was figuring out Halloween on that list?"

"Halloween twenty-five, thirty years ago, wasn't what it is now, nationwide or certainly within Salem. Somewhere around the early 90s it took a big turn where more and more people were coming. It became spring break for us. I think previous administrations didn't really want to own that. I mean, it's never been, and isn't today, an organized effort by a PR or event-planning firm. There's just a bunch of stuff happening that is not really linked, but people are still coming." She told me about previous Halloweens during which stabbings occurred and where the front page of the newspaper on November 1 would have a photo of the SWAT team. "I came on in January, and I said we've got to figure this out. People are coming, so we have to own it. So let's start figuring out what we're going to do. And then we've tried to learn and get better every year."

Some of those efforts at getting better, she told me, include encouraging people to take the train, instead of clogging the streets with cars. They have also outlawed weapons, whether real or fake and accompanying a costume. Rambo's headband? Ok. Rambo's machine gun or Bowie knife? Nope. They created a closing ceremony to remind people when to go home. They've attempted to space out the crowds by strategically placing the food vendors in different areas downtown. And they've created an after-action report process. "I just met last night with the Common Neighborhood Association to talk about some opportunities for building more art and culture into the event and spreading out some of the crowds or moving them to other venues."

"Right now? In February? For the next October?"

"Oh, yeah."

"Is Halloween on the agenda at all meetings?" I started to think of the Mayor of Halloween Town in Tim Burton's *The Nightmare Before Christmas*, running around on November 1 frantically searching for Jack Skellington with an agenda a mile long for planning the next Halloween.

"No, honestly, it's not. But that sort of work is never done, and we're always looking for ways to get better. Continuous improvement is the approach we take in local government."

"By continuous improvement, you're talking about managing the inevitable,"—her "people are coming" phrase kept running through my head—"or are you talking about making this a more lucrative event?"

"We don't want to lose money, but one of the things we do now is track what we bring for resources, what it costs us in extra public services over time." To do that, the city, like Destination Salem, divides the month into two parts: October 1-30 and Halloween itself. "We spend almost as much on Halloween as we spend on October 1-30, especially if it's on a Saturday. I don't want to overstate how much time we spend on it, but it's certainly something that has an impact, and I think we're always trying to communicate and improve it and elevate it." One of the examples she gave was that they jury the Essex Street Pedestrian Mall booths. "We don't want everybody selling light-up fangs and T-shirts. You get your pick of those, of course, but we try to bring in more art and more handmade wares to it."

And then she brought up PEM. "We'd love to figure out how to get the Peabody Essex Museum more engaged. We know they don't like costumes and witches, but there are opportunities there to elevate everything further." She talked about possibly hosting a WaterFire event on the South River. "Sure, maybe it's jack-o-lanterns for us, but still something that recognizes other areas of our city so that it's not all taking place in the same location downtown and inconveniencing the same residents. And we're talking about October, right now, but this continuous improvement applies to every month and every area we have: How are we placemaking in a way that is appealing to both residents and visitors?"

"Because even without October, you still need to be a tourism town."

"Right. And we try to manage the visitor industry and the quality of life for the residents simultaneously. We try to remind visitors that this isn't Williamsburg, we're not a museum, there are actually people living here, sleeping, going to work. And then on the other side, we try to remind the resident community that these are jobs. This is an important part of the local economy. We don't have the manufacturing base that we had at one time in Salem."

But the two groups aren't mutually exclusive, either, Driscoll continued. "The great thing about that is the amenities that you're looking to put in place for visitors are also great for the people who live here. It makes you feel good about the place where you live, even though it might be visitor dollars helping foot the bill for some of that."

We talked a little about the On Point ceremony, and I asked her about the general running of the city that has nothing to do with brooms and masks and crowd control.

"We have a little bit of a push and pull at times, between people who would rather us style ourselves a bedroom community of Boston instead of a city. But we are a city, we are not a town, which means that we are a little grittier, a little more diverse, and we always have been. In the 1700s, we had sea captain mansions on Chestnut Street around the corner from tenement houses on Boston Street for people who worked on the docks. That still exists today, so we've got some of the same challenges of a much larger urban area. But we also don't have as many resources because we don't have a seaport district or the relative wealth and space."

"But you have an international reputation, like the big cities."

"Yes, I could drop down in the middle of China and tell people I'm from Salem, and they'd have some idea of it, some kind of cognitive map for it. You don't have that type of experience if you're the mayor of Peabody or Beverly or Nashua. So we're a little bit higher on the curve than many middle economies because of our tourism." She then explained that it wasn't just the witches, but the fact that so many of Salem's historic buildings downtown weren't bulldozed as part of an urban renewal project. "I credit Sam Zoll in particular for that, one of our former mayors. We're making a living off that preservation right now. We have a place that feels special."

"For a city with such a successful preservation track record, it seems strange that no Witch Trial sites were preserved other than the Corwin House. There must have been some shame involved at some point, right?"

"I agree. The Witch Trials was a notorious part of our history. It happened here and it was awful."

"Looking back across the terrain of your service, more than a decade of it, what are your big successes?"

"I think our tourism and promotion is heading in the right direction. We've had huge fist fights in the past, like between the Witch Museum and the Peabody Essex Museum over which one is the marquee museum. It was crazy. But now we are more tightly aligned in terms of how we want the city to be promoted, we've got some resources to rely on, people are working together on that front." She explained to me that they also have a revenue-sharing program involving the city's hotel/motel taxes. Currently, 50 percent of hotel/motel tax revenue goes to Destination Salem to promote the city. And the city has more than two hundred new hotel rooms being built as of our interview. She also mentioned the development of the waterfront area and the transformation of the power plant.

"Coal's not the best thing in the world, yet we need the power and we rely on the tax revenue. It's our number one taxpayer. Having that come together as a redeveloped, smaller, cleaner natural gas power facility that will still provide revenue and energy, but also enable things like a cruise port and other active development activity there—that's great." Driscoll also mentioned city finances. Her grand prize for winning the mayor's seat was a $6 million deficit. "I'm happy to say we restored more professionalism to our government and got better at financial reporting."

"When October comes, does your routine and to-do list change? Are you constantly in some kind of command center mode, or is it all just happening out there while you're business-as-usual here in your office?"

"Halloween is a working holiday. And it takes a lot of prep. But we're not prepping in October for October." She explained that during the Halloween month, they focus on logistical planning, stuff like checking on traffic, making sure the stage arrived, keeping an eye on the weather. "The team has been doing it for eleven years now. We know people are coming, so it's not overwhelming. Still, it's hard to take an orderly approach to something that doesn't have a lot of order. It's not a ticketed event, it's not a gated area, it's everywhere. When one hundred thousand people are here, they control you more than you control them."

"So what does that witch symbol everywhere in town mean to you?"

"To be honest, I think it is an accurate depiction of Salem, because that is what people identify us with. If we changed that symbol or removed it from the landscape, I don't know that it would change how people view us. There's a part of me that says, 'Own what you are.' That's a strength we have. It is an identity, for better or for worse. But we do want to figure out how to broaden it. We're more than that for the people who live here. We're complicated, but we're fun. Hip and historic, we like to say."

"When you tell somebody that you're the mayor of Salem, and they go, 'You run Witch City!' does that feel belittling at all?" Again, I thought of the triangular, top-hatted mayor of Halloween Town.

"I think it's our personal challenge, for those of us who live here, to make sure people know that there's much more to our community than witches. But it is the first thing that people think of and an important thing, and one I don't think we'll ever change. It's like the Coca-Cola recipe."

"So you don't get tired of people bringing up the witch to you?"

"No, it's the greatest job in the world, it really is. Salem's a great place to be mayor."

14

WITCH CITIZENS

Witch's Brew Cafe

It might be easy to think of Salem as a city populated by Addamses and Munsters and Collinses and Elliotts. But for all the history, all the witchery, all the Halloween hootenanny, it's easy to forget that Salem is a city of forty-two thousand individual stories . . . that I am not going to tell you.

But I did want to tell you a handful of them. I don't claim that the people I interview in this chapter are in any way a representative slice of the population. But they have very Salem stories that I found interesting. This chapter includes people I sought out, people who sought me out, people I met by accident, and one person who was already a friend of mine. I dig her story, so let's start with her. I met Becky Shott at a murder scene about nine years ago.

It was on that same autumn road trip in 2007, when Lindsey and I went to Salem for the first time together. One of our stops was in Fall River, Massachusetts, a city about eighty miles south of Salem. We had rented a room at a bed and breakfast that was the site of one of the most notorious axe murders in New England history. Possibly in the history of the country.

In 1892, two hundred years after the Salem Witch Trials, Lizzie Borden was accused of tenderizing her father and stepmother with an axe. Lizzie was arrested, tried, and found not guilty; however, no other person was ever tried for the crime and doubts about her innocence were so serious that they still linger today.

My wife and I nabbed Lizzie's own room, and the way the house was arranged, we had to share a bathroom with the person staying in the room where the stepmother discovered the secrets of eternity. That was Becky. Becky is from Ohio, and she was on her honeymoon. She has since divorced, but I bring it up because you need to know that Becky is the type of person who sleeps at murder scenes on her honeymoon. Thumbs-up emoji.

We didn't communicate much aside from surreptitious knocks on the bathroom door. We saw each other during the group activities, like the tour and the séance, but that was about it. The next morning we all went back to our respective states.

Later, I wrote an article about our stay, and the owners of the Lizzie Borden House featured it on their website. Soon after that, the article was displaced by a TV clip of a Halloween episode of *The Today Show*. In it, host Natalie Morales, dressed up as Eddie Munster, was interviewing Becky about her time at the Lizzie Borden House and other spooky places she's been.

Turns out, Becky has been featured as an expert in a range of paranormal television programming, including one of my favorite shows in that genre, *Scariest Places on Earth*.

Becky had seen my article, too, and contacted me to be friendly. And then I guess we kept in touch. Because somehow, within the next two years or so, we all found ourselves living in New England. Lindsey and I were in Nashua, Becky in Salem. She lived on Orange Street, right on the heritage trail. At the end of her street towers the *Friendship of Salem*.

"Where else did you go way back in 2007, on that trip where we met you?" I asked her when I was finally able to trap her in a corner to interview her for the project.

"I spent all of my time, other than at the Lizzie Borden House, in Salem."

"I wonder if we crossed paths again without knowing it. Lindsey and I spent some time in Salem on our trip, too. But that was before you knew you were going to live here, right?"

"That was before. I had intentions of moving to Salem down the road at some point, but I didn't expect it to be as soon as it was."

"Why was it even on your radar that you might move here?"

"I've been interested in Salem since I was little, like sixth or seventh grade. I used to watch all those history shows and the haunted shows about Salem, and I knew it was a place I wanted to visit. When I began visiting here regularly and got to know the area, I knew I was going to move here someday. I just didn't know when."

"How often would you come up here when you lived in Ohio?"

"About three times a year. We stayed at the Stepping Stone Inn on the Common and the Morning Glory Bed and Breakfast over on Hardy Street. I ended up being friends with the people who run the Morning Glory because they have a ghost at their place."

Oh, did I forget to mention that Becky is a medium/clairvoyant? She sees ghosts. I think she's crazy. However, despite living in Salem, she doesn't sell her services. She has a normal job doing normal things. Every once in a while, she'll lead a paranormal investigation, but never in October. "I like to do that stuff more quietly," she told me. "You can't do it that way in Salem in October."

"You said you weren't planning on moving here so soon. How'd that switch get flipped?"

"I was in the Salem Library printing out my boarding passes to fly back to Ohio, and I just happened to look on Craigslist for places to rent. I found the apartment on Orange Street, so I took a quick tour and loved it. I gave the landlord a check on my way to the airport. I moved in two or three months later."

"So you liked the idea of Salem and all the spooky stuff, but liking it from afar or while you're on vacation there and permanently moving eight hundred miles away from your birth home to live there are two very, very different things."

"Yeah, but once I moved here, it felt more like home to me than Ohio ever had. And it's not just the spooky stuff. That's obviously interesting, but I love the architecture and the community and the festivals. I love October in Salem, but as soon as November 1 is here and the town is quiet, I feel like it's my town again. And the spooky is still around Salem after October, it's just that not everybody else is looking for it anymore."

"When you first moved here seven years ago, were you surprised by any part of Salem?"

"One of the biggest surprises to me was that more residents downtown didn't decorate for Halloween until maybe the night of. I've always been a huge Halloween fan. I went all-out for Halloween in Ohio. And then I got here, and I was so excited that there would be so many other Halloween people decorating with me. But there weren't."

Keep in mind, Becky's standard for whether a house is decorated or not is a little bit different than most. In October, her house is guarded by a twenty-foot-tall inflatable Grim Reaper (or dead farmer, if you're Esme). Crawling up the side of the house were spiders the size of compact cars. Winged demons dangled from poles. She gave up a driveway worth one hundred times its square footage in parking tickets and garage admission to erect a greenhouse-like shelter just for the purpose of filling it with life-size witches around a cauldron. Many a time in October, we'd be hanging out at her house and see tourists passing by stop and take photos of her place, as if it were one of the official sites on the heritage trail.

But I'd agree with her overall. I didn't see a lot of houses going all out. Businesses, yes. Restaurants, like crazy. But the only other private area in Salem I found that turns itself into a Halloween spectacle in October was an alleyway off Derby Street, a couple numbers down from the Witch's Brew Cafe and In a Pig's Eye. It's actually more like a walkway than an alleyway, as it's formed by the front sides of two houses that are perpendicular to each other and the side of a neighboring florist in one of those weird arrangements like I had at the Essex Street place. A white picket fence where the walkway ends at the sidewalk bars entry to the public, but you can see the whole scene from there.

Every year, the owners turn that area into wall-to-wall Halloween, like a haunted attraction without the walk-through. Giant cockroaches and spiders clamber along the walls, fake corpses bleed to death in bathtubs, a mannequin pukes into a barrel of toxic sludge, graveyard stones pave the ground, bodies wrapped in spiderwebs dangle from windows, a demon clown jack-in-the-box bobs hysterically, scarecrows that would deter human crime are staked into the ground, and blood-covered guillotines and other torture devices add the finishing touch. It's demented and festive at the same time. They need to put it in the Haunted Happenings brochure as a featured attraction.

Back to Becky, here's where her story gets another screw-turn. Not only did she move here all the way from Ohio, but about six years later she convinced her parents, Barbara and Al, to move to Witch City as well, leaving behind the entire life that they'd built out there in the Midwest. She convinced her sister Erica too, but Erica only made it as far east as a tiny, snowy town nestled cozily in the Green Mountains of Vermont, where she's the director of the local library, living, I assume, a life like you see in a Hallmark Channel show.

"Was your family always going to follow you here?"

"No, that wasn't originally the plan. It just worked out that way. But don't listen to them, they enjoy New England a lot more than they let on." They'd told me earlier that day about how bad Massachusetts drivers are and just how different New England is compared to Ohio. At least they're used to snow.

I actually thought Becky would be a constant companion throughout this book—or at least a babysitter—especially because our Essex Street place was mere footsteps away from her Orange Street place. However, right when we moved downtown, she started the messy process of moving to a new house that she and her parents had bought in the Witchcraft Heights district, right up against Gallows Hill Park.

In fact, that's where we were conducting the interview, in her living room, surrounded by unpacked boxes, the water tower with the witch on it visible through the window. She told me that you can hear coyotes out in the park, and that one time a group of them walked down her street like some scene out of *Wolfen*. She also told me with relief that her Witchcraft Heights neighbors decorate for Halloween a lot more than her downtown neighbors.

After seven years, she's not a jaded New Englander yet. When I asked her about the chaos of October, she was proud of it. "I love seeing people come into Salem and having fun in the city I call home and being overwhelmed by it all. At least now that I know what to expect and how to get around."

Being a "resident" changed the character of the chaos for myself as well. There was something about knowing that any second I could leave the crowds by walking two blocks away to a private bed and couch and television that made everything more fun. Of course, often I'd be sitting in the house, comfortable, watching a horror flick, when I would suddenly think, "I need to be out there. I'm missing cool costumes, I'm missing cool events, I'm missing random moments that won't be repeated."

"You've been here now seven years, you've bought a house, you've brought your family from five states away. And you still live less than a mile from downtown. You're more of a Salemite now than you've ever been. What is your favorite thing about Salem today?"

"The history. It just fascinates me. How many hundreds of years people have lived here. What has been moved and changed. I love that. Maybe it's a past-life thing," she added half-jokingly. "You know what my full name is, right?"

"I guess I don't." I knew Becky and I knew Shott.

"It's Rebecca Sara Bridget Shott." That's three Witch Trial victims in one name, give or take a spelling. If only her last name were Hanged instead of Shott.

"So have you seen a ghost in this house yet?"

"One. A lady at the top of the stairs in a pencil skirt like she's from the 1940s."

Seeing ghosts in Salem seems less screwy to me, somehow.

Chris Ricci got in touch with me through the Facebook page for my website. I met him at Rockafellas, where we sat next to a window so that we could see the Essex Street Pedestrian Mall in all of its glory. He was young, like twenty-five, and was carrying a bag of comics that he had just purchased from Harrison's, a comic book and pop culture shop a couple of blocks away. It also didn't take long for me to learn he was a big horror movie fan. He seemed like a very Salem guy. Except that he didn't contact me because he wanted to talk about the spooky side of Salem. What made him excited about the city was its music and arts scene.

Ricci works for Creative Salem, a local online publication dedicated to, according to its website, "Salem and the North Shore as hubs of creativity."

"We don't use the term artist," Ricci explained to me. "But our focus is on any creative person or group—writers, painters, app designers, anyone like that. We try to help them network and give them the proper press that they need in this city."

"What do you mean 'need in this city'?"

"The North Shore can be very sleepy. We want to get people out of their houses to check out galleries, to check out shows. And not just the big stuff that the local news would cover. There's so much that goes on every night in Salem and in Beverly and in Danvers and in Peabody that we want bring to light. And then here, in Salem, a lot of people visit and go up and down this street," he pointed out the window at the pedestrian mall, "and they see it as kind of a one-track thing, like cool curiosity shops and souvenirs. We want people to see everything else that's here."

Ricci grew up next door in Beverly, but spent a lot of time in Salem because his friends all lived here. He ended up going to Salem State for an English degree and then moved to Salem.

"Why Salem for you?"

"I was always more comfortable in Salem. There's always something to do here."

"Did you come to Salem on Halloween when you were growing up?"

"When I was younger, there was a big thrill in going to Salem for Halloween. But as I got older, I kind of viewed it as an inconvenience and it lost its nice, weird shine. You have to do a few Halloweens in Salem to really grasp it, and I did. But after those few times, it wore thin on me."

"Did you just come down and hang out in the streets?"

"I've done Halloween in Salem a couple different ways. I've done the walking-around Essex Street gawking at the costume thing. But I also used to visit my best friend, who lived over on Gallows Hill. There would always be something strange happening in the park around that time. At night, people would go up there to kind of escape what was going on here downtown. It would range from just people in costumes hanging out to very weird things that we couldn't explain. It's a spooky woods, lots of legends."

Ricci told me that he and his friend were sitting out on the porch one Halloween night looking out at the ballfield when they saw what looked like candlelight in the trees. So, being young kids steeped in Steven Spielberg and Joe Dante movies, they decided to check it out. They crept through the forest until they stumbled on what looked like a ritual of some sort, rows and rows of red and black candles and people covered in black robes standing among them.

"Don't the Witches do ceremonies on Gallows Hill on Halloween?"

"That's what we thought it was, too, but this was way late at night and seemed more . . . hidden."

The cloaked figures never moved, so after staring at them for a while, the boys got impatient/terrified and turned to leave, stepping on the clichéd dry stick on the ground in the horror movie that they were creating in real-time. But instead of the figures chasing them or worse (we've all read *Harvest Home*, I assume), the figures scattered, leaving the lit candles where they nestled in the leaf litter. The two ran back to the house, waited a few hours, and then snuck out there again. Nothing remained of the strange vigil they'd witnessed.

I wondered how many kids growing up in Salem had those kinds of stories. Regardless, when I get around to buying the rights to the Hardy Boys, I'm going to rewrite all their books and set them in Salem.

"Did anything surprise you about the city when you moved here?"

"What I didn't realize is the laidback atmosphere Salem has every other month outside of October. Every time I came before I lived here, it was always for an event or Halloween, and it was extremely busy. But on the days where nothing is going on, the city's pretty relaxed."

"Has the city changed much since you were a kid running away from mysterious cults in its parks?"

"Yes, and I think for the better. I see more of a pride of place here now and a progression of things that are going on."

Ricci then listed some specifics, including seeing more people his age in town and the way the city doesn't wait until October to have interesting events anymore. "We're trying to get people to come downtown all the time now. We're telling them, 'Don't be afraid of Salem.'" That should be another motto for Destination Salem.

"Does being a resident of 'Witch City' ever annoy you?"

"No. It's not something you can get mad about when you live here. The family walking around with witch hats and ice cream cones are supporting your town. Otherwise, you're an old man yelling at kids to get off your lawn."

"Do you see yourself staying in Salem for a while?"

"Absolutely. I remember when I was younger I had the typical teenage response that I really wanted to leave the North Shore area. I wanted to see cooler things and people. But I've seen plenty of cool things in this city. Does that mean I'm going to be a townie forever? Hopefully not. But I like being in a progressive town as opposed to a sleepy little town."

Speaking of the arts, required viewing for anybody writing even so much as a tweet about the city of Salem is the locally produced documentary *Witch City*, which hits its twentieth anniversary at the same time that this book hits the streets. The documentary is a hard one to find. A few of Salem's gift shops carry it, but not enough of them. I ended up buying it online from the director himself, Joe Cultrera.

Witch City was filmed in the late '80s and early '90s from the perspective—Cultrera's perspective—of someone who was born in Salem in the 1950s, grew up here, and then, after moving to New York City for a few decades, returned to find a town either transformed or transmogrified, depending on one's perspective. The documentary is full of intense conflict—the past vs. the present, Wiccans vs. Christians, entrepreneurs vs. historians, tourists vs. residents. It's everything I wanted this book to be before I discovered a city that had become, I think, more secure in its identity.

I emailed Cultrera almost immediately after the credits rolled on my TV screen to interview him. He owns a production company in town called Zingerplatz Pictures, but his work schedule as an editor has him in New York half the time. And he purposefully wasn't around in October—"Carney Month" he called it in our email correspondence.

Eventually, months after Salem had rolled up its Haunted Happenings banners, our calendars meshed, and we found ourselves one snowy day in December having tea at the Front Street Coffeehouse, half a block away from the Old Town Hall, and a regular place for Cultrera when he's in town.

"Where in Salem do you live?"

"I live near the police station, in the house where I grew up. It's in an old Italian neighborhood." He told me the house was built after the previous house on the site was destroyed in the Great Salem Fire. He also told me that his mother was born in that house and still lived there. She was ninety-seven years old. Were I not so deep into this book, I'd scrap the concept and make it about her. If only she had a documentarian for a son.

"I haven't talked to anybody with roots that deep in Salem."

"You should, because my viewpoint is that all this stuff you're writing about—Halloween, tourism, Witch shops—it's new. It's not cemented in the long history of Salem. And this whole thing is so centralized to the downtown area. The rest of the town doesn't really have that connection at all. Just people who have been here for generations, different ethnic groups, mainly European and Canadian."

"I haven't heard many people talking about the ethnic areas of Salem, although I have heard people boast of its growing diversity."

He laughed at that. "Sort of, I guess. I spend half of my time in New York at this point, and comparatively, it doesn't seem very diverse when I come here. Maybe compared to the rest of the North Shore."

Cultrera moved to New York for college, where he studied film at the School of Visual Arts in Manhattan and then stayed to work as a film editor. He moved back permanently to Salem in 2007, although these days, he returns to New York for months at a time because most of his clients are there. "But my family is here, so I'd rather be here."

Looking at his CV online, he has only directed three documentaries: *Witch City, Leather Soul,* and *Hand of God. Leather Soul* is about the manufacturing trade that existed in the area at the turn of the century, the same trade that sparked the Great Fire of Salem and took out the house on the site where he was born. *Hand of God* was about his brother and the abuses he suffered at the hands of Catholic clergy. All three were subjects that seemed close to his life.

"I make documentaries when I'm driven to do it. I'm not constantly hunting for a subject, though. Some subjects just pop up and I can't avoid them. That's what happened with the Salem piece." That project started when he and some colleagues got together to create a screenplay about Salem, but discovered the facts of the city to be far more compelling than the fiction they were planning.

The filmmakers had only planned to study the city for three months. However, because it was a side project for them, it ended up taking almost a decade from conception to release. The upside of that, though, was that they got to cover the creation of the Salem Witch Trials Memorial, from Arthur Miller unveiling the plans to Elie Wiesel blessing its installation.

On the back of the case for *Witch City* was a series of blurbs about the movie. The one that stood out the most was from Biff Michaud, the owner of the Salem Witch Museum. It read, "It's a disgusting piece of work. A low-budget piece of trash."

According to Cultrera, Michaud, whom he referred to as the "Donald Trump of Salem," actually threatened to sue him at one point.

"I don't remember the Salem Witch Museum being shown in a bad light," I said.

"I only included statements that he said directly to me," answered Cultrera. He even invited Michaud over to his house for a private screening, because he had the suspicion that Michaud had yet to watch the documentary. "I told him, come over to my house, we'll watch the film, you tell me what the problem is with it, and if it's really something we feel is out of order or out of character, we'll take it out. So he did." While Cultrera's mother was ironing in the background, the two men watched the documentary together. "There was one quote that he really disliked and thought we'd taken out of context, so I took it out of the film."

"So he approved it?"

"Yes, but he still doesn't really like it."

"In my opinion, say what you will about the Salem tourist attractions, but at least they're telling the story of the Witch Trials."

"I think the city should do that," said Cultrera. "If I were the mayor of this town, I'd invest in doing a real museum that is accurate and included some of the stuff from the Peabody Essex Museum so people have access to it. The city should tell the story, as much as it can, anyway. Nobody knows what the hell happened back then. But that's a whole separate issue from October."

"And you dislike October, right? I mean, I think the documentary was pretty clear. It seemed an honest depiction of the city at that time, but your perspective on that certainly came through."

"To me it gets worse and worse, the whole Haunted Happenings thing. I'd be fine with it if it were a week, but now it's like five weeks." Cultrera went on to explain that he makes sure he's working in New York every October so as not to be around all the "inconvenience." I was immediately reminded of the woman at the children's costume parade who was moving away from the city just because of the extreme month-long inconvenience of Haunted Happenings.

"I have a better attitude about the town if I miss all that," continued Cultrera. "I understand people have to make a living, and lot of people I know have restaurants like this coffee house that profit from it and I'd hate to deny them that, but I think that there's enough stuff that's interesting in this town that it could be a more spread-out story instead of all concentrated in one month."

"It seems to me like it's gotten a lot closer to that spread-out story these days, especially compared to when you did the doc."

"Summer and spring, it's gotten better, because it's a beautiful place on the water, but it definitely could have more of a full-time economy if they worked on it. It's like a crutch at this point. It's an easy kind of thing to do. We know that income's coming every year, so why don't we invest in something else."

"The witch's broom as a crutch," I said. "I've been thinking about it in marketing terms, where a marketer would look at the witch angle and say, this is your differentiator. You have great waterfronts, a museum, pretty architecture, and centuries of history, but so do Gloucester and Ipswich and Boston. All these neighbors can compete and in some cases, maybe a lot of cases, beat you on that. But nobody else has the witch."

"I don't deny that. I think it's great. It's just what do you teach them when you get them here? Do people actually walk away thinking about why those people died back then or are they walking away with a black hat on their heads? To me, that's just dishonoring their memory. If we could create a different kind of takeaway, I'd have no problem with them using it as a way to get people here. I just think it's a confused message that they're sending out."

"If the city's biggest problem is that it throws an awesome party for a month, that's kind of a cool problem, though, right?"

"I guess, but if you look at the roots of what that party is, they're kind of troubling. It's a really sad, dark history. Would we be doing this in a town in the south where people were lynched?"

"Valid, but on the other hand, the cheesiness has helped keep the names of the victims alive in a way that most, if not all, other witch sites in the world have not. We know Giles Corey. We know Rebecca Nurse. Some of that is literature and movies, but that all stems from Witch City. People wearing witch hats have had a big part in keeping the names of the victims alive. It might not be the best way to do it, but Salem has done it."

"That's a very American way of doing things, I think," said Cultrera. "The Disneyification of history. In New York, if you go down to the 9/11 memorial, they have their little museum now with a gift shop, and there are venders outside selling stuff. Going there gave me the chills because it started making me think about the connection to Salem and what's going to happen to 9/11 over the centuries. Is it going to get cheesier? Is it going to be a spooky, haunted place?"

"So your biggest thing is just that Salem should be able to marginalize the witch part of its tourism industry. That it has a place, just not on the welcome signs?"

"I mean, it has its own life at this point anyway. I don't know that you need to be putting a lot of dollars in promoting it anymore. That money should go to promote the rest of the city or to get behind the events that locals have pulled together. Like the film festival."

Cultrera is the one who started the Salem Film Fest, doing his part to broaden the appeal of the city beyond Halloween and witches. It's a documentary festival that takes place every March—"in winter when there's nothing to do around here"—and shows some three dozen documentaries from around the world. Over the course of its nine years, it has grown to become the largest documentary festival in New England.

"We have an amazing amount of volunteers putting an amazing amount of time into this stuff, and then you get kind of tired after it all because you don't feel like you're supported. The Film Fest itself has become a real major thing, but we're doing it on our own energy and the support of local businesses. We could really blow it up into a huge thing with the right support."

"So coast on the witches for a while, because they're not going anywhere, and put that money elsewhere."

"They're not going away. You don't have to promote it. Look, if sixty thousand people come on Halloween instead of eighty thousand people, is it really going to make any difference?"

"How does your family respond to it, since they can't flee to New York?"

"They're annoyed by it. Most people I know locally find it annoying. It disrupts their lives, and they don't really get anything out of it. In New York, when they have a festival or a parade, you can easily avoid it, there are many ways to get around. Here you can't. It just clogs up the city. So you're really giving a month a year of your life to the cause." Cultrera then talked about the people and businesses that open up shop for just a few months out of the year. "What do we gain out of that? Those aren't the businesses who are contributing to the local events. They take money, they leave, and then they come back and take more money. They're carnies. I wonder if we've been convinced as citizens that we have to support this. That it's good for the city. I don't know how it's good for the city. I really don't."

It's a sentiment I heard a few times, although Cultrera was the only one who went on the record with me. Another vocal critic of this aspect of Salem is Donna Seger, the Streets of Salem blogger I quoted in the "Fictitious Witches" chapter. She posted regularly on her blog about her distaste for what she feels to be the root cause of the celebration and its dubitable benefit for the city. Seger went so far as to write a letter to *The Salem News* after Halloween: "Just look at what happens to our city. The lack of respect that we have extended to our ancestors is evident in the places that are most connected to them: the Old Burying Point on Charter Street and the adjacent Witch Trials Memorial. All month long I saw people using these sacred places as mere props to showcase their costumes . . . Is this how we want to be remembered?"

"It's the kind of thing that sounds minor, especially if you put it in a book," continued Cultrera. "Oh, it's just locals complaining about nothing, get over it, look what it does for the city. But I don't know what it does for the city."

Hopefully, I'm not portraying Cultrera too cynically. He was a lot of fun to talk to, and it's his bad he's so quotable on the topic. What's probably not coming out in the interview is his genuine affection for his home city. Before our meeting, he had just interviewed someone, a vacuum cleaner repair man, for a series of documentary vignettes he was filming to show before the main features at the upcoming film festival. He sent me a link to a series of about twenty-five of them, and they featured everything from the life of a security guard at PEM to a night at a bingo hall to the musical philosophies of an ancient honky tonk pianist to a shelter dog visit at an elementary school. There was a cobbler, a pasta maker—even the sewage treatment plant got a spotlight. But there wasn't a single kooky tour guide or Witch shop counter in any of them.

And that's probably a good enough segue to the next Salemite.

Margaret Press is a breast cancer–surviving airplane pilot/software designer with a doctorate in linguistics and a bibliography of true crime books and mystery novels, all of which involve Salem. She welcomed me into her home in Salem Willows with, "I don't know why you're here. I'm the least interesting person you could talk to in Salem."

She led me through her house to her back deck, where we settled down into patio chairs to talk. Her yard only extended a few yards past the deck, where it ended at the waters of Collins Cove, the type of place and view that could turn anybody into a writer. Above us, I could hear the seagulls yelling at each other, comparing notes for where to find the parking lots with the most dropped French fries.

Press isn't from Salem originally. She was born in Los Angeles, and her route across the country to Witch City was a strange one. She went to college in Berkeley during the '60s, and later UCLA. "My doctoral thesis was a grammatical analysis of an American Indian language called Chemehuevi. It's probably a dead language now, sadly." While she was getting her degrees, she married an astrophysicist whose first job out of graduate school was across the country at Princeton, in New Jersey. "Going from Venice Beach to Princeton was like being taken out of the sunlight and thrown into an icy pond," she said.

But moving to New Jersey made the subsequent transition to Cambridge, Massachusetts, much easier when her husband transferred to Harvard. Meanwhile, Press kept busy, despite there not being much of a market on the East Coast for an expert in obscure southwestern Native American dialects. She had a daughter, took flying lessons, and learned how to program, which is how she makes her living today.

Later, she would divorce and move to a trailer park in Peabody ("I wanted to be mobile, but it turns out mobile homes are not at all that,"), and then she married her flight instructor and moved to Salem in 1987 because she really wanted to live on the water. At the time, Salem had the most affordable coastal properties on the North Shore.

And then, soon after she moved in, she killed her neighbor.

"One day in March I was walking around the Salem Willows. I'd already started soaking up Salem's specialness, but walking around in that dead park in the winter is just the best time. There's a little building down there that's now a clam shop, but back then it was a men's restroom called the Men's Cottage. It was painted green and all shuttered up then, and it looked like a fabulous place to put a body in." That thought could have taken her down a few roads, I guess, but the one Press chose was to write a mystery novel.

So she did. And then she found a victim.

"We had a neighbor, a former postman, who was really annoying to the neighborhood because he let his dog run round and mess on everybody's lawns every day. One day my husband got into a tussle with him, and after a bit of shoving back and forth, the guy fell down." And it was at that point that they learned something new about their neighbor, that he had a prosthetic leg, which flew off in the fall. It sounded like something straight out of a Flannery O'Connor story. They went to court over the matter, where the postman defended himself with, "I've probably been in a hundred fights with people, and no one's ever taken me to court before."

"I guess I felt a tinge of rage," Press continued. "I own a house, I can't move, and we have a neighbor who is going to come down and fight and be an annoyance? I realized that there's nothing worse than having a problem with a neighbor. So I weaved him into my story." And in 1992, *Requiem for a Postman* became her first novel.

"Did the postman ever find out that you killed him?"

"No, ironically he died before it came out. But I always worried about his wife finding out. People in the neighborhood figured out who it was immediately. One woman invited me to her women's drinking group because they had passed my book around and wanted to grill me about everything in it."

Press would go on to write another mystery using the same Salem cop as her protagonist, but in the process of researching that first book, she befriended members of the Salem Police Department.

"They were great. Every Saturday night for two years I'd go down and hang out with them at the office or on ride-alongs. I was the old lady in an L. L. Bean raincoat and a notebook and purse, and they'd bust in a door and the guys on the other side would say, 'Who's she?' and they'd say, 'She's with us,' or, 'She's from immigration.'"

They let her go through all the old case files—"They don't have a lot of murders in Salem"—and even let her sit in on the interrogation of a career safe-cracker who had been arrested for some scheme around stolen baseball cards. "He was going through heroin withdrawal, and they took him out of his cold cell and let him relax in the detective's warm office, bought him some McDonald's cheeseburgers, and he confessed to fourteen different cases." It all went into her next book *Elegy for a Thief*, right down to some of the exact conversations she had heard the police have.

But that relationship with the Salem police also set her on the course for her true crime book project. While Press was concocting an imaginary crime out of a boardwalk bathroom and a one-legged postman, a real crime happened in the Willows.

In 1991, a Willows resident named Martha Brailsford disappeared. When her husband couldn't find her, it was discovered the last place she was seen was on a sailboat owned by one of her neighbors, a recently fired Parker Brothers employee named Tom Maimoni, who was also married. When questioned about it by police, he claimed she had fallen off the boat when a rogue wave hit it.

When the body didn't turn up, one of the police captains went to Laurie Cabot to see if she could dig up some spectral clues since they lacked any physical ones. But, that same day, in a New England twist, a lobsterman pulled her body up with one of his traps. It had been weighted down with a diving belt and an anchor. Maimoni fled Salem, but was captured days later after breaking into a Maine cabin near the Canadian border. He was found guilty of murder and given a life sentence.

Because she was friends with the detectives working on the case and it was a crime that affected her own neighborhood, Press felt like she should write an account of the crime and investigation. She called it

Counterpoint: A Murder in Massachusetts Bay. Counterpoint was the name of Maimoni's sailboat.

"Tragic case," Press told me. "So sad for the family. Tom Maimoni was a classic sociopath, and the trial was fascinating. I interviewed him a few times. He claimed to be innocent and told me, 'My mistake was coming to Salem. My grandmother always warned me never, never go to Salem.'"

Even though the Maimoni case was a solved mystery, Press's book became the basis for a segment of an *Unsolved Mysteries* episode. Press mentions another Salem missing woman case in the book, so the producers decided to use the Maimoni case as a stepping stone for the second case, and to get Laurie Cabot involved. A murder, a missing woman, and a Witch was the perfect case for Robert Stack to narrate in his spooky, deadpan way. The television crew came to Salem to film a reenactment. Press then found herself in an unmarked cruiser with the lead detective, the captain, and Laurie Cabot, heading to the White Mountains because Cabot had received a vision that the body of the missing girl was there.

It was a cold, rainy day. When they arrived, the film crew rolled some crime scene tape around the wet trunks of a few beech trees and asked Cabot to do her thing. "All I could think," said Press, "was that this is such a hoot, I can't believe we're doing this." On the way back, the Witch, the mystery writer and the two policemen stopped at the house of the captain's mother in New Hampshire for milk and cookies.

"When it aired on Halloween, 300 calls came in, and 298 of them were people wanting to reach Laurie Cabot," said Press. The next spring they re-aired the show, which nabbed them a lead definitive enough for them to close the case. The missing woman had been found in New York, doing fine.

"So we've been talking about Salem for an hour and a half, and you've not brought up October yet. That's interesting to me."

"Well, one of the things about this neighborhood is that it's a pretty quiet one." I guess if you don't count all the shoving matches and murders, real and fictional. "Haunted Happenings doesn't make its way up here. I don't even really get any trick-or-treaters because it's mostly old-timers in this area. The big times for this block are in the summer. Like the Fourth of July or Black Picnic, when we'll have the overflow cars parked all along our street." Black Picnic is an annual Willows event that started in the 1700s when local slaves would congregate on their day off. Over the centuries it became more of a church event sponsored by black congregations in the surrounding cities. These days it's one of Salem's many family festivals.

"Do you like Halloween in general?"

"I love Halloween. I've walked downtown for it for many years. It gives me a great feeling. I think Halloween is as much about the adults as the children these days. It's the only time all year when you're allowed to express yourself, to dress up and be kooky and get away with it."

"Do your neighbors, the 'old-timers,' share that feeling?"

"I think most of the old-timers don't go downtown for it. But Haunted Happenings is a fairly new phenomenon. It started just before I moved here in the late '80s," she said, echoing Cultrera's earlier sentiment.

One phrase she kept using throughout the interview to describe her life in Salem was "stranger in a strange land." "After twenty-eight years," I asked her, "do you still feel that way?"

"Yes, it's still somewhat foreign to me, but sweet. It's like I'm looking into a lit house. The fire's going, but I'm on the outside. That's okay, that's how I was raised. And you don't want to get too comfortable by that fire, anyway. In life you get energy from being a little out of kilter, a little out of step with the people around you. That's part of why I fell in love with Salem. It would be a lot harder for me to write about California, because I grew up there and never really saw it."

The only things that seemed to mar Press's interesting little life in her interesting little city with her idyllic little house on the cove were the cardboard boxes that covered the floors of her house. About four months after our interview, she retired from her programming job and moved back to California so that she could see her daughter and grandchildren more often. "It's breaking my heart to leave," she told me.

We should toast to Margaret Press's interesting life in Salem, so let's hit a bar.

One of the reasons I could never move to Salem myself is the restaurant scene. I would go broke eating out every night. There are enough restaurants downtown to make for a decent variety of choices, but not so many that you'd feel bad for picking just one or two to be your regular places. And then you'd make them your extremely regular places.

In October, most of those restaurants go full Halloween. They paint monsters on their windows, sell Halloween-themed art on their walls, hang ghouls from their ceilings, and cover everything in blood and spiderwebs like there's no such thing as a health inspector. Eating inside a haunted house attraction is one of the delights of Salem in October. Every one of them also does Halloween parties throughout the month, with themes ranging from a Zombie Prom to a Heaven and Hell Party to a Voodoo Ball and a Vampire Masquerade.

And the October-themed cocktails, man. That's the subtext of the reason I couldn't move to Salem. It would escalate my alcoholism far beyond semi-functioning drunk. I wish I had kept a journal of all the spook- and autumn-themed cocktails I tried in those thirty-one nights. Judging by the few, blurry menu photos on my phone, there was at least a Witch's Kettle, a Candy Corntini, about a dozen kinds of pumpkintini and apple cinnamon-tini, a Skeletor Shot, Satan's Cider, a Bobbin' for Apples Fishbowl (which was served in an actual fishbowl . . . with two straws). And I swear I had something called Gary Busey's Spook Juice, but can't find any confirmation of it.

One night when friends came into town, we all went to Rockafellas and did their Helltini, which is a year-rounder for them but especially relevant in October. Ordering those drinks involved signing a "mortality" waiver with Satan's face on it, and then lighting the insides of our faces on fire with a brew of vodka, Fire Water Schnapps, ginger ale, Jagermeister, and something called Hell Water. But we all made it through with only first-degree burns in our throats. The empty glasses on our table entitled us to Helltini T-shirts, which we all promptly threw on and then marched across the street to get our picture taken with the Samantha statue. And that was just the start of that night. Let's just say I haven't been able to even look at my Helltini shirt since, much less wear it.

Another time Lindsey and I were enjoying a night out by ourselves when suddenly we were surrounded by lurching sheet-ghosts. I asked one of them what was happening, and she said, fully three ghost-sheets to the wind, "We're doing a Boo Bar Crawl." She elongated "Boo" for a good fifteen seconds across four octaves. "You want to join us? You have to become a ghost first." It sounded vaguely threatening, but fun.

Oftentimes, I would go out to the restaurants at the end of the night, when the tourist crowds had ebbed, pull up a barstool, and have a drink while I jotted down my notes for the day. I was in the Witch's Brew Café one night when a guy came in and yelled out into the small space, "All the tourists gone?" Everybody cheered (while I ducked deeper into my drink and journal) and then the barkeep passed around a grid for everyone to place their bets on the next Patriots game.

Another night, at the very same restaurant, I found myself either just toasty enough to be friendly or running away from some guy at the bar telling me too many details about his witch victim ancestors—maybe both—but I introduced myself to a man who was drawing in a sketchbook and having a nightcap with his wife. Their names were Lee and Amy Wolf. Lee showed me his sketchbook, which was full of monsters, but I quickly put that down when I found out the pair owned a greasy spoon called The Ugly Mug and a place called the Lobster Shanty.

Now, I'd met a few business and restaurant owners that way, hitting the bars late at night, each one there to let off steam after a wildly busy October day. But this meeting was special because of that second eatery, the Lobster Shanty. This was my favorite place to make a fool of myself in all of Salem.

The shanty is a tiny, nautically themed restaurant on Artists Row, a short stretch of pedestrian walk that connects Derby Street and Front Street, ending at the front steps of the Old Town Hall. The area was deeded to the city in the early 1800s by a Derby and a Pickman and was originally a marketplace. The walk is lined on both sides by little buildings that are barely more than booths that house crafts from local artisans.

The Lobster Shanty is the only restaurant on that strip, a small little place that seats only thirty inside, plus outdoor seating. It's been around since 1980, and I became a temporary regular almost entirely because of something called the Hot and Dirty Pickle Martini, on which I spent most of my book advance.

The Hot and Dirty Pickle Martini is a concoction of pickle juice, gin, and Sriracha, garnished with a pickle spear. The secret is the type of pickle brine, Maitland Mountain Farm, a local Salem product.

In hindsight, maybe that's why I approached the Wolfs. Out of vague recognition. I'd seen Lee at the Shanty more than a few times, but had assumed he was one of the many regulars who frequented the joint, tourists be damned.

Judging from the press I read, Amy is usually the voice of the Shanty, but Lee assented to an interview with the wobbly guy who claimed to be writing a book. We held that interview, not at the Shanty, but at Gulu-Gulu Café, a restaurant in Lappin Park with a coffee-house kind of vibe—couches and open mic nights, you know the place. When we entered, all the staff knew him by name and treated him like the owner instead of a direct competitor. He was wearing a Lobster Shanty T-shirt. "I don't have any other clothes," he joked.

Wolf was born in Yorktown Heights, New York. "Good old Washington Irving country," he told me. "We lived on a street called Ichabod Court." It's about fifteen miles north of Sleepy Hollow, in the Hudson Valley. His family then moved to Windsor, Connecticut, the hometown of Alice Young, the first person to be executed for witchcraft in the Colonies.

Wolf attended the Rhode Island School of Design and became a freelance illustrator. His work has appeared in *The New Yorker* and *Rolling Stone* and newspapers like the *Washington Post* and *Los Angeles Times*. "My two biggest influences are Cubism and Dr. Seuss."

Lobstertinis from the Lobster Shanty

Wolf moved to Cambridge to continue working as an artist, but soon found himself employed at a restaurant for the regular paycheck. "And then I kind of got sucked into the culture, which is very easy to do." He was a regular at the Cambridge Brewing Company, and then ended up getting hired there. Before he knew it, he had thirteen years of restaurant experience.

"What's the order of wife, Salem, restaurant owner for you?"

"I met my wife in Cambridge. She's from Marblehead, which is why we ended up this way. We saw an ad for an apartment on Chestnut Street, and my wife had always wanted to live on Chestnut Street. So that was our first place in Salem."

His wife attended the culinary school at Johnson and Wales in Providence, the same place Emeril Lagasse graduated from. Meanwhile, Wolf plied his twin trades of artist and restaurant employee. He worked for Rockafellas for a time, and so had a front row seat when the Samantha statue was installed across the street.

Once the Wolfs found themselves one part restaurant man and one part chef, they decided to become restauranteurs. When they found out that a restaurant they frequented was up for sale, they went there and ordered beers and the deed to the place.

The Lobster Shanty opened under the management of the Wolfs in 2007, making 2015 their eighth season. But it was in 2010 that the restaurant really took off thanks to a visit from a guy with wraparound sunglasses, bleached hair, and a goatee.

The Food Network show *Diners, Drive-Ins and Dives,* hosted by Guy Fieri, featured the Lobster Shanty on its show solely on the rumor of the Lobstertini. The Lobstertini is a vodka cocktail mixed with lobster "essence" and garnished with a lobster claw. That's the actual signature drink of the Shanty. I tried the Lobstertini—a drink I later heard one regular call a "tourist-tini." It was fine, a good Instagram opportunity. But it was no Hot and Dirty Pickle Martini.

"Sometimes I would order the Hot and Dirty Pickle," I told Wolf, "and then people around the bar would see this weird pink cocktail with a pickle sticking out of it and start ordering it."

"There's a name for that," he told me. "I mean, it probably has a real name in psychology, but we call it the Nacho Effect. The theory goes that when a plate of nachos goes out, everybody who sees it suddenly wants nachos."

"What is the restaurant culture like in Salem? I mean, you own the Shanty, I met you at the Witch's Brew, and here we are at Gulu-Gulu. I assume it's not steak knives at dawn here."

"My take is, the more the merrier. The more restaurants we have up here, the more it makes Salem a destination."

The Shanty closes down for about ten weeks every year, from the middle of January to April 1. "Historically, it's always been that way. Being in a New England town, especially near the water, there are places that are just seasonal. It really is a shanty. The floor outside the building is the same floor inside."

"Do you guys make most of your year in October?"

"We do really well pretty much all summer. But October, there's a line out the door."

"So what's changed since you moved here?"

"The downtown is much more vibrant. That pretty much started with Rockafellas, I think. There were so many buildings on Essex Street that were just burnt out, old buildings, nothing in them, and now they're all condos and shops and restaurants. They still turn over, and Essex Street still kind of suffers and you'll see some empty storefronts, but when we came here in 2001, it was a lot more barren."

"You've lived here, you've worked here, you own here, you can't be more here."

"I can't imagine living anywhere else."

We got on the topic of witches briefly. "Does the Witch City reputation annoy you at all?"

"Oh no, not at all. It's Salem. I say Witch City all the time. I mean, yes, it's commercialized, and yes, you can only have so many T-shirts, but at the same time as much as I kind of don't like that I still want to embrace it, because if people find it fun, great. And there's something about living in a place where you see people wear costumes all year round, well, for one it's fucking insane, but it never stops being entertaining. I don't like when people get worked up about it." He paused. "But it can drive anybody crazy who lives here after a while just because you want to be able to live in a normal place sometimes."

"And that'll never happen in October."

"You just plod through it. But then next thing you know, it's over. As a business owner, you're disappointed that it's over, but I like to think we're a city that doesn't rely entirely on October like it's a month-long Black Friday here."

Eventually, the conversation turned back to the Lobster Shanty.

"I think the Shanty is a unique place," he told me. "So unique, in fact, that if it can't be where it is, there's not going to be a shanty. The Shanty is not something you can pick up and move. We kind of have a theory that we're not really its owners, we're just the stewards of it. We are going to be very careful about who gets it after us."

And I hope that one of the requirements for its next owners is that they keep the Hot and Dirty Pickle Martini on the menu.

But there you go. Some of the people in your neighborhood when you live in Salem. They couldn't be more different from each other, except that looming large over the landscape of each one's psyche—whether they want it there or not, whether they've lived in Salem a year or all of their lives—is a crooked-nosed creature with scraggly hair and a pointy hat. Witch cackle goes here.

15

H-DAY

"It feels like Christmas morning," said Lindsey as we awoke in our Essex Street house on Saturday, October 31st, in Salem, Massachusetts.

I didn't need her to explain. I felt it, too. As if something momentous had arrived, and the world had shut down for it. As if time was standing still. As if we couldn't leave the city because there was nowhere else to go except Chinese restaurants.

However, outside our windows, the ones that faced Essex Street, as they had done for more than 160 years, we could already see a steady trickle of people arriving in costume, monsters and movie characters and superheroes and animals and less identifiable things. It definitely wasn't Christmas morning.

We had so far experienced what seemed like thirty days of Halloween. But now it really was Halloween outside the walls of the house. When I opened the door that morning, I felt like I was Neil Armstrong and the moon was full of uninhibited and strangely clad beings.

We knew we were in for a busy, exhausting, awesome day, so we decided to pace ourselves, to spend the morning carving our hard-won pumpkins into jack-o'-lanterns.

Acquiring them had been a suburban adventure. Our normal Halloween rhythms were completely shattered by Salem. I didn't have a caramel apple until a few days before the actual holiday. I don't think I made popcorn balls at all. We missed the animated version of *The Halloween Tree* completely. We didn't drive into the mountains up north to check out the foliage. And we didn't get pumpkins until October 30.

We drove to three different grocery stores looking for those pumpkins. All we found were red and green decorations and Christmas cookies. Maybe that's another reason why the next day felt like Christmas morning. Every time, I had to come out to face Esme and her heartbreakingly hopeful question, "Did they have pumpkins?"

Finally, we found a small farm nearby. Strewn across the ground like they had been dropped there in disgust were small piles of soft, undergrown pumpkins ready to be pulped for fertilizer for next year's crop. We sorted through them and grabbed four of the least rotted ones, not making eye contact with the cashier as we placed them on the counter with a series of squelches. Mine wasn't even orange, it was pale yellow, like the color of the inside of a banana peel.

The pumpkins lasted until morning, though, and I walked over to the convenience store near the house to get some newspapers on which to gut them. When I approached the rack, there, on the front page of the *Salem News*, was a large picture of me and Esme. She was in her peacock costume, I was in more boring clothes, and we were both blissfully smiling while behind us Steve the Vampire, his fangs bared, raised his arms in attack.

The previous day, we had gotten our traditional photo with Steve. While Lindsey was taking it, I saw a guy with a camera the size of a dishwasher standing behind her taking his own photo of us. It didn't strike me as odd. This was the Essex Street Pedestrian Mall, after all. Every person has eight cameras aimed at them at all times. But after we were done with our photo, he explained that he was a newspaper photographer and asked for our names in case they used it. I didn't think anything of it. I'm sure he took scores of photos that day.

I grabbed the convenience store's entire stock of newspapers and dropped them face-down on the store counter. "We're carving pumpkins on them," I explained to the cashier. I returned home, threw the newspapers on the table, and told Lindsey, "Our visit is front-page news."

While we were carving the pumpkins, letting the softer parts of their rinds dictate the shape of the faces, I got an email from Michael Vitka, the tour guide I shut down the Hawthorne Hotel bar with. "Happy Halloween!" it said. "If you get caught in the crowd tonight let me know, there is a Halloween party for the tour guides we could sneak you into." That's a show somebody should make. Salem tour guides doing their weird jobs and then partying afterwards. It could be done as a reality show. Call it *Witch City Walkers*. Or as a quirky independent movie, in which case, they could call it, I don't know, *A Season with the Witch*.

Finally, around lunch, we realized it was probably time to dive into the deep end. And that meant costumes. Because for this, our Halloween in Salem, I had to dress up. Obviously.

The kids were easy, of course. They both had already worn their costumes plenty of times throughout the month, Esme in her peacock-inspired dress and mask and Hazel in a green triceratops outfit.

As for me and Lindsey, at some point we decided not to do a couple's costume, and that point was right around the time I figured out what I wanted to be: Vincent Price from the 1964 Edgar Allan Poe–inspired Roger Corman flick, *The Tomb of Ligeia*. His character, Verden Fell, wore a top hat, a long black overcoat, a black cravat, and these strange sunglasses that had side panels. I figured that it didn't matter if it was too obscure a reference for a costume, that if people thought I was an old-fashioned undertaker or a Salem tour guide, it would work.

Lindsey went as a ghost bride. She wore an antique bridal dress and painted her face white, with dark circles around her eyes. "I picked the costume," she told me one day in consternation before the Halloween weekend, "because I just happened to have an old wedding dress lying around and thought it was a good idea. But I've already seen like half a dozen ghost brides since we moved here."

And that's how a peacock, a ghost bride, a sun-sensitive bigamist, and a triceratops in a stroller ended up on the streets of Salem. And, man, was it a party.

The pedestrian mall was packed, but not really in a claustrophobic way—at least not yet—and not so much that it was impossible to get a stroller through. The hardest part of making our way through the downtown, though, was that every few steps, somebody stopped us so that they could take a picture of the Ghost Bride. But we had gotten used to that, too. That had started the night before.

We wore our costumes for the first time on October 30. Marshall and Elaine had invited us to a Halloween party that night. The landlord for their office was a local drywall magnate who threw a big Halloween party for his company and friends. "There will be some good food and a high-end rock band. We'll put you on the guest list. You should come," said Marshall.

We had tickets to a Halloween party on Halloween night already, but we figured it only made sense that as part of our massive Salem Halloween weekend we attend two different parties. So we had our babysitter watch the kids and took off into the night of All Hallows' Eve eve. The site of the party was about a mile and a half from the house, but the route would take us directly through the pedestrian mall. We decided to walk there, stopping at the halfway point—Rockafellas—for drinks.

But, man, did we get stopped on that first leg a lot. There must be dozens of photos of Lindsey on the socials of people from all over the world. Every once in a while they asked for me to jump in, but mostly they wanted to get their photo taken with Lindsey. It wasn't until somebody asked me specifically, "Can I borrow your bride for a photo?" that I realized what Lindsey had done. She'd co-opted my costume.

I think the real reason she picked a ghost bride for her costume after I'd gone my own way with mine was that it transformed my costume from *Tomb of Ligeia* Vincent Price to Groom of Ghost Bride. My black coat, cravat, hat, and walking stick suddenly became old-fashioned wedding-day finery. It was a fantastic feat of marital manipulation on her part as I suddenly found myself part of a couple's costume.

Eventually we made it to Rockafellas, where we sat at a table near the bar and drank Candy Corntinis and didn't at all feel out of place. And that, let me tell you, is a magical thing.

We eventually arrived at the warehouse where the party was already in progress. Salem police officers guarded the entrance, and our names were on the list. It was a great, classic kind of Halloween party. Everyone was in costume, from the guy dressed as the classic vampire—the tuxedo of the Halloween party scene—to the couple dressed as matching boobs that of course somebody immediately motorboated for a photo. I really hope, for their sakes, that they didn't come to the party via the pedestrian mall.

The host himself was dressed as a post-accident bicyclist, and there were Marshall and Elaine in wizard hats and robes. A stage was set up on one side of the warehouse, and when the band came out, that high-end rock group turned out to comprise founding members of Boston, Steely Dan, and Bob Marley's Wailers, guys who used to sell out stadiums and had probably seen some serious stuff in their rock and roll lives, all inches away from us on stage enthusiastically playing their hits for this private party like they had just written them the day before.

For us, the whole thing was kind of a dry run for Halloween itself.

For lunch that Halloween afternoon, instead of fighting the crowds in the restaurants, we ate carnival food on the Common, while people took surreptitious photos of the Ghost Bride and her nachos. The Ghost Bride and her candy apple. The Ghost Bride and Groom of Ghost Bride sharing a Coke Zero. Meanwhile, Esme and Hazel ran through the kid's carnival on the Common.

Eventually the kids were tired, so we took them back to the hosue. They had to rest up for trick-or-treating, after all. I then ran back out into the fray solo and took photos like I was paid by the click. Even in the short amount of time it took me to go back to the house and come back out, the crowd had increased. Like I had been warned, most people weren't in costume. But even if the ratio was one to ten, the numbers were still huge enough that it meant a lot of costumes. Now it was my turn to stop everybody on the pedestrian mall to take their photos. I think my favorite of the day was the zombie holding a cake with a severed head on it from the "Father's Day" segment of the 1984 movie *Creepshow*. But, man, some people went so far out, they were less in costume and more putting on one-person special effects shows for the crowd.

The police presence was noticeably thicker as well, though even their yellow smocks were swallowed up by the crowd. The biggest change in their presence, though, the one that showed that the alert state had risen from smoldering porch-step jack-o'-lantern to full-on flaming Headless Horseman pumpkin missile, was a mobile observation tower erected by the MBTA Transit Police at the intersection of Essex Street and Washington Street. It was a white box about the size of a ticket booth, raised about twenty or thirty feet into the air on hinged metal stilts. It was called a Skywatch Tower, and cameras sent a live feed back to the command center at the police station. But even in that atmosphere it looked less like Big Brother and more like a carnival ride. Another Skywatch Tower was set up on Lafayette Street near the Salem Fire Department.

But so far, the only violence I saw was contained within the costumes themselves. Lots of people covered in blood.

The only agitators I saw were the street preachers, who were out in force for the weekend. The previous night, a group of them aimed a megaphone at Crow Haven Corner from about twenty feet away, yelling through it at the tourists about to embark on a Witch tour with Sammy. "You gotta love the First Amendment," I heard a passerby say.

On Halloween itself, street preachers were decrying the sinful scam

of Salem through microphones and speakers set up in Lappin Park, beside the Samantha statue and in the shadow of the Skywatch Tower. Beside them, a woman dressed as Deadpool held up a sheet of cardboard hastily scribbled with, "Thor is God! Read Mighty Thor #5" while she danced with a pair of blue and white sharks from the Katy Perry Super Bowl half-time show. A large bald man painted red from the neck up with horns on his head stood nearby and applauded.

Eventually, I returned home to rest and reload my camera with a new card. We were getting close to crossing that strange shadow border between Halloween day and Halloween night. I next took off—still in costume—for Pickering Wharf, where, right in front of Gypsy Ravish's Nu Aeon store, her temple was gathering. A thin man in glasses wearing a long gold cloak with a red hood was directing the crowd around him, handing out large signs with mystical images on them. A column formed full of cloaked and masked figures. Drummers stood on either side of a purple banner at the front of the group adorned with a gold pentacle and the words, "The Temple of Nine Wells, A.T.C."

"Is this a parade?" someone shouted at the man in the gold cloak.

"This is not a parade. It's a procession," he explained. "If anyone wants to join us, feel free to follow."

The procession was headed to Gallows Hill for its twenty-fourth annual Samhain magic circle. All over the city of Salem, similar Samhainic rites were being performed to welcome in the new year on the Witch's Wheel and to commune with those across the veil.

I wanted to follow them to the ceremony, but I didn't want to add the two-mile round trip to my odometer, especially since my costume demanded dress shoes, and we had miles to walk before we slept.

I raced back to the house, where our friend Kathleen had arrived. She had been kind of enough to come in from New Hampshire to watch our kids so that we could stay out late to get involved in whatever depravity it took to fully experience a Salem Halloween. And because she's awesome. And because I told her I'd put her name in the book and call her awesome.

Next on our agenda was another Witch ritual. Lindsey and I took off for the Common, where we found hundreds of people wrangled into forming a large circle about five people deep. In the middle was a small table, a portable sound system, and a handful of Witches engaged in casting a circle. Like the movie *Bio-Dome,* remember? Christian Day and Brian Cain led the proceedings, both in full Witch regalia like they'd brought their own wardrobe department from New Orleans. Drummers

Samhain Gallows Hill Procession

at the edges of the circle kept things pagan. Lorelei Stathopoulos was also inside the circle, her accent unmistakable when she took the microphone to decry animal abuse. Another Witch walked the inner circumference of the circle, sweeping an extremely witchy-looking broom in a symbolic cleaning. Many in the crowd raised their hands and closed their eyes like they were at a Pentecostal church service. Above it all, a drone hovered, its insect-engines barely audible above the din below.

But that din wasn't totally from the microphone-amplified spellcasting or the echoing chants of "So mote it be" from the crowd. Walking around the outside perimeter of the circle was a group three people, the leader of which held an amplifier over his shoulder like a purse and a microphone clutched tightly in his hand. His black sweatshirt said "Jesus is Love" and his microphone was set to disrupting and discrediting the ceremony. In reality, it just made it seem like the circle had been successfully cast to keep the negative energy outside of it.

"I think we know how this ends," Lindsey said to me. "Ready to trick-or-treat . . . in Salem?"

It was just past 5:30, the official trick-or-treat starting time for Salem. I imagined our kids butting at the front door with their plastic jack-o'-lantern pails like anxious horses in stalls at the start of a race. We walked the four blocks home, the bones in my legs aching as though they were ready to snap at any step.

Our original plan was to trick-or-treat Chestnut Street, the site of our original digs. Marshall and Elaine had told us that Chestnut Street was a trick-or-treater's paradise, that they'd sit out on their front stoop with a bottle of wine and hand out candy like they were factory workers on a conveyor belt. "Last year, we gave out nine hundred pieces of candy," Marshall had told me. At one point he asked one of the trick-or-treating parents from out of town why they chose this street. They replied, "We asked the police where to trick-or-treat in Salem, and they sent us here."

However, we were already hitting an exhaustion point, and Chestnut Street was on the other side of the downtown. So instead of having the kids make the long trek and really earn their candy, we trick-or-treated in the neighborhoods around the Common.

We were in hour six of wearing our costumes at that point, although we had switched Hazel to a bulky, one-piece dragonfly costume since it was warmer and the weather was turning cold. The hood with the antennae flopping atop it swallowed her tiny head. It was her second-ever trick-or-treating, the first on her own two feet. One of my best memories of Salem is watching her put her head down, isolated in the unwieldly costume like an astronaut on a spacewalk, and trudging along the even, undulating sidewalks of Salem, dragging her plastic jack-o'-lantern behind her, surprised every time somebody tried to stick candy in it.

And so the five of us—me, Lindsey, Hazel, Esme, and Kathleen—headed off to trick-or-treat a town full of Witches and costumed monsters on a night when the veil was so thin, dead people could hand out candy.

Trick-or-treating is one of the last few truly neighborly activities we have in our culture, and nothing illustrates that better than trick-or-treating in somebody else's neighborhood. Everybody was sitting on their porches and stoops, meeting all the trick-or-treaters halfway and having as much of a blast handing out candy as the kids were filling their bags with it. One woman was marking a notepad when we approached. "So far I have five different states and two different countries. Where are you guys from?"

"New Hampshire."

"Six different states!"

Another house gave the kids candy and then asked if we wanted any adult treats. They handed Lindsey, Kathleen, and me pumpkin spice Jell-O shots in plastic, lidded condiment containers like you'd find at a fast food joint. I was familiar with trick-or-drinking. Previous Halloweens back home we had gotten into the habit of taking "walking margaritas" with us in plastic cups, and I'd heard tales of other neighborhoods setting up beer kegs on porches to keep all the adult chaperones in high Halloween spirits.

We trick-or-treated until night fell and the kids' shoulder sockets were loose from the weight of their hauls. Had the holiday ended there, it would have been a satisfying one, maybe even a spectacular one. But it was far from over. We walked Kathleen and the kids back to the house, and then Lindsey and I jumped out on our own deeper into the dark . . . the very loud dark.

A Beatles tribute band jammed on the Common—because Screamin' Jay Hawkins tribute bands are hard to come by—and a DJ set up on Hawthorne Boulevard turned the street into a dance party as Hawthorne himself looked on stone-faced and obviously wondering why Salem wasn't this fun during his day.

The Essex Street Pedestrian Mall had moved even further from the pedestrian. It was teeming, boiling, overflowing at the edges with monstrous revelers. We held our breaths and dived in. The ratio of those in costume to those not seemed higher than during the day, but there were still many there who were too cool for it. Which was fine. Monsters need victims. And now that it was night-time, those monsters took on new levels of menace. One creepy scarecrow leaned against a lamppost long enough for people to gather around to see if it was a decoration. When enough came close, it would leap from the pole to the satisfying sounds of screams and shutterclicks. A group of Grim Reapers, their scythes held high despite the prohibition against fake weapons, strutted around like some ancient cult fresh from their hidden chambers looking for new adherents to add to their ranks. An evil clown and a skull-headed demon with a Mohawk of horns, both on stilts, loomed over the chaos, somehow deftly navigating the cobblestones and curbs of the street. Every bump into somebody elicited a cry of fright or a shout of delight as you found yourself close enough to smell the latex of some of the more creative costumes. And many of the costumes were works of art, for sure, from

people whose supreme moment on the planet obviously happens every October 31st.

And nobody was going anywhere. They were just walking, just hanging out, just taking pictures like it was the law. Some partied at the stage set up at East India Square, knee-deep in the Salem map of the fountain basin. Some squeezed into bars that were throwing their own mini–Halloween parties, the attendees ebbing and flowing in and out from the vaster one outside.

In the tumult, I don't remember any street preachers at that point megaphoning into the void. Maybe they were there, I don't know, but I can guarantee their efforts were futile against the full might of Halloween. At one point we passed a group of Hare Krishna, who were singing and playing instruments. One jumped out at Lindsey and I, clapped me on the back, and said, with obvious joy in his bearing, "Great costumes." He handed us a card with the Maha Mantra printed on it.

Many of the streets downtown were closed to vehicular traffic, creating a network of pedestrian malls all across downtown Salem. Suddenly, we could walk down the middle of wide, multi-laned road that is Derby Street, past the Haunted Neighborhood and the carnival and the food venders and Count Orlok's. The world had finally been taken over by monsters, and all the post-apocalyptic movies had lied to us. It was a blast. The Charter Street Cemetery was shut down—I expected Mr. St. Amour must've had to use a snow plow to remove everyone on this night—and a massive light on a pole towered over it to ensure no trespassing among the tombstones.

In addition to enjoying and exploring Salem's Halloween, we were also killing time. In my pocket was a pair of high-priced tickets to the Witches' Ball. This is one of the Festival of the Dead events thrown by Day and Cain. It was being held at the Hawthorne Hotel. Eventually, we made our way back there. Inside was a dance floor with lights and a pentacle projected onto the ceiling. Giant balloon sculptures that matched the theme of the party, Dance of the Tarot. On stage, a belly dancer writhed, followed by the loud rhythm of a pagan troupe called the Dragon Ritual Drummers—the same gents who had been in the circle on the Common earlier. And there were Witches everywhere. Day and Cain circulated through. Laurie Cabot was there, as well, in a small VIP area reserved for the founding Witch of Salem. I've seen estimates of 650 people at that particular party. The night before, when we were party crashing with Boston and Steely Dan, the Hawthorne Hotel had thrown its own elaborate party, it's attendance estimated at about a thousand costumed revelers.

However, despite the unique vibe of spending Halloween night partying with Witches, we only stayed long enough to down a couple of gin and tonics and catch a couple of the more elaborate costumes. We wanted to go back outside. Partly, that's because the party from the previous night had scratched our Halloween party itch, but also, in the end, a Halloween party is still just a Halloween party (even one thrown by Witches), while the streets of Salem at Halloween are something else entirely. The Witches' Ball was a back-up plan for us anyway, in case we wanted to stay out past curfew.

Because Halloween in Salem had a curfew. Shortly after 10:30, police start directing people to Salem's exits. If you weren't at a party or inside a bar when the music stops, you had to go home. And the city-wide signal wasn't a witch on a broom projected into the night sky overhead. It was fireworks. Because Halloween is Salem's Fourth of July, too.

Shortly before the curfew, the city starts shooting the fireworks out over the North River. The best place to see them from is Washington Street . . . which just happens to lead right to the train station. Strategy.

We made our way to Washington Street to find another Essex Street Pedestrian Mall. A sea of people were waiting on the fireworks or trying to escape to the trains before the mass exodus started. On the spot of the old Salem courthouse was a wizard, elevated above the crowd on either stilts or the shoulders of friends—I couldn't tell from the distance I was at. I mentally overlaid a Colonial-era courtroom over the site. The dancing of the Halloween revelers merged with the writhing of the afflicted Puritans.

Finally, the fireworks went off. There were no Halloween shapes in the airborne explosions—I guess modern fireworks technology isn't quite there yet—but it was still a show, made all the stranger for illuminating the masks and face paint of the partiers below. Shortly before the sizzling finale, we started meandering away from Washington Street. As our hearing returned, we heard the rumble of motorcycle engines. It was followed by a phalanx of motorcycle cops who sped through the crowd to hit their positions for enforcing the imminent curfew.

As we walked back toward the direction of both the Witches' Ball and our house beyond, unsure which one we'd end up at, I didn't feel too pushed out of the city by the police, so we meandered a bit to see some old haunts one last time during this strange, strange October.

Eventually, we neared the Roger Conant statue, all bronze and proud and dark and completely oblivious to what his acres of virgin forest had become. At that moment we decided to skip the rest of the ball, to forego any final toast to the night and the season, to head home for one last sleep on Essex Street. We'd had thirty-one days of Salem Halloween, and it would be sad to witness the dates on our phones changing to November 1. We tried to cut through the Common but police officers surrounded it.

"Common's closed, sir," one said to me.

"But I live here." I'd been waiting all of October to use that line.

"Common's closed, sir."

We took the long way home, shed our Ghost Bride and Groom of Ghost Bride personas, and were in bed before November.

EPILOGUE: SALEM AFTER THE SPELL

It was March 12, 2016, more than four months since my family and I had driven away from Salem on that surreal first morning of November. Had it been March 12, 2015, the witch town would have been a ghost town, huge humps of snow swallowing entire parts of the city, salt staining the cobblestones, residents bundled up indoors in front of the cold warmth of LED television screens, visitors far away in warmer climes. But on the late-winter day that we found ourselves there, it was close to sixty degrees. I would call that unseasonably warm for a New England March, but the entire season had been unreasonably unseasonable. Pathetic amounts of snow, random short-sleeve days throughout, records for suckiest winter ever broken every week. Hardly the white-out, snowed-in winter I wanted as an excuse to barricade myself inside my study to finish the book that you are now also finishing and, I assume, hoping for a good payoff to.

It was the first time all four of us—myself, Lindsey, Esme, and Hazel—had been downtown together since we had left. I had been back by myself a handful of times in the interim to pick up a few outstanding interviews once everybody's schedules recovered from October, but that was about it. As we passed the shuttered Dairy Witch, a hand-made sign that promised "See You in the Spring" blocking its window, I asked Esme what she remembered most about her time in Salem. "Witches," was her response. Hazel piped in with something unintelligible. She's still getting the hang of talking. When she sees Mary, Ray Bradbury's witch, in my study, she just puts her hand on her head and says, "Hat."

We drove past the Roger Conant statue and the Salem Witch Museum, both doing their part to represent their city regardless of the season. After we parked in the garage on New Liberty Street, we stepped out onto the Essex Street Pedestrian Mall. A nearby street performer blew deep notes from his saxophone across the air. He wasn't wearing a costume, and I had no idea if he was the near-spring alter ego of the demon clown saxophonist we had seen every weekend in October. Patrick Dougherty's *What the Birds Know* still survived on the lawn of the Crowninshield-Bentley House, albeit a few shades of gray deeper into decay and its form slumping as the dead saplings loosened. Both the Old Town Pump fountain and the East India Square fountain were dry.

In every window of the stores and restaurants, the jack-o'-lanterns and ghosts that I remembered and which seemed like permanent adornments had been replaced by shamrocks and eggs. St. Patrick's Day was a mere five days away, and Easter was only fifteen. Both were in March this year, leading to a bit of theme-confusion for retailers. Generally, the bars and restaurants stuck to St. Paddy's, while other stores went full Easter.

Still, I didn't have to look very close to see witches. Among all the green Boston Irish T-shirts at Witch Tee's were the usual black Salem witch shirts. Here and there I spotted full-on Halloween decorations sitting in the sills of windows. And if this had been any other city on the planet, I would say that all the gift shops looked like their stock hadn't been touched since October. At one point we walked past the only other street performer out besides the sax man, this one a musician as well. He was compressing and extending an accordion as he slowly drew from its bellows "Sally's Song" from *The Nightmare Before Christmas*. You can cover the city in clover and pastel, but you can't completely cover up the Halloween.

Still, the Witch History Museum was closed, as was the Witch Mansion haunt. The Salem Time Machine was also closed, and a paper sign had been taped to its window: "Attraction for Lease."

The rest of the stores seemed open. And that included every Witch shop on the mall. From Crow Haven Corner to The Magic Parlor, Tarot decks were snapping across tables, "boring" crystal balls were polished shiny, and hand sanitizer was at the ready.

The streets were neither crowded nor empty, with a pleasant flow of people walking the mall and lunching at Rockafellas and the Red Line Café and the Village Tavern. We even saw a tour bus drive up Hawthorne Boulevard.

We walked our old routes, from our Chestnut Street digs to our Essex Street ones. We cut through Artists Row, passing a closed-down Lobster Shanty, which wouldn't open for another three weeks. Otherwise, the Hot and Dirty Pickle Martini would have made an appearance in this epilogue. Oh, look, it did anyway. Lee Wolf later told me about Halloween 2015 at the Lobster Shanty: "It was our best day ever. We broke our record. And without incident, too . . . which is a rarity."

We followed Derby Street along the water. The *Friendship of Salem* was topless, its masts and rigging and spars removed as if it had gone too fast under a low bridge. The Witch's Brew Café had Windexed Michael Myers and Chucky and Twisty off its window and replaced them with leprechauns. The last smokestack from the power plant that had stood lonely over Salem during October had been demolished. The House of the Seven Gables looked as dark and eternal as it always does. We stopped into the Ye Old Pepper Companie across the street, which was full of Easter candy. Chocolate bunnies had replaced chocolate witches and skull pops. All the candy corn had been scooped out for jelly beans. I saw not a single witch, edible or otherwise, inside the small, crammed space.

You can't fit a city into a book. I knew that going in. But I thought I could squeeze a single season of a city into one. I'm not sure how I did. The book feels like one of those suitcases in the cartoons, so packed that you have to sit on top of it to close it, but the moment someone opens it, everything flies out—hanging nooses and broom bristles and rubber bats and gravestones and multi-attraction tickets. I probably should have warned you on the cover.

I'd been to a few cities between October and March. Like Austin, Texas, which, by comparison to Salem, isn't weird in the least, despite its popular slogan. I'd also spent a few days in New Orleans, which has both everything and nothing in common with Salem. I even spent a week in exotic Barcelona, an entire ocean away. But I was really always in Salem. Always pecking away at the manuscript, always looking at the thousands of photos we took, always thinking about the questions and controversies and paradoxes that surround the city and come to a high cauldron boil in October.

The November morning we left was surreal. Like the last day of a college semester when your home is eight hundred miles away. We didn't have anybody to say goodbye to, just packed and left, texting an IOU to our Essex Street landlords for breaking one of their wine glasses. It was time for us to stop pretending to be Salemites. But I did see one familiar face before we drove off.

As I stood in the driveway packing the trunk, Richard St. Amour, the Charter Street Cemetery security man walked past. I waved, but he didn't seem to recognize me and just kept going. I'm not sure if I imagined it, but there seemed to be a bounce in his step. My Salem was ending, but his Salem was just starting, the one in which he didn't have to be an asshole anymore.

We drove out of a city that was dead calm, like everybody had gone overboard at sea and all that was left was a ghost ship. No orange and black streamers clogged the sewer drains, no cast-off masks littered the streets, nobody slumped miserably on benches or against storefronts. The cleaning crews had come in and scoured the place. The only clue to the massive Halloween party hours before were the Halloween decorations still hung throughout the city. And that isn't really a clue in Salem—it's almost a state of being.

I'd find out later that week that what we had experienced in Salem on Halloween night was a record crowd. We had partied in the midst of more than one hundred thousand people. Chief Mary Butler would tell me it had been a record night at the station, as well . . . for the low number of arrests. There had been eleven total, three of which weren't related to the downtown Halloween festivities, and twenty people had been taken into temporary protective custody for intoxication. It was a mere drop in the apple-bobbing tub for such a massive number of people. The police force that night had numbered two hundred uniformed officers, with fifty to sixty more in plainclothes, which on Halloween is pretty funny.

On the way out of town we stopped at Proctor's Ledge behind the Walgreens for a last look at the Witch Trials execution site. Lindsey and the girls hadn't been with me on my own trek, and I wanted them to see the reason why we personally ended up in Salem, why we can now draw a direct line from Bridget Bishop to a month of our lives.

And that's where the big questions start, right? We had a magnificent time in Salem. Loved Haunted Happenings. I was, of course, particularly susceptible to its charms. Steve McCaw had described himself to me as "a spooky person" at Witch's Brew Café, and that applies to me as well. But people had to die in a horribly unjust manner so that we could dress up as monsters and party with Witches and revel in thirty-one days of commonality with other spooky people and people allowing themselves to be spooky once a year.

And that seems like a big jump, because, as was pointed out to me multiple times over the course of this book, Halloween is a completely separate thing from the Salem Witch Trials. Except that it's not. Not any more at least. The reverberations of both have rippled out across the American timeline and met in a Venn diagram, right at the point where a hunched hag throws amphibian parts into a scarlet brew to curse her enemies. There's a reason why Halloween just sticks to this city better than anywhere else on the planet, regardless of what the *USA Today* polls say.

One night, while I was trying to find a synonym for spooky that I hadn't used twenty times already, an author/illustrator acquaintance of mine named Jamison Odone messaged me. He asked, "Would you trade the Salem Witch Trials for the Salem that you love? Would you stop their executions or preserve the legend and mystique of the place? Twenty-four deaths is basically Sandy Hook." He had once lived not too far from the elementary school tragedy.

It wasn't a flippant question. He himself had tackled it. About a year previously, he—under the pen name Jakob Crane—had published a graphic novel called *Lies in the Dust: A Tale of Remorse from the Salem Witch Trials* that dramatized the events using Ann Putnam's statement of apology as a lens.

It was an easy answer, technically. Of course, lives take priority. Sure, I'd miss the Salem story, but we have billions of other stories in the world to obsess over (and thousands of other witch trials). But it's not really the right question. The question isn't trading the tragedy for Witch City. It's trading Witch City for Pepper City after the tragedy happens.

Had Salem become Pepper City, the state as a whole, the nation as a whole, the world as a whole, forgets about it. And by "it" I mean both the tragedy and the city. The Witch Trial victims become witch trial victims, anonymous in the ranks of tens of thousands of others. And Salem's glory days aren't enough to glorify it today. It takes Salem's darkest days to keep the street lights on. Honestly, maybe even Pepper City itself forgets about the tragedy. Maybe the Witch Trials victims get a plaque on a boulder on the Common. That's it. We know this because it's happened at other witch trial sites in the world.

The other thing is, everything in the entire world is founded on tragedy. Our country, every country. There's not a society on the planet that doesn't have ancient tragedies clawing at its back. The past is a giant corpse—right, Hawthorne? But life isn't a perpetual state of regret and mourning over those tragedies, it's taking those tragedies, giving them their due in proportion, learning from them (or not), working to prevent them from happening again (or not), and then we all party because we only have so many holidays in our lives.

I mean, you cringed a little at Odone's comparison of Sandy Hook to the Salem Witch Trials, right? Or maybe even Joe Cultrera's comparison to 9/11. Or Richard Trask's comparison to Auschwitz. Part of that is because these tragedies, and all tragedies, are incomparable in a sense. Each one has its own texture of tragedy, each one is horrible in its own way. But really, it's more a case of old wounds vs. new. And we have much more latitude with old wounds. And 324-year-old wounds are hardly wounds at all, anymore. Those have been covered up by scar tissue thick enough to build on.

Because even better than memorializing a tragedy is making something positive out of it. And being able to support an entire economy, to have people want to come to your city, to be unique in a world where cities are just so many glass buildings and chain stores. That's positive.

But that happens only after you've dealt honestly with the tragedy. After you've asked yourself and come to terms with Odone's question. Every writer and artist inspired by the Witch Trials and every tourist inspired to visit the city needs to do that at some point.

And I believe Salem has. It has officially memorialized the victims. It's now going to memorialize their execution site. It still tells their full story through the attractions, even if it's not at a city level. It has steadfast and concerned citizens like Joe Cultrera and Donna Seger to help us never forget whose dust we're dancing on. It even finally completed the business of exonerating all the victims. In 2001—the year Arthur C. Clarke and Stanley Kubrick predicted we would be among the stars—the acting governor of Massachusetts signed into law the exoneration of five victims who had somehow been overlooked over the centuries: Bridget Bishop, Susannah Martin, Alice Parker, Wilmot Redd, and Margaret Scott.

If that late date or random slice of victims sound strange, that's because over the years, various acts have cleared various victims, not always by name. The last act was signed into law on Halloween itself. That's an exhibit for the case I've tried to build in the preceding paragraphs. But all those things show Salem dealing with that part of its past. And, once you get past the past, you can expand your vision. The bosses at PEM are right about that.

But 1692 is only part of the puzzle of Witch City.

I mean, 1692 simply isn't enough. I've seen all the explainations for how these witch trials were different than any the world has seen thus far. Like its duration of months instead of days and weeks. The number of people involved. The high proportion of accused men. The power of teenage girls in the story. The high-ranking accused. How over fifty people confessed. And the trove of documentation that survives.

But it took more than documentation to create Witch City.

For sure, it started with an odd tragedy that was never really righted. But then it took the death of a major industry, the maritime industry, for "Witch City" to gain a foothold, one that could easily have slipped over time. Then a second industry, manufacturing, died, robbing the city of another identity. Then a popular sitcom decided to film there. The horror genre grew in popularity. A single woman moved there while committing herself to an esoteric religion. And that had to catch on. Then a minor holiday became a major one. All those steps are important in making the Witch City we know today.

And the common denominator in all of that? A single word: Witch.

And this is the real difference between the tragedy of 1692 and tragedies like 9/11. That word. That word is magic. Without that word, that exact word, that particular word, Witch City doesn't happen. Put it this way: What if the people of Salem had hanged run-of-the-mill religious heretics, instead of what they believed to be supernatural witches? What does Salem 2016 look like then?

Today, I think, the "Witch" of Witch City has transcended all of that.

That shape on the patches of the police officer uniforms, on the doors of the cabs and the fire engines, on the Dairy Witch. That shape doesn't represent the victims of 1962. If it did, the shape would be a Puritan on a noose. It doesn't stand for the religious Witch community. Otherwise, the witch wouldn't be astride a broom or look like a monster. It doesn't even stand for the Halloween witch. Salem adopted the witch back when Halloween was a mere kid's night and not a multi-billion-dollar industry.

So which witch is on the police officer's patch? Which witch? (I ask so that I can write that phrase twice.)

It's the Salem witch. It owes its existence to all three witches, but it has transcended them all, too, and become its own thing. And in a world where civic symbols are often boring and where cities are too often defiend by a sports mascot, to define one's community with something that has actual resonance—good, bad, and fun—is impressive and unique.

So did I get sick of October in Salem? No. Not after a month. On November 1, I was done with Halloween, as I am every November 1. Part of the specialness of a holiday is the ephemeral nature of it. Even Jack Skellington tired of Halloween. But in March, as Lindsey, Esme, Hazel, and I walked down the familiar, uneven sidewalks of Salem, eating bunny-shaped candies and looking at the patterned eggs hanging in the windows, I did miss the October Salem. March Salem felt like a nice city, one certainly worth settling down in and being proud of. But I never would have discovered that city, never wouldn't have written a book about that city.

The last place we went on that warm March day was the Charter Street Cemetery, the Old Burying Point—the dark, dead heart of Salem. It wasn't empty. Maybe half a dozen other people were meandering among the headstones. The cemetery trees were all leafless, their hanging branches looking even spookier than they had in autumn.

I leaned against a tomb and asked Lindsey what she took from Salem. She told me, "It just feels like a unique place. I liked saying that we were living in Salem." It took me an entire book to say that. As we hung out there in the cemetery, a tour group of high school students entered. We watched them being led through the graves, past the Grimshawe House and Judge Hathorne's stone.

Eventually, we left, and I made it as far as the parking garage before I realized that I had left my camera on the 1797 tomb of one Mr. William Orne. By the time I dashed back, it was gone. But that's fine. The camera is replaceable, most of the memory card backed up, the few pictures I took that day unnecessary. I already had thousands of photos of Salem. It was like the city was telling me that it was done with me documenting it.

And I am done with that. But not with Salem.

I'll see you next Halloween Season, Witch City. And hopefully every one after that. Although I do want to check out Anoka, Minnesota, and Derry, Ireland, at some point.

ACKNOWLEDGMENTS

Some forty people took time out of their personal lives and workdays to become part of this book. I'm indebted to each.

Everybody involved in the Great Salem House Hunt of 2015, from Jennifer and Nic Kiefer to Claudia Paraschiv and Michael Jaros, the latter of whom rented us our Essex Street home. Most important in this area are Marshall Strauss and Elaine Gerdine.

Others who deserve acknowledgement are Rob Velella, Penny Cabot, Jim Dempsey, Genesis Brito, Jacob Strunk, and Dan Crissman at The Countryman Press. Richard Beck for his copyediting support. Also, Esme's teacher Darlene Travis, who put in extra work so we could continue Esme's schooling.

I'd like to thank all my friends from OTIS who showed enthusiasm for the project.

Many family and friends visited our temporary Salem homes and made it that much more fun. My parents, Edward and Nancy, my aunt and uncle Norma and Karl Cranston, Lindsey's parents, Jim and Pat Jennings, Alison and Jeff and their family, Tessa Anganes, Will Webster, Ben Alcorn, Zach Sanzone, Kathleen Costello, Kathryn O'Shields, and Burke Blackman.

Of course, Lindsey, Esme, and Hazel, the loves of my life.

And, finally, all the participants, willing and otherwise, in the Witch Trials of 1692.

INDEX